Progressive Business Plan for a Subscription Clothing Rental Company

Copyright © 2019 by Progressive Business Consulting, Inc.
Pembroke Pines, FL 33027

Subscription Clothing Rental Company
Business Plan
_____ (date)

Business Name: _____
Plan Time Period: 2019 - 2021

Founding Directors:
Name: _____
Name: _____

Contact Information:
Owner: _____
Address: _____
City/State/Zip: _____
Phone: _____
Cell: _____
Fax: _____
Website: _____
Email: _____

Submitted to: _____
Date: _____
Contact Info: _____

This document contains confidential information. It is disclosed to you for informational purposes only. Its contents shall remain the property of _____ (business name) and shall be returned to _____ when requested. This is a business plan and does not imply an offering of securities.

NON-DISCLOSURE AGREEMENT

_____ (Company)., and _____ (Person Name), agrees:

_____ (Company) Corp. may from time to time disclose to _____ (Person Name) certain confidential information or trade secrets generally regarding Business plan and financials of _____ (Company) corp.

_____ (Person Name) agrees that it shall not disclose the information so conveyed, unless in conformity with this agreement. _____ (Person Name) shall limit disclosure to the officers and employees of _____ (Person Name) with a reasonable "need to know" the information and shall protect the same from disclosure with reasonable diligence.

As to all information which _____ (Company) Corp. claims is confidential, _____ (Company) Corp. shall reduce the same to writing prior to disclosure and shall conspicuously mark the same as "confidential," "not to be disclosed" or with other clear indication of its status. If the information which _____ (Company) Corp. is disclosing is not in written form, for example, a machine or device, _____ (Company) Corp. shall be required prior to or at the same time that the disclosure is made to provide written notice of the secrecy claimed by _____ (Company) Corp..
_____ (Person Name) agrees upon reasonable notice to return the confidential tangible material provided by it by _____ (Company) Corp. upon reasonable request.

The obligation of non-disclosure shall terminate when if any of the following occurs:
(a) The confidential information becomes known to the public without the fault of _____ (Person Name), or;
(b) The information is disclosed publicly by _____ (Company) Corp., or
(c) a period of 12 months passes from the disclosure, or;
(d) the information loses its status as confidential through no fault of _____ (Person Name).

In any event, the obligation of non-disclosure shall not apply to information which was known to _____ (Person Name) prior to the execution of this agreement.

Dated: _____

_____
_____ (Company) Corp.
_____ (Person Name)

Business and Marketing Plan Instructions

1. If you want the digital file for this book, please send proof-of-purchase to probusconsult2@yahoo.com

2. Complete the Executive Summary section, as your final step, after you have completed the entire plan.

3. Feel free to edit the plan and make it more relevant to your strategic goals, objectives and business vision.

4. We have provided all the formulas needed to prepare the financial plan. Just plug in the numbers that are based on your particular situation. Excel spreadsheets for the financials are available on the microsoft.com website and www.simplebizplanning.com/forms.htm http://office.microsoft.com/en-us/templates/

5. Throughout the plan, we have provided prompts or suggestions as to what values to enter into blank spaces but use your best judgment and then delete the suggested values (?).

6. The plan also includes some separate worksheets for additional assistance in expanding some of the sections, if desired.

7. Additionally, some sections offer multiple choices and the word 'select' appears as a prompt to edit the contents of the plan.

8. Your feedback, referrals and business are always very much appreciated.

Thank you

Nat Chiaffarano, MBA
Progressive Business Consulting, Inc.
Pembroke Pines, FL 33027
ProBusConsult2@yahoo.com

Subscription Clothing Rental Company Business Plan: Table of Contents

Section	Description	Page
1.0	**Executive Summary**	___
1.1.0	Tactical Objectives	___
1.1.1	Strategic Objectives	___
1.2	Mission Statement	___
1.2.1	Core Values Statement	___
1.3	Vision Statement	___
1.4	Keys to Success	___
2.0	**Company Summary**	___
2.1	Company Ownership	___
2.2	Company Licensing and Liability Protection	___
2.3	Start-up To-do Checklist	___
2.4.0	Company Location	___
2.4.1	Company Facilities	___
2.5.0	Start-up Summary	___
2.5.1	Inventory	___
2.5.2	Supply Sourcing	___
2.6	Start-up Requirements	___
2.7	SBA Loan Key Requirements	___
2.7.1	Other Financing Options	___
3.0	**Products and Services**	___
3.1	Service Descriptions	___
3.1.1	Product Descriptions	___
3.2	Alternate Revenue Streams	___
3.3	Production of Products and Services	___
3.4	Competitive Comparison	___
3.5	Sale Literature	___
3.6	Fulfillment	___
3.7	Technology	___
3.8	Future Products and Services	___
4.0	**Market Analysis Summary**	___
4.1.0	Secondary Market Research	___
4.1.1	Primary Market Research	___
4.2	Market Segmentation	___
4.3	Target Market Segment Strategy	___
4.3.1	Market Needs	___
4.4	Buying Patterns	___
4.5	Market Growth	___

Section	Description	Page
4.6	Service Business Analysis	____
4.7	Barrier to Entry	____
4.8	Competitive Analysis	____
4.9	Market Revenue Projections	____
5.0	**Industry Analysis**	____
5.1	Industry Leaders	____
5.2	Industry Statistics	____
5.3	Industry Trends	____
5.4	Industry Key Terms	____
6.0	**Strategy and Implementation Summary**	____
6.1.0	Promotion Strategy	____
6.1.1	Grand Opening	____
6.1.2	Value Proposition	____
6.1.3	Positioning Statement	____
6.1.4	Distribution Strategy	____
6.2	Competitive Advantage	____
6.2.1	Branding Strategy	____
6.3	Business SWOT Analysis	____
6.4.0	Marketing Strategy	____
6.4.1	Strategic Alliances	____
6.4.2	Monitoring Marketing Results	____
6.4.3	Word-of-Mouth Marketing	____
6.5	Sales Strategy	____
6.5.1	Customer Retention Strategy	____
6.5.2	Sales Forecast	____
6.5.3	Sales Program	____
6.6	Merchandising Strategy	____
6.7	Pricing Strategy	____
6.8	Differentiation Strategies	____
6.9	Milestone Tracking	____
7.0	**Website Plan Summary**	____
7.1	Website Marketing Strategy	____
7.2	Development Requirements	____
7.3	Sample Frequently Asked Questions	____
8.0	**Operations**	____
8.1	Security Measures	____
9.0	**Management Summary**	____
9.1	Owner Personal History	____

Section	Description	Page
9.2	Management Team Gaps	____
9.2.1	Management Matrix	____
9.2.2	Outsourcing Matrix	____
9.3	Employee Requirements	____
9.4	Job Descriptions	____
9.4.1	Job Description Format	____
9.5	Personnel Plan	____
9.6	Staffing Plan	____
10.0	**Business Risk Factors**	____
10.1	Business Risk Reduction Strategies	____
10.2	Reduce Customer Perceived Risk Strategies	____
11.0	**Financial Plan**	____
11.1	Important Assumptions	____
11.2	Break-even Analysis	____
11.3	Projected Profit and Loss	____
11.4	Projected Cash Flow	____
11.5	Projected Balance Sheet	____
11.6	Business Ratios	____
12.0	**Business Plan Summary**	____
13.0	**Potential Exit Strategies**	____
	Appendix	____
	Helpful Resources	____

"Progressive Business Plan for a Subscription Clothing Rental Company"

Copyright Notice
Copyright © 2019   Nat Chiaffarano, MBA
Progressive Business Consulting, Inc
All Rights Reserved.   **ISBN:** 9781792196911

This program is protected under Federal and International copyright laws. No portion of these materials may be reproduced, stored in a retrieval system or transmitted in any manner whatsoever, without the written consent of the publisher.

Limits of Liability / Disclaimer of Warranty
The author and the publisher of "Progressive Business Plan for a Subscription Clothing Rental Company", and all accompanying materials have used their best efforts in preparing this program. The author and publisher make no representations and warranties with respect to the accuracy, applicability, fitness or completeness of the content of this program. The information contained in this program is subject to change without notice and should not be construed as a commitment by the author or publisher.

The authors and publisher shall in no event be held liable for any loss or damages, including but not limited to special, incidental, consequential, or other damages. The program makes no promises as to results or consequences of applying the material herein: your business results may vary in direct relation to your detailed planning, timing, availability of capital and human resources, and implementation skills.

This publication is not intended for use as a source of legal, accounting, or professional advice. As always, the advice of a competent legal, accounting, tax, financial or other professional should be sought. If you have any specific questions about your unique business situation, consider contacting a qualified business consultant. The fact that an organization or website is referred to as a 'resource' or potential source of information, does not mean that the publisher or authors endorse the resource. Websites listed may also have been changed since publication of the book.

1.0 Executive Summary

Industry Overview

According to a report published by Allied Market Research, titled, "Online Clothing Rental Market by End User and Clothes Style: Global Opportunity Analysis and Industry Forecast, 2017-2023", the global online clothing rental market was valued at $1,013 million in 2017, and is estimated to reach $ 1,856 million by 2023, registering a CAGR of 10.6% from 2017 to 2023. In 2017, some women online clothing rental and ethnic wear segments dominated the global market share. Additionally, the men end user and western clothing style segments are anticipated to grow at a robust rate in terms of market share.

Source: alliedmarketresearch.com/press-release/online-clothing-rental-market.html

Fashion-conscious individuals who lack the financial resources to purchase the designer clothing of their choice are expected to make most use of online clothing rental services. Rental services are proved to be a cost-effective option for these end users especially women, who are also thriving on the growth showed in the global online clothing rental market. The primary drivers of the global online clothing rental market are the increase in ease of use of online retail and the rising of household debt levels. Moreover, the growing popularity of online shopping portals over the last decade has boosted this market. The advancement in mobile internet technology has further driven the demand for online rental by making the process even more convenient. The subscription clothing rental industry has arisen in the middle of a massive shift in consumer demand, as the traditional retail model is fading away. In its place, the companies that are thriving provide convenience, personalization, affordability, free shipping both ways, no laundering requirements, designer access, fashion guidance, and the ability to try new upscale things, in the comfort of their homes, on a temporary rental basis, without a long-term commitment or substantial financial risk. Consumers are joining subscription clubs because they have found it to be a better way to get what they want, when they want it, for a pre-arranged price, and are willing to pay for these benefits on an automatic recurring monthly billing basis. Research shows that the average American woman buys 64 new pieces of clothing each year, and of these purchases, only wears 50% of them more than once. Companies in this industry are capitalizing on millennials decreasing emphasis on ownership and increasing focus on individual experiences and access to a wide array of items.

Source:
www.businessoffashion.com/articles/intelligence/can-subscription-services-work-for-fashion

Business Overview

_____ (company name) will be a fashion subscription rental service that lets our subscribers rent clothing and accessories for a flat, recurring monthly membership fee, and to purchase at a discounted rate, any special or favorite pieces they want to add to their long-term or permanent collection. The basic market need that we will be satisfying is providing the ability to rent complete outfits or designer dresses as opposed to the customary practice of having to purchase them for a limited period of usage or just one special occasion or event. For these reasons, it has been wasteful to have to buy a new dress every time a person attends a special event. We plan to capitalize on the fact, that common sense is beginning to prevail, as people are becoming more careful with their hard-earned money and choosing to rent instead of buy.

We will rent out items for up to a _____ (month/week?) and charge a ____ (#) percentage of the retail price as the fee. The rental fee charged will cover the service charges, dry cleaning, and other minor expenditures. When the order is placed, the product will be dispatched from our company's inventory with pre-paid pre-addressed package to return the item. There will also be the option of holding an extra amount as insurance during the rental period to cover any sort of accidental damage.

Members will start their subscription membership by completing an extensive personal fashion preferences questionnaire or quiz to arrive at their subscriber profile. Our style consultants will then use the information contained in this profile to make proposed selections for our subscribers. Selections will become more personalized as the 'Customer Profile' continues to be updated, the subscriber supplies feedback on items received and returned, and our computer algorithms analyze actual transaction data overtime, looking for consumption and fit patterns.

_____ (company name) has a unique opportunity to be the only _____ (specialty?) clothing rental service provider in ___ region. _____ (company name) plans to seize this opportunity and is forecasted to reach profitability by the end of year ___ (one/two?) and achieve profits of $_____ by year ___ (two/three?).

The owner, _____, will run the business full-time and hire style consultants as well as _____ (tailors/seamstresses/alterations?) specialists to keep the clothing looking new and in an excellent state of repair. The business has the potential of employing up to ___ (#) full-time employees, estimating a minimum of ___ (#) to start. We will also need ___ (#) people to staff our in-house laundering facility and ___ (#) people to staff our outgoing shipments and 'returns' receiving departments. The hours will be _____ (8:00?) a.m. to ____ (6:00?) p.m. Monday through Saturday. All daily bookkeeping will be done by a dedicated bookkeeper. An accountant will take care of the necessary month-end work, year-end reporting and business ratios analysis.

_____ (company name) will be located on _____. We are currently negotiating a lease on a commercial property of _____ (#) square feet. The rent on the space is only $_____ per month plus approximately $_____ per month for utilities. This is a good price, compared to other less desirable locations, because of the easy roadway access, certified sprinkler system and high ceilings. We plan to invest $_____ (50,000?) in building renovations to meet the special clothing racking needs of our Subscription Clothing Rental Company. The renovations will be free-standing, and the racking system can be easily taken with us to another location, if need be. _____ (company name) will open in mid to late _____ (month).

The Subscription Clothing Rental Company will compete on the following basis:

1. Product variety, including new designer dresses, accessories and jewelry.
2. Facility organization that makes it easy to locate specific inventory items.
3. Superior level of attentive customer service.
4. Affordable rentals fees amounting to about ___ (15?) % of the retail value.
5. Wraparound services, including spotting, laundering, style consulting, free shipping and special event clothing rentals.

We believe that we can become the Subscription Clothing Rental Company of choice in the _____ area for the following reasons:

1. We will develop a training program to create a competent staff, dedicated to continuously improving their skill sets to better assist our members in making informed rental decisions.
2. We will develop a questionnaire to survey changing customer needs and wants, regularly update the customer preference profiles with 'returns' data and enable members to override programed selections within 48 hours of shipment, continually express their level of satisfaction and welcome constructive feedback.
3. We will become a one-stop destination for members in need of affordable clothing for any occasion.
4. We will offer quality clothing rental services, using the latest technological advances, at value-based prices with convenient 24/7 access hours.

In order to succeed, _____ (company name) will have to do the following:

1. Conduct extensive market research to demonstrate that there is a demand for a Subscription Clothing Rental Company with our aforementioned differentiation strategy.
2. Make superior customer service our number one priority.
3. Stay abreast of developments in the Subscription Clothing Rental Industry.
4. Precisely assess and then exceed the expectations of all members.
5. Form long-term, trust-based relationships with members and designers to secure profitable repeat business and referrals.
6. Develop process efficiencies to achieve and maintain profitability.

Mission Statement   (optional)

Our Mission is to address the following customer pain points or unmet needs and wants, which will define the opportunity for our subscription clothing rental business:
_____
In order to satisfy these unmet needs and wants, we will propose the following unique solutions, which will create better value for our customers:
_____

Target Market

Our target market will be educated, style-conscious men and women who want to rent designer dresses and accessories, to make luxury clothing affordable again, while using the opportunity to rebrand their images. Our subscription service will be for any adult who wishes to dress and look fabulous at their place of employment or while attending a job interview, church socials, galas, parties, festivals, weddings, funerals, business meetings, and other special occasions. Our rental business model will offer _____ (men/women/pregnant women/children?) a more economical way to look fashionable.

Budget-conscious fashion lovers will be an ideal target market for our subscription clothing rental company. Another ideal customer base will consist of individuals going through temporary stages of rapid size change. This includes pregnant women and small children. Rather than paying full price for clothing that won't fit in just a few months, these consumers will be able to simply rent items in their current size.

Marketing Strategy

The foundation for this plan is a combination of primary and secondary research, upon which the marketing strategies are built. Discussions and interviews were held with a variety of individuals and other area retail small businesses to develop financial and proforma detail. We consulted census data, county business patterns, and other directories to develop the market potential and competitive situation.

Our market strategy will be based on a cost-effective approach to reach this defined target market. The basic approach to promote our clothing rental services will be through establishing relationships with key influencers in the community and then through referral activities, once a significant client base has been established.

____(company name) will focus on developing loyal client relationships by offering clothing rental services based on the customer's need for time-saving convenience, selection recommendation support, and economic savings. The newest wraparound service offerings, stylist and customer service staff accessibility and value-based rental fee pricing will all serve to differentiate our company from the other providers. With the help of an aggressive marketing plan, ____ (company name) expects to experience steady growth. __ (company name) also plans to attract its members through the use of fashion magazine advertisements, circulating flyers, a systematic series of direct mailings, press releases in newspapers and on the internet, an interactive content-based website, and online Yellow Page and review directories. We will also become an active member of the local Chamber of Commerce.

Marketing Objectives
1. Maintain steady, high rates of growth each month.
2. Generate a __ percent increase in referrals monthly.
3. Expand the rental industry into a legitimate alternative to clothing purchases.

Critical Risks

Management recognizes there are several internal and external risks inherent in our business concept. Quality, selection, cash savings, value pricing and convenience will be key factors in the consumers' decision to utilize our rental services. Consumers must be willing to accept our one-stop clothing rental services and become repeat and referral members for the business to meet its sales projections. Building a loyal and trusting relationship with our members, suppliers and referral partners will be a key component to the success of _____ (company name). Furthermore, we must stay in touch with changes in consumer acquisition and usage trends.

Customer Service
We will take every opportunity to help the customer, regardless of what the revenue might be. We will outshine our competition by doing something "extra" and offering added-value services in a timely manner. We will take a long-term perspective and focus on the client's possible lifetime value to our business. By giving careful consideration to customer responsiveness, _____ (company name) goal will be to meet and exceed every service expectation. Quality service, and quick and informed responsiveness will be the philosophy guiding a customer-centric approach to our Subscription Clothing Rental Company.

Business Plan Objectives
This business plan serves to detail the direction, vision, and planning necessary to achieve our goal of providing a superior Subscription Clothing Rental Company shopping experience. The purpose of this document is to provide a strategic business plan for our company and to support a request for a $ _____, five-year bank loan to purchase inventory and supplies, as part of the financing for a start-up Subscription Clothing Rental Company. The plan has been adjusted to reflect the particular strengths and weaknesses of _____ (company name). Actual financial performance will be tracked closely, and the business plan will be adjusted when necessary to ensure that full profit potential and loan repayment is realized on schedule. The plan will also help us to identify and quantify objectives, track and direct growth and create benchmarks for measuring success.

The Company
The business ____(will be/was) incorporated on ____ (date) in the state of ___, as a _____ ("S/C" Corporation/LLC), and intends to register for Sub-chapter 'S' status for federal tax purposes. This will effectively shield the owner(s) from personal liability and double taxation.

Business Goals
Our business goal is to continue to develop the _____ (company name) brand name. To do so, we plan to execute on the following:
1. To provide high quality. designer clothing rental services to our members.
2. Focus on quality controls and ongoing operational excellence.
3. Recruit and train the very best ethical employees and talented stylists.
4. Create a marketing campaign with a consistent brand look and message content.
5. To grow at a steady and manageable rate.

Location
_____ (company name) will be located in the ___ (complex name) on _____ (address) in __ (city), __ (state). The __ (purchased/leased) _____ (warehouse/commercial/retail?) space will be easily accessible and provides ample parking for __ (#) members and ___ (#) support staff. The location is attractive due to the area demographics, which reflect

our middle to upper-middle class target customer profile.

Competitive Edge

_____ (company name) will compete well in our market by offering competitive rental prices on an expanded line of quality, designer clothing brands, creating other innovative services, training a knowledgeable and approachable staff, and by using the latest software to manage inventory and improve member satisfaction, and enable convenient online ordering and returns. Furthermore, we will maintain an excellent reputation for trustworthiness and integrity with the communities we serve.

Recap of competitive advantages accruing to members:
- Able to try a variety of clothes that are not readily available in local retail boutiques.
- Able to try outfits on, in the comfort of own home.
- Do not have to do laundry (ever again?).
- Faster service possible by email advising company of planned return items.
- Free online chats with a Professional Style Consultant
- Able to prioritize 'favorites' in virtual closet containing 25 selected items.
- Can wear and buy items for significantly less than the suggested retail price.
- Able to get the latest fashion trends and update wardrobe with items delivered direct to home.
- Never have to wear the same outfit twice.
- Free shipping on all transactions.
- Unlimited 'returns' policy.
- No hidden fees.
- Provide standardized pattern sizes or 'straight sizes' and distribution channels for plus-size designers.
- Expanding the clothing options for plus-size and _____ (pregnant?) women.
- Members not responsible for normal wear and tear on garments.
- Able to post notes on previously rented items.
- Allows members to familiarize themselves with the sizes of different brands and find what works best for them before committing to an investment.
- Bringing in styles that our members say, in their feedback, are not readily accessible in the standard _____ (plus-size?) market.
- Developed partnerships with emerging designers, such as those launching a new _____ (business-wear?) line, to bring in new exclusive products and sustain a competitive edge in the marketplace.
- Work with designers to translate their patterns into proper-fitting _____ (plus-size) patterns to match our customer fit needs.
- Able to review contents of next proposed shipment to make personalized swap-out/in decisions.

Member Retention Strategies

We will pursue the following primary member retention strategies:
1. The use of data to understand our customers, their likes and dislikes, their shopping behavior patterns, etc., and personalize our rental services accordingly.
2. The use of style consultants to enrich the personalized fashion discovery process.

3. The carrying of exclusive private label or designer branded garments.
4. The removal of the fear of commitment to a subscription because of an easy cancellation process, no late fees, a free and assisted 'returns' process, and curated fashion proposals, with the member making the ultimate rental decisions.
5. The giving to subscribers the following easy options: rent, buy, return or cancel.
6. The building of a dimension of fun and surprise subscriber rewards or bonus extras into the shipment receiving process.
7. The offering of 'Live Chats' with stylists to enable more member input.
8. The offering of the same item in two sizes so that customers may try them on and choose the better fit.

Source:
https://blog.oceanx.com/7-factors-driving-subscription-acquisition-and-retention

The Management Team

_____ (company name) will be led by _____ (owner name) and _____ (co-owner name). ____ (owner name) has a _____ degree from _____ (institution name) and a _____ background within the ____ (fashion?) industry, having spent ____ (#) years with ____ (former employer name or type of business). During this tenure, ___ (he/she) helped grow the business from $_____ in yearly revenue to over $___. ____ (co-owner name) has a ___ (IT?) background, and while employed by __ was able to increase operating profit by __ percent. These acquired skills, work experiences and educational backgrounds will play a big role in the success of our Subscription Clothing Rental Company. Additionally, our president, _____ (name), has an extensive knowledge of the ___ area and has identified a niche market retail opportunity to make this venture highly successful, combining his __(#) years of work experience in a variety of businesses. ____ (owner name) will manage all aspects of the business and service development to ensure effective customer responsiveness while monitoring day-to-day operations. Qualified and trained clerks personally trained by ___(owner name) in customer service skills will provide additional support services. Support staff will be added as seasonal or extended hours mandate.

Recap of Past Successful Accomplishments

_____ (company name) is uniquely qualified to succeed due to the following past successes:

1. **Entrepreneurial Track Record**: The owners and management team have helped to launch numerous successful ventures, including a _____.

2. **Key Milestones Achieved**: The founders have invested $___ to-date to staff the company, build the core technology, acquire starting inventory, test market the _____ (product/service), realize sales of $_____ and launch the website.

Start-up Funding

_____ (owner name) will financially back the new business venture with an initial investment of $_____ and will be the principal owner. Additional funding in the amount of $_____ will be sought from _____, a local commercial bank, with a SBA loan guarantee. This money will be needed to start the company. This loan will provide start-up capital and financing for a selected site lease, leasehold improvements, designer clothing inventory purchases, pay for permits and licensing, staff training and certification, equipment and working capital to cover operational expenses during the first year of operation.

Financial Projections

We plan to open for business on ___(target date). __ (company name) is forecasted to gross in excess of $___ in sales in its first year of operation, ending ___ (month/ year). Profit margins are forecasted to be at about __ percent. Second year operations will produce a net profit of $__. This will be generated from an investment of $__ in initial capital. It is expected that payback of our total invested capital will be realized in less than __ (#) months of operation. It is further forecasted that cash flow becomes positive from operations in year __ (one?). We project that our net profits will increase from $___ to over $ __ over the next three years.

Financial Profile Summary

Key Indicator	2019	2020	2021
Total Revenue			
Expenses			
Gross Margin			
Operating Income			
Net Income			
EBITDA			

EBITDA = Revenue - Expenses (excluding tax, interest, depreciation and amortization)
    EBITDA is essentially net income with interest, taxes, depreciation, and amortization added back to it, and can be used to analyze and compare profitability between companies and industries because it eliminates the effects of financing and accounting decisions.
Gross Margin (%) = (Revenue - Cost of Goods Sold) / Revenue
Net Income = Total revenue - Cost of sales - Other expenses - Tax

Exit Strategy

If the business is very successful, _____ (owner name) may seek to sell the business to a third party for a significant, earnings multiple. Most likely, the Company will hire a qualified business broker to sell the business on behalf of _____ (company name). Based on historical numbers, the business could generate a sales premium of up to __(#) times earnings.

Summary

Through a combination of a proven business model and a strong management team to guide the organization, _____ (company name) will be a long lasting, profitable business. We believe our ability to create future subscription apparel and accessories rental service opportunities and growth strategies will only be limited by our imagination and our ability to attract talented people who understand the concepts of branding, customer profiling and 'big data' analysis.

1.1.0 Tactical Objectives (select -3)

The following tactical objectives will specify quantifiable results and involve activities that can be easily tracked. They will also be realistic, tied to specific marketing strategies and serve as a good benchmark to evaluate our marketing plan success. (Select Choices)

1. Earn and maintain a rating as one of the best Subscription Clothing Rental Companies in the ___ (city).
2. Establish and maintain ___ (30?) % minimum gross profit margins.
3. Achieve a profitable return on investment within ___ (two?) years.
4. Earn a ___ (15?) % internal rate of return for investors over the life of the lease.
5. Recruit fashion-oriented and motivated staff by ___ (date).
6. Capture an increasing share of the commuter traffic passing through_____.
7. Offer our members superior subscription rental plan options at affordable prices.
8. Create a company whose primary goal is to exceed member expectations.
9. To develop a cash flow that is capable of paying all salaries, as well as grow the business, by the end of the _____ (first?) year.
10. To be an active networking participant and productive member of the community by _____ (date).
11. Create over _____ (40?) % of business revenues from repeat members by _____ (date).
12. Achieve an overall member satisfaction rate of ____ (98?) % by _____ (date).
13. Get a business website designed, built and operational by _____ (date), which will include an online shopping cart.
14. Achieve total sales revenues of $_____ in _____ (year).
15. Achieve net income more than ___ percent of net sales by the ____ (#) year.
16. Increase overall sales by _____ (20?) percent from prior year through superior service and word-of-mouth referrals.
17. Reduce the cost of new customer acquisition by ___ % to $ ___ by _____ (date).
18. Provide employees with continuing training, benefits and incentives to reduce the employee turnover rate to _____ %.
19. To pursue a growth rate of ____ (20?) % per year for the first ____ (#) years.
20. Enable the owner to draw a salary of $ _____ by the end of year _____ (one?).
21. To reach cash break-even by the end of year _____ (one?).
22. Increase market share to ___ percent over the next ___ (#) months.
23. Become one of the top ___ (#) players in the emerging subscription rental category in ___ (#) months.
24. Increase Operating Profit by ___ percent versus the previous year.
25. Achieve market share leadership in the clothing rental category by _____ (date).

1.1.1 Strategic Objectives

We will seek to work toward the accomplishment of the following strategic objectives, which relate back to our Mission and Vision Statements:
1. Improve the overall quality of our subscription clothing rental services.
2. Make the buyer experience better, faster and more customer friendly.
3. Strengthen personal relationships with members.
4. Enhance affordability and accessibility.
5. Foster a spirit of innovation.
6. Get the average total costs per order spent on operations, such as logistics and dry-cleaning, below __ (40?) percent.
7. In Year 3, to have sales more than double first year level and net income of at least 10% of sales.

1.2.0 Mission Statement   (select)

Our Mission Statement is a written statement that spells out our organization's overall goal, provides a sense of direction and acts as a guide to decision making for all levels of management. In developing the following mission statement, we will encourage input from employees, volunteers, and other stakeholders, and publicize it broadly in our website and other marketing materials.

Our mission is to help members to find the outfit of their dreams, at a very affordable rental fee. We want to make certain the experience of renting a special occasion dress is a pleasurable one. Our mission is to make fashion readily accessible for everyone. Our mission is to help empower women to buy less and wear more. Our mission is to apply our fashion rental model to more-personal items and enable unprecedented, affordable access to the more expensive fashion items and accessories.

Our mission is to provide superior customer service and create a shopping experience that is relaxed, hassle-free and pleasurable. We also believe in providing a working environment for our employees that is professional and fun, and that empowers our employees to be trustworthy and valuable resources to our members.

____ (company name) will strive to provide quality rental apparel and accessories that appeal to a more sophisticated modern woman, combined with excellent customer service to encourage positive public response and create a loyal customer base. We will organize our location, hours, products, rental terms, staffing and staff schedule to create a positive and effective environment to achieve our mission and to ensure future growth. Our goal is to set ourselves apart from the competition by making customer satisfaction our number one priority and to provide customer service that is responsive, informed and respectful.

1.2.1 Mantra

We will create a mantra for our organization that is three or four words long. Its purpose will be to help employees truly understand why the organization exists. Our mantra will

serve as a framework through which to make decisions about product and business direction. It will boil the key drivers of our company down to a sentence that defines our most important areas of focus and resemble a statement of purpose or significance.
Our Mantra is _____

1.2.2　　Core Values Statement

The following Core Values will help to define our organization, guide our behavior, underpin operational activity and shape the strategies we will pursue in the face of various challenges and opportunities. We will fulfill our mission through our commitment to:

    Being respectful and ethical to our members and employees.
    Building enduring relationships with members by fine-tuning our assessment of their fashion needs and wants.
    Seeking innovation in our subscription clothing rental industry.
    Practicing accountability to our colleagues and stakeholders.
    Pursuing continuous improvement as individuals and as a business entity.
    Performing tasks on time to satisfy the needs of our internal staff and external members.
    Taking active part in the organization to meet the objectives and the establishment of continuous and lasting relationships.
    Offering professional treatment to our members, employees, shareholders, and the community.
    Continuing pursuit of new technologies for the development of the projects that add value for our members, employees, shareholders, and the community.
    Personal and professional improvement through education and training.
    Teamwork to achieve our goals and vision for the future.
    Honesty and integrity in all areas of our professional relationships.
    Loyalty to the team and dedication to achieving our mission.

1.3　Vision Statement　　　　　　　　　　　　　　　(select)

The following Vision Statement will communicate both the purpose and values of our organization. For employees, it will give direction about how they are expected to behave and inspire them to give their best. Shared with members, it will shape members' understanding of why they should work with our organization.

___ (company name) will strive to become one of the most respected and favored Subscription Clothing Rental Companies in the __ area. It is our desire to become a landmark business in _____ (city), ____ (state), and become known not only for the quality of our designer products and subscription clothing rental services, but also for our community outreach and charity involvement.

_____ (company name) will be dedicated to operating with a constant enthusiasm for learning about the subscription clothing rental business, being receptive to implementing new ideas, and maintaining a willingness to adapt to changing fashion trends, and customer needs and wants. To be an active and vocal member of the community, and to provide continual reinvestment through participation in community activities and financial contributions. To incorporate the use of more state-of-the-art technologies to provide high-quality services, and thereby improve the effectiveness, efficiency and competitiveness of the subscription business.

1.4 Keys to Success

In broad terms, the success factors relate to providing what our members want and doing what is necessary to be better than our competitors. The following critical success factors are areas in which our organization must excel in order to operate successfully and achieve our objectives:

1. Must develop a close working relationship with members and designers.
2. Generate and preserve a reputation of being a one-stop-shop for clothing and accessories rentals.
3. Establish a strong referral network among others in the fashion industry.
4. Provide exceptional customer service to generate referrals.
5. Maintain a fresh mix of updated, trend conscious inventory.
6. Contact each designer to set up an account and establish a working relationship.
7. Use creativity to design web garment display pages.
8. The style consultants should have knowledge about the fashion trends, have sense of style, and should be able to assist the members on their selection of clothes.
9. New product and service innovation is seen as the key to attracting and retaining members.
10. Computerized inventory and sales records will allow the company to identify and exploit best-selling products, match volumes and profitability to service levels, anticipate demand, manage cash flows, assist with revenue growth plans, and optimize supplier/distributor relationships.
11. Offer garment rentals specifically tailored for the tastes of the area.
12. Secure regular and ongoing customer feedback.
13. The offering of good quality clothing at competitive rental prices.
14. Launch a website to showcase our services and customer testimonials, provide helpful information and facilitate online rental order placement.
15. Local community involvement and strategic business partnerships with other fashion industry service providers.
16. Conduct a targeted and cost-effective marketing campaign that seeks to differentiate our one-stop, convenient services from competitor offerings.
17. Institute a pay-for-performance component to the employee compensation plan.
18. Control costs and manage budgets at all times in accordance with company goals.
19. Institute management processes and controls to insure the consistent replication of operations.
20. Recruit screened employees with a passion for delivering exceptional service.
21. Institute an employee training to ensure the best techniques are consistently practiced.
22. Network aggressively within the community, as word of mouth will be our

most powerful advertising asset.
23. Retain members with added-value to generate repeat purchases and initiate referrals.
24. Utilize competitive pricing in conjunction with a differentiated service business model.
25. Build our brand awareness, which will drive members to increase their usage of our services and make referrals.
26. Business planning with the flexibility to make changes based on gaining new insightful perspectives as we proceed.
27. Build trust by circulating to our Code of Ethics and Service Guarantees.
28. Partner with producers and designers who can offer unique products.
29. Work with a lawyer to develop a well-conceived rental agreement.
30. Offer a wide selection of clothing styles and designer brands.
31. Attentive customer attention is required to make each customer feel like this is their special occasion.
32. Develop the systems so that the garments arrive on time and in perfect condition or suffer the reverberating negative consequences.
33. Must build a robust customer relationship management (CRM) strategy to capture the millennial user and make them repeat customers.
34. Ask members to provide feedback on how each and every garment fits, to collect significant amounts of data, and use that data to really personalize and recommend items to each and every member on an individual basis, based on likelihood of fit and sense of fashion match.
Source: www.fastcompany.com/3064748/how-gwynnie-bee-is-personalizing-the-plus-size-fashion-experience
35. Must continually add new items to the collection to maintain subscriber interest.
36. Continually work to perfect the algorithm, which functions as a virtual stylist, by fine-tuning how it understands customer needs based on their measurements, age, life stage, gender, location, season, fashion aspirations, the choice of items they put into their "closet", customer feedback and returns.
37. Assemble an analytics team to look at ideal rental periods and best shipping methods, and garment rental statistics, such as what dress styles, colors and sizes are seeing the most rentals to make good future inventory purchase decisions.
38. Find a shipping company that can deliver on time and at the right cost.
39. Enable subscribers to leave detailed reviews of their rentals on the website, including bedroom-mirror or office-bathroom selfies, along with intimate information, like weight, bust and waist measurements.
40. Collect data how many times a rental was worn and to what sort of occasion, and whether she liked it, loved it, or didn't care for it at all.
41. Create a personalized home page for each user, offering suggestions for future selections.
42. Make certain that every returned item goes through an extensive cleaning and sanitation process, and finally a 'smell test'.
43. Key plan components include: members can decide if they want to opt-out, pick products with recommendations based on data but let the customer ultimately pick the items they want, when they want.

44. Capitalize on the fact that 'Google Search' is the biggest source of customers for subscription companies and 'Social Media' is second.
Source: www.forbes.com/sites/richardkestenbaum/2017/08/10/subscription-businesses-are-exploding-with-growth/#3c8253666678
45. Because there is so much competition in the subscription market, continually need to assess price points, value proposition, value-added benefits, assortments, and ability to meet the customer's changing needs and preferences.
46. Seize every opportunity to surprise, delight, learn from quizzes, transaction histories (big data), feedback, and then curate shipments and educate subscribers.
47. Must learn how to sustain the experiential sense of a personalized surprise, and to do that by constantly broadening the knowledge of the subscribers and range of fashions offered.
Source: www.retaildive.com/news/why-retailers-are-going-all-in-on-subscription-services/445971/
48. Use A/B Testing to quickly determine which website design features are most likely to get visitors to click on our subscriber registration button.
49. Issue regular 'style tips' via blogs, articles and e-newsletters to keep members engaged.

2.0 Company Summary

_____ (company name) will be a subscription clothing rental company that will ride the popularity of the new 'sharing economy'. It will be able to service the continental United States via the internet, big data analysis and the US Postal Service.

Our goal is to be the one-stop-shop for all items related to the fashion world, and to provide a fulfilling, hassle-free, cash saving experience for our members. The consumers of our subscription service will get affordable access to high fashion garments, by well-known designers, the way they want it, that is, with a minimal cash outlay and with the ability to return it when the event is over, the fascination wears off (the thrill is gone) or the trend moves on. Our goal will be to offer a great selection of basics and statement pieces from contemporary designer brands, such as NYDJ and London Times.
Our appeal will rest on the fact that we will provide a personalized, curated and guided or professional stylist supported subscription clothing rental experience, based on personal style quiz responses, transaction 'big data' analysis, virtual closet selections, proposed shipment items being swapped in/out by members, software algorithmic calculations, fashion trends and local geographic influences, including near-term weather forecasts.

_____ (company name) is a start-up _____ (Corporation/Limited Liability Company) consisting of _____ (#) principle officers with combined industry experience of _____ (#) years. The owner of the company will be investing $ ___ of _____ (his/her) own capital into the company and will also be seeking a loan of $ __ to cover start-up costs and future growth. __ (company name) will be located in a ____ (purchased/rented) _____ (suite/complex) in the _____ on _____ (address) in _____ (city), __ (state). The owner, _____, has ___ (#) years of experience in managing _____ (retail businesses?).

The company plans to use its existing contacts and customer base to generate short-term revenues. Its long-term profitability will rely on focusing on referrals, networking within community organizations and a comprehensive marketing program that includes public relations activities and a structured referral program.

Sales are expected to reach $_____ within the first year and to grow at a conservative rate of _____ (20?) percent during the next two to five years.

Facilities Renovations

The necessary renovations are itemized as follows:	Estimate
Partition of space into private offices.	_____
Build garment storage racks.	_____
Painting and other general cosmetic repairs	_____
Install work tables and shelving units.	_____
Install communication lines and computer equipment	_____
Install laundering equipment.	_____
Other _____	_____
Total:	_____

Hours of Operations
_____ (company name) will open for business on _____ (date) and will maintain the following business hours:
- Monday through Thursday: _____ (7 AM to 6 PM?)
- Friday: _____
- Saturday: _____
- Sunday: _____

The company will invest in customer relationship management software (CRM) to track real-time sales data and collect customer information, including names, email addresses, key reminder dates and preferences. This information will be used with email, e-newsletter and direct mail campaigns to build personalized fulfillment programs, establish customer loyalty and drive revenue growth.

2.0.1 Test Marketing (optional)

We will use the following methods to help test market our subscription clothing rental service and make an informed 'go/no-go' business decision before investing larger sums of money:

1. Solicit justified feedback from industry experts and other investors.
2. Track the response rate from free classified ads placed on Craigslist.
3. Gain insights from a clothing rental companies in other geographic markets.
4. Build a prototype and use a survey to ask potential buyers for feedback.
5. Purchase a limited quantity of goods to be marketed through online sales channels, such as amazon and online auctions such as eBay.
6. Exhibit at festivals, fairs, trade shows and flea markets to obtain reaction to products and services.
6. Offer a special beta release or pre-release version of the service to a select group of members in exchange for feedback.
7. Make an offer through social networking portals like Twitter or Facebook noting that the first people to reply will get access to special limited time benefits.
8. Release the service to a test group at a drastically reduced price to gauge interest for the rental service and learn how to refine it.
9. Make the discounted sales strategy offer contingent on a response to surveys or questions about the service.
10. Hire or form a market research group to conduct focus groups with prospective members.
11. Compare the service to others on the market to make sure that something about the new service either improves on an existing service or meets a need better than it can be met by something that's currently available.
12. Use a commissioned sales representative to sample the local market demand and secure future sale dates.
13. Offer the rental service through an appropriate end user outlet and price the service as though it were in production, even though each rental may result in a loss.

14. Issue a press release to appropriate fashion trade publications to gauge response to the subscription clothing rental service.
15. Encourage comments to a Youtube.com video about our business model concept.

2.0.2 Traction (optional)

We will include this section because investors expect to see some traction, both before and after a funding event and investors tend to judge past results as a good indicator of future projections. It will also show that we can manage our operations and develop a business model capable of funding inventory purchases. Traction will be the best form of market research and present evidence of customer acceptance.

Period _____
Product/Service Focus _____
Our Sales to Date: _____
Our Number of Users to Date: _____
Number of Repeat Users _____
Number of Pending Orders: _____
Value of Pending Orders: _____
Reorder Cycle: _____
Key Reference Sites _____
Mailing List Subscriptions _____
Competitions/Awards Won _____
Notable Product Reviews _____
Actual Percent Gross Profit Margin _____
Industry Average: GPM _____
Actual B/(W) Industry Average _____

Note: Percent Gross Profit Margin equals the sales receipts less the cost of goods sold divided by sales receipts multiplied by 100.

2.1 Company Ownership

_____ (company name) is a _____ (Sole-proprietorship /Corporation/Limited Liability Corporation (LLC)) and is registered to the principal owner, _____ (owner name). The company was formed in _____ (month) of ____ (year). It will be registered as a Subchapter S to avoid double taxation, with ownership allocated as follows: ____ (owner name) __ % and ____ (owner name) ____ %.

Resources:
www.businessnewsdaily.com/8163-choose-legal-business-structure.html
www.nerdwallet.com/blog/small-business/online-legal-tools/
www.legalzone.com

The owner is a _____ (year) graduate of _____ (institution name), in _____ (city, ____ (state), with a _____ degree. He/she _____ has a second

degree in _____ and certification as a _____. He/she also has ____ years of executive experience in the _____ (?) industry as a _____, performing the following roles: _____.
His/her major accomplishments include: _____

Ownership Breakdown:

Shareholder Name	Responsibilities	Number and Class of Shares	Percent Ownership

The remainder of the issued and outstanding common shares are retained by the Company for ___(future distribution / allocation under the Company's employee stock option plan).

Shareholder Loans

The Company currently has outstanding shareholder loans in the aggregate sum of $_____. The following table sets out the details of the shareholder loans.

Shareholder Name	Loan Amount	Loan Date	Balance Outstanding

Directors

The Company's Board of Directors, which is made up of highly qualified business and industry professionals, will be a valuable asset to the Company and be instrumental to its development. The following persons will make up the Board of Directors of the Company:

Name of Person	Educational Background	Past Industry Experience	Other Companies Served

2.2 Company Licensing & Liability Protection

Our Subscription Clothing Rental Company business will consider the need to acquire the following types of insurances. This will require extensive comparison shopping, through several insurance brokers, listed with our state's insurance department:

1. Workers' Compensation Insurance
2. Business Policy: Property & Liability Insurance
3. Health insurance.
4. Commercial Auto Insurance
5. State Unemployment Insurance
6. Business Interruption Insurance (Business Income Insurance)
7. Disability Insurance
8. Life Insurance

9.	Cyber Liability Insurance

We will carry business liability and property insurance and any other insurance we deem necessary after receiving counsel from our lawyer and insurance agent. Health insurance and workers' compensation will be provided for our full-time employees as part of their benefit package. We feel that this is mandatory to ensure that they do not leave the company for one that does offer these benefits. Workers' Compensation covers employees in case of harm attributed to the workplace. The Property and Liability Insurance protects the building from theft, fire, natural disasters, and being sued by a third party. Life and Disability Insurance may be required if a bank loan is obtained.

Liability Insurance includes protection in the face of day-to-day accidents, unforeseen results of normal business activities, and allegations of abuse or molestation, food poisoning, or exposure to infectious disease.

Property Insurance - Property Insurance should take care of the repairs less whatever deductible you have chosen.

Loss of Income Insurance will replace our income during the time the business is shut-down. Generally, this coverage is written for a fixed amount of monthly income for a fixed number of months.

Product Liability Insurance covers injuries caused by products that are designed, sold or specified by the practice.

Cyber Liability Insurance will protect our website from cyber-crimes, such viruses, hackers stealing confidential information, and identity theft. So if a hacker steals a customer's identity, and the customer sues our business, the legal costs are covered by cyber liability.

Resource: www.boltinsurance.com

To help save on insurance cost and claims, management will do the following:
1.	Stress employee safety in our employee handbook.
2.	Screen employees with interview questionnaires and will institute pre-employment drug tests and comprehensive background checks.
3.	Videotape our equipment and inventory for insurance purposes.
4.	Create an operations manual that shares safe techniques.
5.	Limit the responsibilities that we choose to accept in our contracts.
6.	Consider the financial impact of assuming the exposure ourselves.
7.	Establish loss prevention programs to reduce the hazards that cause losses.
8.	Consider taking higher deductibles on anything but that which involves liability insurance because of third-party involvement.
9.	Stop offering services that require expensive insurance coverage or require signed releases from members using those services.
10.	Improve employee training and initiate training sessions for safety.
11.	Require Certificate of Insurance from all subcontractors.

12. Make members and staff responsible for a portion of any damages they cause.
13. We will consider a partial reimbursement of health club membership as a benefit.
14. We will find out what employee training will reduce rates and get our employees involved in these programs.
15. We will investigate the setting-up of a partial self-insurance plan.
16. Convince underwriters that our past low claims are the result of our ongoing safety programs and there is reason to expect our claims will be lower than industry averages in the future.
17. At each renewal, we will develop a service agreement with our broker and get their commitment to our goals, such as a specific reduction in the number of incidents.
18. We will assemble a risk control team, with people from both sides of our business, and broker representatives will serve on the committee as well.
19. When an employee is involved in an accident, we will insist on getting to the root cause of the incident and do everything possible to prevent similar incidents from re-occurring.
20. At renewal, we will consult with our brokers to develop a cost-saving strategy and decide whether to bid out our coverage for competitive quotes or stick with our current carrier.
21. We will set-up a captive insurance program, as a risk management technique, where our business will form its own insurance company subsidiary to finance its retained losses in a formal structure.
22. Review named assets (autos and equipment), drivers and/or key employees identified on policies to make sure these assets and people are still with our company.
23. As a portion of our business changes, that is, closes, operations change, or outsourcing occurs, we will eliminate unnecessary coverage.
24. We will make sure our workforce is correctly classified by our workers' compensation insurer and liability insurer because our premiums are based on the type of workers used.
25. We will become active in Trade Organizations or Professional Associations, because as a benefit of membership, our business may receive substantial insurance discounts.
26. We will adopt health specific changes to our work place, such as adopting a no smoking policy at our company and allow yoga or weight loss classes to be held in our break room.

The required business insurance package will be provided by _____ (insurance carrier name). The business will open with a _____ (#) million-dollar liability insurance policy, with an annual premium cost of $ _____.

The business will need to acquire the following special licenses, accreditations, certifications and permits:
1. A Sales Tax License is required through the State Department of Revenue.
2. Use Tax Registration Certificate
3. A County and/or City Occupational License.

4. Business License from State Licensing Agency
5. Permits from the Fire Department and State Health Department.
6. Building Code Inspections by the County Building Department.
7. Building Sign Permit.

Note: In most states, you are legally required to obtain a business license, and a dba certificate. A business license is usually a flat tax assessment and a percentage of your gross income. A dba stands for Doing Business As, and it is the registration of your trade name if you have one. You will be required to register your trade name within 30 days of starting your business. Instead of registering a dba, you can simply form an LLC or Corporation and it will have the same effect, namely register your business name.

Note: Check with your local County Clerk and State Offices or Chamber of Commerce to make sure you follow all legal protocols for setting up and running your business.

Resources:
Insurance Information Institute   www.iii.org/individuals/business/
National License Directory   www.sba.gov/licenses-and-permits
National Association of Surety Bond Producers   www.nasbp.org
Independent Insurance Agents & Brokers of America   www.iiaa.org
Find Law   http://smallbusiness.findlaw.com/starting-business/starting-business-licenses-permits/starting-business-licenses-permits-guide.html
Business Licenses   www.iabusnet.org/business-licenses
Legal Zoom   www.legalzoom.com
Business Filings   www.bizfilings.com

Resources:
Workers Compensation Regulations
   http://www.dol.gov/owcp/dfec/regs/compliance/wc.htm#IL
New Hire Registration and Reporting
   www.homeworksolutions.com/new-hire-reporting-information/
State Tax Obligations
   www.sba.gov/content/learn-about-your-state-and-local-tax-obligations
Resource:
www/sba.gov/content/what-state-licenses-and-permits-does-your-business-need

2.3 Start-up To-Do Checklist

1. Describe your business concept and model, with special emphasis on planned multiple revenue streams and services to be offered.
2. Create Business Plan and Opening Menu of Products and Services.
3. Determine startup costs of bridal boutique business, and operating capital and capital budget needs.
4. Seek and evaluate alternative financing options, including SBA guaranteed loan, equipment leasing, social networking loan (www.prosper.com) and/or a family loan (www.virginmoney.com).

5. Do a name search: Check with County Clerk Office or Department of Revenue and Secretary of State to see if the proposed name of business is available.
6. Decide on a legal structure for business.
Common legal structure options include Sole Proprietorship, Partnership, Corporation or Limited Liability Corporation (LLC).
7. Make sure you contact your State Department of Revenue, Secretary of State, and the Internal Revenue Service to secure EIN Number and file appropriate paperwork. Also consider filing for Sub-Chapter S status with the Federal government to avoid the double taxation of business profits.
8. Protect name and logo with trademarks, if plan is to go national.
9. Find a suitable location with proper zoning for a Subscription Clothing Rental Company.
10. Research necessary permits and requirements your local government imposes on your type of business. (Refer to: www.business.gov & www.ttb.gov)
11. Call for initial inspections to determine what must be done to satisfy Fire Marshall, and Building Inspector requirements.
12. Adjust our budget based on build-out requirements.
13. Negotiate lease or property purchase contract.
14. Obtain a building permit.
15. Obtain Federal Employee Identification Number (FEIN).
16. Obtain State Sales Tax ID/Exempt Certificate.
17. Open a Business Checking Account.
18. Obtain Merchant Credit Card /PayPal Account.
19. Obtain City and County Business Licenses
20. Create a prioritized list for equipment, furniture and décor items.
21. Comparison shop and arrange for appropriate insurance coverage with product liability insurance, public liability insurance, commercial property insurance and worker's compensation insurance.
22. Locate and purchase all necessary equipment and furniture prior to final inspections.
23. Get contractor quotes for required alterations and rack installations.
24 Manage the alterations process.
25. Obtain information and price quotes from possible fashion distributors and designer manufacturers.
26. Set a tentative opening date.
27. Install 'Coming Soon' sign in front of building and begin word-of-mouth advertising campaign.
28. Document the ordering, rental, returns, data analysis and payment process flows.
29. Create your member profiling, accounting, purchasing, payroll, marketing, loss prevention, employee screening and other management systems.
30. Start the employee interview process based on established job descriptions and interview criteria.
31. Contact and interview the following service providers: uniform service, security service, trash service, utilities, telephone, credit card processing, bookkeeping, cleaning services, etc.
32. Schedule final inspections for premises.

33. Correct inspection problems and schedule another inspection.
34. Set a Grand Opening date after a month of regular operations to get the bugs out of the processes.
35. Make arrangements for website design.
36. Train staff.
37. Schedule a couple of practice sessions for friends and interested prospects.
38. Be accessible for direct customer feedback.
39. Distribute comment cards and surveys to solicit more constructive feedback.
40. Remain ready and willing to change the business concept and offerings to suit the needs and wants of the actual customer base.

2.3.1   EMPLOYER RESPONSIBILITIES CHECKLIST

1. Apply for your SS-4 Federal Employer Identification Number (EIN) from the Internal Revenue Service. An EIN can be obtained via telephone, mail or online.
2. Register with the State's Department of Labor (DOL) as a new employer. State Employer Registration for Unemployment Insurance, Withholding, and Wage Reporting should be completed and sent to the address that appears on the form. This registration is required of all employers for the purpose of determining whether the applicants are subject to state unemployment insurance taxes.
3. Obtain Workers Compensation and Disability Insurance from an insurer. The insurance company will provide the required certificates that should be displayed.
4. Order Federal Tax Deposit Coupons – Form 8109 – if you didn't order these when you received your EIN. To order, call the IRS at 1-800-829-1040; you will need to give your EIN. You may want to order some blanks sent for immediate use until the pre-printed ones are complete. Also ask for the current Federal Withholding Tax Tables (Circular A) – this will explain how to withhold and remit payroll taxes, and file reports.
5. Order State Withholding Tax Payment Coupons. Also ask for the current Withholding Tax Tables.
6. Have new employees complete an I-9 Employment Eligibility Verification form. You should have all employees complete this form prior to beginning work. Do not send it to Immigration and Naturalization Service – just keep it with other employee records in your files.
7. Have employees complete aW-4 Employees Withholding Allowance Certificate.

2.4.0   Company Location

_____ (company name) will be located in the _____ (residential/commercial?) area in _____ (city). The site is one of the densest and _____ (affluent?) markets in the state. Our outlet storefront will be _____ (warehouse/retail?) space in the _____ (northeast?) corner of the _____ Avenue building, facing ___, a main artery for vehicles and city buses coming and going from the complex. The facility is centered within a cluster of _____ (#) (commercial/residential?) _____ (buildings?).

_____ (company name) will be located in the _____ (complex name) in _____ (city), ___ (state). It is situated on a _____ (turnpike/street/avenue) just minutes from _____ (benchmark location), in the neighborhood of _____. It borders a large parking lot which is shared by all the businesses therein. There is parking available for _____ (#) vehicles. Important considerations relative to shop location will be competition, visibility, accessibility, signage, community growth trends, demographics, walk by foot traffic, and drive by traffic patterns.

The location has the following advantages: (Select Choices)
1. It is easy to locate and accessible to a number of major roadways.
2. Easy access from public transportation.
3. Ground level access.
4. Good neighborhood visibility and traffic flow.
5. Plentiful parking.
6. Proximity to _____ and _____ income growth areas.
7. Proximity to businesses in same affinity class with same ideal client profiles.
8. Reasonable rent.
9. Conveniently located to _____ (millennial?) customer base.
10. Proximity to the growing residential community of _____.
11. Low crime rate with good police and fire protection.
12. Outlet store located within a strip mall or shopping center with excellent foot traffic.
14. Zoning approved for a _____ (warehouse/retail?) business.

2.4.1 Company Facilities

_____ (company name) signed a _____ (#) year lease for _____ (#) square foot of space. The cost is very reasonable at $____/sq. foot. We also have the option of expanding into an additional _____ sq. ft. of space. A leasehold improvement allowance of $___ /sq. ft. would be given. Consolidated area maintenance fees would be $____/month initially. _____ (company name) has obtained a _____ (three) month option on this space effective _____ (date), the submission date of this business plan, and has deposited refundable first and last lease payments, plus a $_____ security deposit with the leasing agent.

The facilities will incorporate the following room parameters into the layout:

		Percentage	Square Footage
1.	Reception Area	_____	_____
2.	Garment Repair Workroom	_____	_____
3.	Laundering Workroom	_____	_____
4.	Supplies Storage	_____	_____
5.	Garment Display Rack Area	_____	_____
6.	Staff Room		

7. Conference Room/Classroom _____ _____
8. Shipping/Receiving Areas _____ _____
9. Admin Offices _____ _____
10. Data Center _____ _____
11. Restrooms _____ _____
Totals: _____ _____

2.5.0 Start-up Summary

The start-up costs for the Subscription Clothing Rental Company will be financed through a combination of an owner investment of $ _____ and a short-term bank loan of $ _____. The total start-up costs for this business are approximately $ _____ and can be broken down in the following major categories:

1. Leasehold and Improvements $ _____
2. Equipment and Installation Expenses $ _____
3. Development Expense $ _____
4. Office Furniture: Work Tables and Cabinets $ _____
5. Initial Product Inventory (Garments/Accessories) $ _____
6. Working Capital (6 months) $ _____
   For day-to-day operations, including payroll, etc.
7. Renovate Warehouse Space $ _____
   Includes architect, lighting update, flooring, etc.
8. Marketing/Advertising Expenses $ _____
   Includes sales brochures, direct mail, opening expenses.
8. Utility/ (Rent?) Deposits $ _____
9. Licenses and Permits $ _____
10. Contingency Funds $ _____
11. Other (Includes training, legal expenses, etc.) $ _____

The company will require $_____ in initial cash reserves and additional $_____ in assets. The start-up costs are to be financed by the equity contributions of the owner in the amount of $ _____, as well as by a ____ (#) year commercial loan in the amount of $ _____. The funds will be repaid through earnings.
These start-up expenses and funding requirements are summarized in the tables below.

2.5.1 Inventory

Inventory will typically be purchased in two seasons: fall and spring. The fall buying season is typically for items that will be displayed in the winter and spring, which will then be worn in the spring and summer. The spring buying season is typically for items that will be displayed in the summer and fall, which will then be worn in the fall and winter. Inventory audits will be conducted on a regular basis to determine the best-selling and most profitable product lines, and to reduce stock in slower moving items.

Inventory:	Supplier	Qty	Unit Cost	Total
Bags and Supplies				
Formal Gowns				
Casual Dresses				
Shirts and Blouses				
Denim and Pants				
Shirts				
Cardigans and Sweaters				
Jackets and Outerwear				
Handbags				
Jewelry				
Bubble Wrap				
Pre-paid Return Envelopes				
Shipping Boxes				
Shipping Labels				
Cleaning Supplies				
Dry-cleaning Supplies				
Spot Removers				
Fabric Fragrances				
Plastic Bags				
Garment Repair Supplies				
Ribbons				
Sequins				
Buttons				
Zippers				
Various Thread Colors				
Sewing Needles				
Office Supplies				
Marketing Materials				
Business Forms				
Rental Contracts				
Misc. Supplies				
Totals:				

Sample Clothing Rental Agreement/Contract:
https://lendingluxury.com/rental

2.5.2   Supply Sourcing

Initially, _____ (company name) will purchase its equipment from _____, inventory from _____ and supplies from _____, the _____ (second/third?) largest supplier in _____ (state), because of the discount given for bulk purchases. However, we will also maintain back-up relationships with two smaller suppliers, namely _____ and _____. These two suppliers have competitive prices on certain fashion brands.

Online Wholesale Fashion Marketplaces
    FashionDomino.com
    LAShowroom.com
    FashionGo.net
    TopTenWholesale.com
    JoorAccess.com   USA, high-end fashion
    Uppler.com   Western Europe/USA, Mass Market Fashion
    Nuorder.com   USA, Mass market fashion

Wholesale Fashion Distributors in the USA:
- Wholesale Fashion Square   www.wholesalefashionsquare.com
- Bloom Wholesale   www.bloomwholesale.com
- Sugarlips Wholesale   www.sugarlipswholesale.com
- Magnolia Fashion Wholesale   www.magnoliafashionwholesale.com
- Tasha Apparel   www.tashaapparel.com

Wholesale Fashion Distributors in China
    Chinabrands.com
    AliExpress.com
    AliBaba.com
    US.Shein.com
    Wholesale7.net
    Modlily.com

Spotting Chemicals
A.L. Wilson Chemical Company   www.alwilson.com/

Pre-used Wedding Dress Suppliers
Tradesy.com
Preownedweddingdresses.com
Nearlynewlywed.com
Bravobride.com

2.5.3   Supplier Assessments

We will use the following form to compare and evaluate suppliers, because they will play a major role in our procurement strategies and significantly contribute to our profitability.

	Supplier #1	Supplier #2	Compare
Supplier Name			
Website			
Address			
Contacts			
Annual Sales			

Distribution Channels _____
Memberships/Certifications _____
Quality System _____
Positioning _____
Pricing Strategy _____
Payment Terms _____
Discounts _____
Delivery Lead-time _____
Return Policy _____
Rebate Program _____
Technical Support _____
Core Competencies _____
Primary Product _____
Primary Service _____
New Products/Services _____
Innovative Applications/Uses _____
Competitive Advantage _____
Capital Intensity _____
State of Technology _____
Capacity Utilization _____
Price Volatility _____
Vertical Integration _____
References _____
Overall Rating _____

2.5.4 Equipment Leasing

Equipment Leasing will be the smarter solution allowing our business to upgrade our equipment needs at the end of the term rather than being overly invested in outdated equipment through traditional bank financing and equipment purchase. We also intend to explore the following benefits of leasing some of the required equipment:

1. Frees Up Capital for other uses.   2. Tax Benefits
3. Improves Balance Sheet   4. Easy to add-on or trade-up
5. Improves Cash Flow   6. Preserves Credit Lines
7. Protects against obsolescence   8. Application Process Simpler

Our leasing strategy will also be shaped by the following factors:
1. Estimated useful life of the equipment.
2. How long our business plans to use the equipment.
3. What our business intends to do with the equipment at the end of the lease.
4. The tax situation of our business.
5. The cash flow of our business.
6. Our company's specific needs for future growth.

List Any Leases:
Leasing Company   Equipment Description   Monthly   Lease   Final

Payment   Period   Disposition

Resources:
LeaseQ   www.leaseq.com
Innovative Lease Services   www.ilslease.com/equipment-leasing/

2.5.5   Funding Source Matrix

Funds Source   Amount   Interest Rate   Repayment Terms   Use

2.5.6   Distribution or Licensing Agreements   (if any)

Note: These are some of the key factors that investors will use to determine if we have a competitive advantage that is not easily copied.

Licensor   License Rights   License Term   Fee or Royalty

2.5.7   Trademarks, Patents and Copyrights (if any)

Our trademark will be virtually our branding for life. Our choice of a name for our business is very important. Not only will we brand our business and services forever, but what may be worthless today will become our most valuable asset in the years to come. A trademark search by our Lawyer will be a must, because to be told down the road that we must give up our name because we did not bother to conduct a trademark search would be a devastating blow to our business. It is also essential that the name that we choose suit the expanding product or service offerings that we plan to introduce.

Note: These are some of the key factors that investors will use to determine if we have a proprietary position or competitive advantage that is not easily copied.

Resources:
Patents/Trademarks   www.uspto.gov
Copyright   www.copyright.gov

2.5.8   Innovation Strategy   (optional)

____ (company name) will create an innovation strategy that is aligned with not only our firm's core mission and values, but also with our future technology, supplier, and growth strategies. The objective of our continuous innovation strategy will be to create a sustainable competitive advantage. Our education and training systems will be designed to equip our staff with the foundations to learn and develop the broad range of skills

needed for innovation in all of its forms, and with the flexibility to upgrade skills and adapt to changing market conditions. To foster an innovative workplace, we will ensure that employment policies facilitate efficient organizational change and encourage and reward the expression of creativity, engage in mutually beneficial strategic alliances and allocate adequate funds for research and development. Our radical innovation strategies include _____ to achieve first mover status. Our incremental innovation strategies will include modifying the following _____ (products/services/processes) to give our customers added value for their money.
Resource: https://hbr.org/2015/04/the-5-requirements-of-a-truly-innovative-company

2.5.9   Summary of Sources and Use of Funds

Sources:
Owner's Equity Investment $ _____
Requested Bank Loans $ _____
Total: $ _____

Uses:
Capital Equipment $ _____
Beginning Inventory $ _____
Start-up Costs $ _____
Working Capital $ _____
Total: $ _____

2.5.9.1   Funding to Date   (optional)

To date, _____'s (company name) founders have invested $_____ in _____ (company name), with which we have accomplished the following:
1. _____ (Designed/Built) the company's website
2. Developed content, in the form of ___ (#) articles, for the website.
3. Hired and trained our core staff of __(#) full-time people and ___ (#) part-time people.
4. Generated brand awareness by driving ___ (#) visitors to our website in a ___(#) month period.
5. Successfully _____ (Developed/Test Marketed) ___ (#) new _____ (products/services), which compete on the basis of _____.
6. _____ (Purchased/Developed) and installed the software needed to _____ (manage _____ operations?)
7. Purchased $_____ worth of _____ (supplies)
8. Purchased $_____ worth of _____ equipment.

2.6 Start-up Requirements

Start-up Expenses: Estimates
    Legal   _____   500

Accountant	_____	300
Accounting Software Package	_____	300
State Licenses & Permits	_____	
Store Set-up	_____	15000
Unforeseen Contingency	_____	3000
Market Research Survey	_____	300
Office Supplies	_____	300
Sales Brochures	_____	300
Direct Mailing	_____	500
Other Marketing Materials	_____	2000
Logo Design	_____	500
Advertising (2 months)	_____	2000
Consultants	_____	5000
Insurance	_____	
Rent (2 months security)	_____	3000
Rent Deposit	_____	1500
Utility Deposit	_____	1000
DSL Installation/Activation	_____	100
Telecommunications Installation	_____	3000
Telephone Deposit	_____	200
Expensed Leasehold Improvements	_____	10000
Expensed Equipment	_____	1000
Website Design/Hosting	_____	2000
Computer System	_____	12000
Used Office Equipment/Furniture	_____	2000
Organization Memberships	_____	300
Cleaning Supplies	_____	200
Staff Training	_____	5000
Promotional Signs	_____	7000
Security System	_____	8000
Other	_____	
Total Start-up Expenses	_____ (A)	

Start-up Assets:

Cash Balance Required	_____ (T)	15000
Start-up Equipment	_____	See schedule
Start-up Inventory	_____	See schedule
Other Current Assets	_____	
Long-term Assets	_____	
Total Assets	_____ (B)	
Total Requirements	_____ (A+B)	

Start-up Funding

Start-up Expenses to Fund	_____ (A)
Start-ups Assets to Fund	_____ (B)
Total Funding Required:	_____ (A+B)

Assets
Non-cash Assets from Start-up _____
Cash Requirements from Start-up _____ (T)
Additional Cash Raised _____ (S)
Cash Balance on Starting Date _____ (T+S=U)
Total Assets: _____ **(B)**

Liabilities and Capital
Short-term Liabilities:
Current Borrowing _____
Unpaid Expenses _____
Accounts Payable _____
Interest-free Short-term Loans _____
Other Short-term Loans _____
Total Short-term Liabilities _____ **(Z)**

Long-term Liabilities:
Commercial Bank Loan _____
Other Long-term Liabilities _____
Total Long-term Liabilities _____ **(Y)**
Total Liabilities _____ (Z+Y = C)

Capital
Planned Investment
Owner _____
Family _____
Other _____
Additional Investment Requirement _____
Total Planned Investment _____ **(F)**
Loss at Start-up (Start-up Expenses) (-) _____ **(A)**
Total Capital (=) _____ **(F+A=D)**
Total Capital and Liabilities _____ **(C+D)**
Total Funding _____ (C+F)

2.6.1　　Capital Equipment List　　　　　　(select)

Equipment Type	Model No.	New/Used	Lifespan	Quantity	Unit Cost	Total Cost
Security System						
Electronic Safe						
Counter Merchandiser						
Display Racks						
Bagging Machines						

Sewing Machines _____
Steamer _____
Spot Remover Guns _____
Dry Cleaning Equipment _____
Computer System _____
Fax Machine _____
Copy Machine _____
Security System _____
Video Surveillance System _____
Electronic Cash Register _____
Answering Machine _____
TV and DVD Player _____
Office Furniture _____
Waiting Room Furniture _____
Accounting Software _____
Microsoft Office Software _____
Shelving Units _____
Lockers _____
Hand Truck _____
Mop Station _____
Marquee Sign _____
Sewing Machine _____
Iron _____
Refrigerator _____
Microwave _____
Assorted Signs _____
Telephone headsets _____
Calculator _____
Filing & Storage Cabinets _____
Conveyer System _____
Cabinetry _____
Credit Card Verification Machine _____
Pricing Guns _____
Paper Shredder _____
Other _____

Total Capital Equipment _____

Note: Equipment costs are dependent on whether purchased new or used or leased.
All items that are assets to be used for more than one year will be considered a long-term asset and will be depreciated using the straight-line method.

2.7.0   SBA Loan Key Requirements

To be considered for an SBA loan, we must meet the basic requirements:

1. Must have been turned down for a loan by a bank or other lender to qualify for most SBA Business Loan Programs. 2. Required to submit a guaranty, both personal and business, to qualify for the loans. 3. Must operate for profit; be engaged in, or propose to do business in, the United States or its possessions; 4. Have reasonable owner equity to invest; 5. Use alternative financial resources first including personal assets.

All businesses must meet eligibility criteria to be considered for financing under the SBA's 7(a) Loan Program, including: size; type of business; operating in the U.S. or its possessions; use of available of funds from other sources; use of proceeds; and repayment. The repayment term of an SBA loan is between five and 25 years, depending on the lift of the assets being financed and the cash needs of the business. Working capital loans (accounts receivable and inventory) should be repaid in five to 10 years. The SBA also has short-term loan guarantee programs with shorter repayment terms.

A Business Owner Cannot Use an SBA Loan: To purchase real estate where the participant has issued a forward commitment to the developer or where the real estate will be held primarily for investment purposes. To finance floor plan needs. To make payments to owners or to pay delinquent withholding taxes. To pay existing debt, unless it can be shown that the refinancing will benefit the small business and that the need to refinance is not indicative of poor management.

SBA Loan Programs:
Low Doc: www.sba.gov/financing/lendinvest/lowdoc.html
SBA Express www.sba,gov/financing/lendinvest/sbaexpress.html
Basic 7(a) Loan Guarantee Program
For businesses unable to obtain loans through standard loan programs. Funds can be used for general business purposes, including working capital, leasehold improvements and debt refinancing.   www.sba.gov/financing/sbaloan/7a.html
Certified Development Company 504 Loan Program
Used for fixed asset financing such as purchase of real estate or machinery.
    www. Sba.gov/gopher/Local-Information/Certified-Development-Companies/
MicroLoan 7(m) Loan Program
Provides short-term loans up to $35,000.00 for working capital or purchase of fixtures. www.sba.gov/financing/sbaloan/microloans.html

2.7.1   Other Financing Options

1. Grants:
   Health care grants, along with education grants, represent the largest percentage of grant giving in the United States. The federal government, state, county and city governments, as well as private and corporate foundations all award grants. The largest percentage of grants are awarded to non-profit organizations, health care agencies, colleges and universities, local government agencies, tribal institutions, and schools. For profit organizations are generally not eligible for

grants unless they are conducting research or creating jobs.
- A. Contact your state licensing office.
- B. Foundation Grants to Individuals: www.fdncenter.org
- C. US Grants www.grants.gov
- D. Foundation Center www.foundationcemter.org
- E. The Grantsmanship Center www.tgci.com
- F. Contact local Chamber of Commerce
- G. The Catalog of Federal Domestic Assistance is a government-wide compendium of Federal programs, projects, services, and activities that provide assistance or benefits to the American public. It contains financial and nonfinancial assistance programs administered by departments and establishments of the Federal government. . https://www.cfda.gov/
- H. The Federal Register is a good source to keep current with the continually changing federal grants offered.
- I. FedBizOpps is a resource, as all federal agencies must use FedBizOpps to notify the public about contract opportunities worth over $25,000.
- J. Fundsnet Services http://www.fundsnetservices.com/
- K. SBA Women Business Center www.sba.gov/content/womens-business-center-grant-opportunities

Local Business Grants
Check with local businesses for grant opportunities and eligibility requirements. For example, Bank of America sponsors community grants for businesses that endeavor to improve the community or protect the environment.
Resource: www.bankofamerica.com/foundation/index.cfm?template=fd_localgrants

Green Technology Grants
If you install green technology in the business as a way to reduce waste and make the business more energy efficient, you may be eligible for grant funding. Check your state's Economic Development Commission.
Resource: www.recovery.gov/Opportunities/Pages/Opportunities.aspx

2. Friends and Family Lending www.virginmoney.com
3. National Business Incubator Association www.nbia.org/
4. Women's Business Associations www.nawbo.org/
5. Minority Business Development Agency www.mbda.gov/
6. Social Networking Loans www.prosper.com
7. Peer-to-Peer Programs www.lendingclub.com
8. Extended Credit Terms from Suppliers 30/60/90 days.
9. Consignment Terms from Suppliers Contract statements.
10. Community Bank
11. Prepayments from Members
12. Seller Financing: When purchasing an existing Subscription Clothing Rental Company.
13. Business Funding Directory www.businessfinance.com
14. FinanceNet www.financenet.gov

15. SBA Financing www.sbaonline.sba.gov
16. Micro-Loans www.accionusa.org/
17. Private Investors http://ActiveCapital.org
18. Use retirement funds to open a business without taxes or penalty. First, establish a C-corporation for the new business. Next, the C-corporation establishes a new retirement plan. Then, the owner's current retirement funds are rolled over into the C-corporation's new plan. And last, the new retirement plan invests in stock of the C-corporation. Warning: Check with your accountant or financial planner. Resource: http://www.benetrends.com/
19. Business Plan Competition Prizes
www.nytimes.com/interactive/2009/11/11/business/smallbusiness/Competitions-table.html?ref=smallbusiness
20. Unsecured Business Cash Advance based on future credit card transactions.
www.merchantcreditadvance.com
21. Kick Starter www.kickstarter.com
22. Tech Stars www.techstars.org
23. Capital Source www.capitalsource.com
www.msl.com/index.cfm?event=page.sba504
Participates in the SBA's 504 loan program. This program is for the purchase of fixed assets such as commercial real estate and machinery and equipment of a capital nature, which are defined as assets that have a minimum useful life of ten years. Proceeds cannot be used for working capital.
24. Commercial Loan Applications www.c-loans.com/onlineapp/
www.wellsfargo.com/com/bus_finance/commercial_loans
25. Sharing assets and resources with other non-competing businesses.
26. Angel Investors www.angelcapitaleducation.org
27. The Receivables Exchange http://receivablesxchange.com/
28. Bootstrap Methods: Personal Savings/Credit Card/Second Mortgages
29. Community-based Crowd-funding www.profounder.com
www.peerbackers.com
A funding option designed to link small businesses and entrepreneurs with pools of prospective investors.
30. On Deck Capital www.ondeckcapital.com/
Created the Short-Term Business Loan (up to $100,000.00) for small businesses to get quick access to capital that fits their cash flow, with convenient daily payments.
31. Royalty Lending www.launch-capital.com/
With royalty lending, financing is granted in return for future revenue or company performance, and payback can prove exceedingly expensive if a company flourishes.
32. Stock Loans Southern Lending Solutions, Atlanta. GA.
Custom Commercial Finance, Bartlesville, OK
A stock loan is based on the quality of stocks, Treasuries and other kinds of investments in a businessperson's personal portfolio. Possession of the company's stock is transferred to the lender's custodial bank during the loan period.
33. Lender Compatibility Searcher www.BoeFly.com

34. Strategic Investors
    Strategic investing is more for a large company that identifies promising technologies, and for whatever reason, that company may not want to build up the research and development department in-house to produce that product, so they buy a percentage of the company with the existing technology.
35. Bartering
36. Small Business Investment Companies   www.sba.gov/INV
37. Cash-Value Life Insurance
38. Employee Stock Option Plans   www.nceo.org
39. Venture Capitalists   www.nvca.org
40. Initial Public Offering (IPO)
41. Meet investors through online sites, including LinkedIn (group discussions), Facebook (BranchOut sorts Facebook connections by profession), and CapLinked (enables search for investment-related professionals by industry and role).
42. SBA Community Advantage Approved Lenders
    www.sba.gov/content/community-advantage-approved-lenders
43. Small Business Lending Specialists
    https://www.wellsfargo.com/biz/loans_lines/compare_lines
    http://www.bankofamerica.com/small_business/business_financing/
    https://online.citibank.com/US/JRS/pands/detail.do?ID=CitiBizOverview
    https://www.chase.com/ccp/index.jsp?pg_name=ccpmapp/smallbusiness/home/page/bb_business_bBanking_programs
44. Startup America Partnership   www.s.co/about
    Based on a simple premise: young companies that grow create jobs. Once startups apply and become a Startup America Firm, they can access and manage many types of resources through a personalized dashboard.
45. United States Economic Development Administration   www.eda.gov/
46. Small Business Loans   http://www.iabusnet.org/small-business-loans
47. Tax Increment Financing (TIF)
    A public financing method that is used for subsidizing redevelopment, infrastructure, and other community-improvement projects. TIF is a method to use future gains in taxes to subsidize current improvements, which are projected to create the conditions for said gains.
48. Gust   https://gust.com/entrepreneurs
    Provides the global platform for the sourcing and management of early-stage investments.
49. Goldman Sachs 10,000 Small Businesses   http://sites.hccs.edu/10ksb/
50. Earnest Loans   www.meetearnest.com
51. Biz2Credit   www.biz2credit.com
52. Funding Circle   www.fundingcircle.com
    A peer-to-peer lending service which allows savers to <u>lend</u> money directly to small and medium sized businesses
53. Lending Club   www.lendingclub.com
54. Equity-based Crowdfunding   www.Indiegogo.com
    www.StartEngine.com
    www.SeedInvest.com

55. National Funding   www.nationalfunding.com
    Their customers can to get working capital, merchant cash advances, credit card processing, and, equipment leasing.
56. Quick Bridge Funding   www.quickbridgefunding.com
    Offers a flexible and timely financing program to help assist small and medium sized businesses achieve their goals.
57. Kabbage   www.kabbage.com
    The industry leader in providing working capital online.
58. Female Founders Fund   https://femalefoundersfund.com/
59. Community Sourced Capital
    Ex: www.communitysourcedcapital.com/squareholder/campaigns/help-us-bring-urban-boxing-to-firebrand?quantity=2
60. Start Engine   www.startengine.com
    Built a community of 145,000+ registered investors and launched 150+ companies. Leveraging its experience and expertise in crowdsale and regulation, StartEngine delivers a one-stop ICO solution for companies of all sizes.

Funding Resources for Women Entrepreneurs

Female Founders Fund	https://femalefoundersfund.com/
BBG Ventures	www.bbgventures.com
500 Women	https://angel.co/500-women
Bella Capital USA	http://www.bellevc.com/
Golden Seeds	https://goldenseeds.com/
Women's Venture Capital Fund	www.womensvcfund.com/
Tory Burch Foundation	www.toryburchfoundation.org/
Pipeline Angels	http://pipelineangels.com/
iFund Women	https://ifundwomen.com/
Amber Grant	www.ambergrantsforwomen.com/get-an-amber-grant/
Idea Café Grant	www.businessownersideacafe.com/business_grants/index.php
Grants for Women	www.grantsforwomen.org/
FedEx Small Business Grants	https://smallbusiness.fedex.com/grant-contest.html
Open Meadows Foundation	https://sites.google.com/site/openmeadowsfoundation/
Girl Boss Foundation Grants	www.girlboss.com/foundation/apply
Cartier Women's Initiative	www.cartierwomensinitiative.com/
Eileen Fisher Grants	www.eileenfisher.com/grants/grants-overview/
Innovate Her Challenge	www.sba.gov/offices/headquarters/wbo/resources/1465581

Community Action Grants
www.aauw.org/what-we-do/educational-funding-and-awards/community-action-grants/
Example: https://fundersclub.com/companies/letote/

Resources: www.sba.gov/category/navigation-structure/starting-managing-business/starting-business/local-resources
http://usgovinfo.about.com/od/moneymatters/a/Finding-Business-Loans-Grants-Incentives-And-Financing.htm

3.0 Products and Services   (Select)

In this section, we will not only list all our planned subscription products and rental services, but also describe how our proposed subscription clothing rental services will be differentiated from those of our competitors and solve a real problem or fill an unmet need in the marketplace.

_____ (company name) will provide a deep inventory of clothing rentals and accessories in a wide variety of styles and price-ranges that are of good quality and from many reputable designers. We will also seek to bring in styles that we hear from our members are not readily accessible in the standard _____ (plus-size?) market. We will look to develop partnerships with emerging designers, such as those launching a new _____ (business-wear?) line, to sustain a competitive edge in the marketplace.

We will promote more affordable options than our competitors, including a monthly fee of as little as $____ (39.00?) for a single item rental plan. Members will also be allowed to rent more than one item at a time, depending on the subscription plan they choose. Our tiered monthly plans will enable subscribers take out up to ___ (ten?) items at a time, with unlimited exchanges and free shipping. The brands carried in our inventory will come from big names like Vince Camuto or ASOS, as well as small upstarts and straight-size companies looking to expand their offerings.

We will use the following types of Subscription Plan Sign-up Incentives:
First Order Incentive: Sign-up by _____ (date) to Get Up to ___ % Off… Plus Free Surprise Goodies in the First Shipment Box.

We will track the "success rate" (the number of times a particular dress is rented), and if a dress style is renting poorly, it will be discounted, sold off the rack, and replaced with a new designer garment. We will continue to ask subscribers to provide feedback on how each and every garment fits to collect significant amounts of data. We will then use that data to really personalize and recommend items to each and every member on an individual basis, based on the likelihood of fit and sense of fashion match. To encourage the much-needed feedback, we will list every item rented and create a scoring system for the many qualities of a garment, including fit, garment condition, wrinkles, sanitary cleanliness, fragrance, style, fashion trendiness, usage adaptability, ready-to-wear, seam quality, fabric quality, fabric preference, designer favorability, and color and pattern likeability. We will provide incentives for the submission of this critical feedback, including discount coupons and submissions into contests.

To better service the fashion needs of our subscribers, we will develop the following quiz, which will provide a _____ (virtual) _____ (assistant/stylist) with the information needed to make informed clothing recommendations:
1. What is your gender?
2. What is birthday?
3. What is your height
4. What is your weight?

5. Hair, eyes and skin colors?
6. Describe your body type: slim/average/hour-glass/athletic/well-built/stocky/pregnant
7. Primary reason for becoming a subscription member: too busy to shop/seeking style advice/want to discover new products/other.
8. What aspects of clothing and shopping are you most passionate about: fashion trends/sustainable products/ethical manufacturing/other?
9. What is the best description of your overall style: casual/classic/conservative/creative/fashion-forward/glamorous?
10. Do you dress more for style or comfort?
11. How do you usually dress on: weekdays/weekends/evenings out?
12. Please select which occasions you would like our service to focus on and how often: Work/Business, Casual, Weekend Casual, or Date Night/Night Out. Indicate: Rarely/Sometimes/Often.
13. What is your normal size, in your favorite brand, for the following variety of garments, including suits, gowns, cocktail dresses, casual dresses, blouses, T-shirts, pants, jeans, underwear, bras, panties, socks, gloves, shoes, belts, etc.?
14. Please indicate style preferences in each category:
    Top styles: ruffles, tanks, off the shoulder, flowy, tunics, sweatshirts, collared shirts, and boho.
    Sweater styles: drape front, dusters, oversized, ponchos, turtlenecks, cardigans, cold shoulder, or graphic.
    Jacket styles: faux leather, bombers, blazers, carcoats, vests, cropped, denim, or trench coats.
    Pant styles: skinny jeans, trousers, joggers, wide leg, cropped, boyfriend jeans, jumpsuits, and leggings.
    Dress styles: slip dresses, wrap dresses, shirt dresses, sheath dresses, fit and flare, bodycon, maxi dresses, and elastic waist.
    Jewelry style: Everyday jewelry style or Statement jewelry style.

Other Profiling Questions:
1. What are your proportions, e.g. short arms, long torso, etc.?
2. How do you prefer your clothing to fit, with five options from tailored to lose?
3. What are your preferences for different styles of jeans, including fit and length?
4. What body features do you like to flaunt, with a sliding scale for each area? Back, butt, cleavage, hips, legs, shoulders, other.
5. What features do you like to hide?
6. What are your favorite brands?
7. Who are your favorite designers?
8. Which celebrities do you share a common sense of style with?
9. What do you want your clothes purchases to help you to achieve?
10. In which retail outlets do you most often shop for clothes?
11. In which online websites do you shop for clothes?
12. In what type of climate will your clothes be worn?
13. How often do you wear formal versus casual attire, such as business or business casual, laid back clothing, cocktail dresses or dress up for date night?

14. How adventurous do you want your selections to be in terms of trends?
15. Which styles of trend, such as preppy, casual, classic, etc., would you like to focus on incorporating more into your wardrobe?
16. What styles would you like to avoid, in terms of color and pattern, type of garment, levels of formal dress (business, laid back, cocktail, etc.)
17. What categories would you like to avoid, including accessories and shoes.
18. Preferred price range for each garment type.
19. What is your total monthly budget for clothing rentals?
20. What is your budget for each item?
21. In what price category do you prefer to receive items?
22. How often would you like to receive shipments?

After answering questions specific to their size and fit preferences, members will be shown ____ (seven?) sets of styled wardrobes, which include three similarly styled outfits in each, and asked to rate each set on a scale of 'hate it' to 'love it'.
Examples: https://lendingluxury.com/easysearch/search/form/

Services:
We will also rent dresses for the following wedding related occasions in a separate department that will be driven by event type and date:

Bachelorette party dresses	Bridesmaids dresses
Fall wedding dresses	Honeymoon dresses
Rehearsal dinner dresses	Summer wedding dresses
Winter wedding dresses	

3.1 Service Descriptions

In creating our service descriptions, we will provide answers to the following types of questions:
1. What does the service do or help the customer to accomplish?
2. Why will people decide to subscribe to the service?
3. What makes it unique or a superior value?
4. How expensive or difficult is it to copy our business model by a competitor?
5. How much will the subscription clothing rental service be sold for?

Rapid Spotting and Dry-Cleaning Services
Our goal will be to get returned clothing cleaned and sent back out the same day to reduce in-transit down-time. Stains will be pretreated with special cleaners before the garment is immersed in solvents. If invisible stains aren't pre-treated, they will become set with the heat of dry cleaning. Perspiration and alcohol are water soluble and won't be removed completely by dry cleaning solvents unless they are pretreated. Alcohol dries clear, but the sugar found in alcohol turns brown with age. We will check for tears and examine the areas which came in contact with skin for stains and grime. We will also inspect the skirt and/or train for stains and decide whether or not the garment can be perfectly restored.

Packaging
We will use packaging that has been developed, selected, and tested to meet the specifications set by the common carriers and our insurance company. Every component of our storage materials will be of archival quality to avoid the yellowing of garments. These boxes will be selected and produced with meticulous care to rigorous standards. A return postage-paid label will be included in the boxed shipment. We will hire a graphic artist to print our company name, logo, website and company mantra on every box.

Shipping
The shipping of rental garments to any destination outside the continental United States will be available upon request but may require additional fees. This also applies to overnight shipments. Shipments to and from subscribers of rental clothing in the continental United States will be free. Subscribers will be able to send us an email notification to advise us a return shipment, so that we can expedite the readying and the shipping of another collection of curated rental clothing.

Style or Fashion Consulting Service
A style consultant will be available online to assist subscribers with garment and accessories selection and fashion coordination, and jewelry rentals or purchases. They will use their knowledge of trends and fashion principles to assist subscribers in the realm of appropriate, personalized fashion selection. They will also post helpful articles and tutorial videos about fashion trends on our website and YouTube.

Personal Shopper Service
We will train our Personal Shoppers to provide advice, guidance, and buying services to customers. This service will involve communicating with clients to determine what they are looking for, offering advice and knowledge of the best products to purchase, processing orders, and assisting with exchanges or returns. The scope of this service will range from gift buying for clients to providing advice for a complete change of image.

Clothing Redesign, Restyle, Upcycle or Refashion Service
We will redesign, upcycle or refashion some garments to create designs that are unique to our business. We will refashion garments in a new style or shape to fit another purpose and to extend the useful life of some items and/or to create uniquely designed items to create a sustainable competitive advantage. We will develop efficient ways to make these changes to hundreds of similar garments.
Examples:
www.attitudeclothing.co.uk/restyle-m123
www.etsy.com/market/redesigned_clothing
www.pinterest.com/salsa913/redesigned-clothing/
www.trashtocouture.com/p/before-after.html

3.1.1 Subscription Membership Benefits

Wardrobe Convenience

Members can wear it once and exchange or keep it as long as they want.

Guaranteed Free Shipping
> Unlimited USPS Priority Shipping, both ways, in the Continental U.S.

Overnight Shipping Service
> This service will be made available at the carrier's cost, plus a nominal rush handling fee.

Unlimited Exchanges
> Postage-paid return shipping labels are included in every box.

Free Style Consulting Services
> The fashion, style and/or image consulting services will be available at no cost to our subscribers.

Free Dry Cleaning or Laundry Services
> Return it and we will take care of the rapid cleaning and sanitizing of all garments.

The Love it and Keep it (Buy) Option
> If the customer finds an item they want to keep, they can just buy it right from their at-home closet at a significant discount off the retail price.

Reduced Wardrobe Clutter
> Just return the items that are no longer being used to fee up valuable wardrobe space.

Wardrobe Organizing Service
> We will produce video tutorials on how to organize and maximize closet space.

Lower Monthly Clothing Expenses
> The cost of purchasing new designer clothing is much higher, by a factor of nearly x10 times, than the rental fees.

No Buyers Remorse
> If the member or the style consultant made the wrong choice, the subscriber can just send it back, with no penalties.

No Textile Waste
> Instead of discarding old clothes and negatively impacting the environment, we will find ways to resell, donate or recycle them.

No Discarding Clothes Due to a Changing Waistline.
> Subscribers can simply make the transition to the 'right' size and send the wrong size back for a replacement garment.

3.1.2   Brands Carried   (select)

We plan to carry the following brands:

- Gilli
- KUT
- Hutch
- NYDJ
- Bobeau
- Jessica Howard
- Karen Kane

Johnny WAS
Democracy
Leota
Tahari
Rachel Roy
Catherine Malandrino
Taylor Dresses

- Adrianna Papell
- London Times
- Vince Camuto
- Frank Agostino
- Eliza J
- Fever
- Anne Klein
- Levi's
- Sangria
- City Chic
- INC
- Lucky
- Rachel Antonoff
- Tocca
- Lucky Brand
- BCBGeneration
- Brass
- For Love & Lemons
- Alice + Olivia
- Jovani
- _____

Kensie
eShakti
Lucky Brand
Gabby Skye
Drew
Vision
Yumi
Lotus
Calvin Klein
Clementine
American Rag
IGIGI
Melissa McCarthy Seven7
Kiyonna
Free People
Zuri
Self-portrait
Reformation
Zimmermann
Adrianna Papell

Examples:
https://www.armarium.com/designers
https://www.armoire.style/collection/
https://thefashionpass.com/pages/brands
https://closet.gwynniebee.com/pages/size-chart

3.2 Alternative Revenue Streams

1. Classified Ads in our Newsletter
2. Vending Machine Sales
3. Product Sales.
4. Website Banner Ads
5. Content Area Sponsorship Fees
6. Online Survey Report Fees
7. Style Consulting Services
8. Facilities Sub-leases
9. Feedback Reports to Designers
10. Tailoring Services
11. Rush or Emergency Shipments
12. Referral Commissions

3.3 Production of Products and Services

We will use the following methods to locate the best suppliers for our business:
- Attend fashion shows and other fashion related trade shows to understand the latest trend in fashion.
- Magic Las Vegas — https://ubmfashion.com/shows/magic
- Project Las Vegas — https://ubmfashion.com/shows/project
- Dallas Market Center — www.dallasmarketcenter.com

- Fame New York https://ubmfashion.com/shows/project
- Stylemax (Chicago) www.stylemaxonline.com
- AmericasMart Atlanta www.americasmart.com
- Accessories the Show (NY/Vegas) www.ubmfashion.com/shows/ATS-1
- NW Trend Show (Seattle) www.nwtrendshow.com
- OffPrice (Las Vegas and NY) www.offpriceshow.com
- dg expo www.dgexpo.net
- Kingpins Show www.kingpinsshow.com

- Attend trade shows and seminars to spot upcoming trends, realize networking opportunities and compare prices.

Subscription Summit https://subsummit.com/
Connects industry leaders, innovators and partners that are driving the rapid evolution of how consumers discover, buy and experience new products.

- Subscribe to appropriate trade and consumer magazines, journals, newsletters and blogs.

Real Simple
www.realsimple.com/beauty-fashion/clothing/shopping-guide/clothing-subscription-boxes
Business of Fashion
www.businessoffashion.com/articles/news-analysis/soon-you-may-be-renting-your-work-clothes
Glamour Magazine
www.glamour.com/story/womens-work-clothing-subscription-box-reviews
In-Style Magazine
www.instyle.com/holidays-occasions/gift-guides/best-fashion-subscription-boxes-women
Fashion Magazine Directory
https://en.wikipedia.org/wiki/List_of_fashion_magazines

Clothing and Textiles Research Journal https://journals.sagepub.com/home/ctr
Conde Nast Bridal Group www.condenast.com
Fairchild Bridal Group www.fairchildpub.com

- Join our trade association to make valuable contacts, get listed in any online directories, and secure training and marketing materials.

Subscription Trade Association
https://subta.com/subscription-trade-association-subta-launches-help-subscription-companies-learn-connect-grow/

International Textile & Apparel Association https://itaaonline.org/
American Rental Association www.ararental.org/
National Cleaners Association www.nca-i.com
Association for Wedding Professionals www.afwpi.com
Resources: www.marketingsource.com/associations/

53

3.4 Competitive Comparison

There are only ___ (#) other Subscription Clothing Rental Companies in the ___ area. ____ (company name) will differentiate itself from its local competitors by offering a broader range of designer brands and style consulting services, maintaining a database of customer preferences and transaction history, offering membership club benefits to qualifying members, using a monthly e-newsletter to stay-in-touch with members and offering an array of new innovative wraparound services, including _____ (mobile pick-up and delivery services).

We will also place a heavy emphasis on the development of a staff training program to meet member information demands, while also serving to control operational costs. We will especially establish training programs for style consultants, spotters (stain removers) and seamstresses. We will use surveys to solicit customer feedback and obtain information why some members have cancelled their subscriptions. We will also encourage members to make special order requests with regard to preferred designers and trending fashions.

____ (company name) does not have to pay for under-utilized staff. Our flexible employee scheduling procedures and use of part-timers will ensure that are operations are never overstaffed during slow times. We will also adopt a pay-for-performance compensation plan, and use referral incentives to generate new business. We will reinvest major dollars every year in professional and educational materials. We will participate in online webinars to bring members the finest selection of clothing rental services, and industry trend information.

Our rental fees will be competitive with other Subscription Clothing Rental Companies that offer far less in the way of eco-friendly benefits, innovative services, and designer garment selection, and we will offer an unconditional satisfaction guarantee.

3.5 Sales Literature

____ (company name) has developed sales literature that illustrates a professional organization with vision. ____ (company name) plans to constantly refine its marketing mix through a number of different literature packets. These include the following:
- direct mail with introduction letter and product price sheet.
- product information brochures
- press releases
- new product/service information literature
- email marketing campaigns
- website content
- corporate brochures

A copy of our informational brochure is attached in the appendix of this document. This brochure will be available to encourage referrals, hand out at seminars, and use for direct mail purposes.

3.6 Fulfillment

The key fulfillment and delivery of services will be provided by our cross-trained and internally certified associates. The real core value is the industry expertise of the founder, and staff experience and company training programs for style consultants.

3.7 Technology

_____ (company name) will employ and maintain the latest technology to enhance its office management, inventory management, shipping and returns monitoring, payment processing, customer profiling and record keeping systems. This business will need to set up expensive technology tools. To satisfy customers, we will need to implement technologies that will consistently ensure hassle-free deliveries and returns, and in terms of customer 'big data' analysis, it will be essential to fully understand changing customer fashion and fit expectations and to be relevant to the specific requirements of designer clothing rentals.

We will acquire a secure, reliable and robust recurring revenue billing system. We will need to work with the right gateway and set up our account to ensure that payments will be efficiently processed every month. We will also need an easy, highly automated means to rectify failed payments and minimize churn. We will need the ability to correctly bill for changes to a customer's plan, such as an upgrades or downgrade in the middle of the billing cycle, and to collect the right taxes.

Resources:
Subscription Billing Software
CaaStle   www.caastle.com

Gwynnie Bee has packaged its e-commerce software and began licensing a white-label version to traditional retailers. The company name is derived from: 'Clothing as a Service'. It is a technology platform enabling retailers and brands to offer an unlimited-access clothing subscription service to complement existing business models. The platform handles all aspects of the subscription business, including the website, databases, customer service, and more. This platform will handle all logistics of clothing rentals, including cleaning, packing, shipments, and returns. CaaStle has been managing the rental businesses of Ann Taylor (Infinite Style) and New York & Company (NY&C Closet). Basically, this platform opens up a new channel for the distribution of product and getting the unsold merchandise off the store floor. This solves the real estate space problem and gives retailers and brands a new way to sell clothes that doesn't interfere with their mainstream businesses. Research indicates that what sells well are the basic, staple items and what rents well is all the upscale designer fashions.

With CaaStle, retailers send Gwynnie Bee their inventory, and the platform takes care of everything else. It builds the front-end site under the retailer's name, processes returns and takes care of the cleaning, inspecting, restocking and picking, packing and shipping

— all from its multi-tenant warehouses in Columbus and Phoenix. The retailers pay Gwynnie Bee on a per-customer basis when they use CaaStle. There are basic, premium and enterprise tiers available, with additional services, such as fit-and-size recommendations, personalization technology, algorithms that price clothes and more. The service works for both retailers looking to expand its customer base, as well as those that simply want their current members to spend more money. CaaStle can also help those with excess inventory they're looking to unload.
Source:
www.pymnts.com/news/retail/2019/gwynnie-bee-clothing-subscription-caastle/

Zuora www.zuora.com

Creates cloud-based software on a subscription basis that enables any company in any industry to successfully launch, manage, and transform into a subscription business. Zuora provides a SaaS platform that automates all subscription order-to-revenue operations in real-time for any business. Zuora Central sits in between the CRM and ERP and a solution that orchestrates all subscription order-to-cash processes in real-time. Growth companies use Zuora's multi-tenant cloud platform to launch, scale, and monetize their subscription services. Zuora's applications work for subscription pricing, quoting, orders, billing, payments, and renewals.

Vindicia www.vindicia.com

Provides SaaS-based subscription billing and recurring revenue solutions to various brands across the globe. Its solutions include Vindicia CashBox, a subscription billing platform to speed time to market and drive recurring revenue streams; Vindicia Select, a cloud-based recurring payment solution that works to resolve failed payment transactions; and Vindicia Trial, a solution to grow subscription and recurring revenue overnight. The company serves SaaS and services, OTT and entertainment, media and content, Internet of Things, and other industries. Vindicia, Inc. was founded in 2003 and is based in Redwood City, California. It also has offices in London, United Kingdom; Singapore; Polanco, Mexico; and Sao Paulo and Rio de Janeiro, Brazil. As of September 14, 2016, Vindicia, Inc. operates as a subsidiary of Amdocs Limited.

Chargebee www.chargebee.com

Provide more options and flexibility to manage varied billing use-cases. Chargebee is built with a focus on delivering the best experience to provide a seamless and flexible recurring billing experience to customers and manage customer subscriptions. Commercially available since mid-2012, Chargebee is trusted billing partner for SaaS, Subscription eCommerce and Membership Services of various sizes, globally. It helps small businesses quickly implement best practices and compliance requirements. Some of the features that help differentiate Chargebee are the ability to use custom fields, custom domain support with mobile compatible check-out pages, apart from a highly stable REST API for extended flexibility.

Chargify www.chargify.com

A subscription billing software service that offers a recurring billing and subscription management space. Chargify Elastic Billing turns billing into a competitive edge for modern recurring revenue-based businesses that need to personalize and differentiate their offerings for the Relationship Economy. Elastic Billing is transforming the way that businesses package, price, and promote offers and manage change over time. It was founded in 2009 and is headquartered in San Antonio, TX.

Directory of Subscription Management Software
www.g2crowd.com/categories/subscription-management

Clever Bridge www.cleverbridge.com
Provides global commerce, billing and payment solutions for leading digital goods, services and SaaS companies across a variety of industries. Relying on their flexible platform and unique consultative approach, their clients grow their digital businesses by building long-term customer relationships and maximizing global recurring revenue.

Brightpearl www.Brightpearl.com
An omnichannel retail management system.

Directory of Predictive Analytics Software
https://financesonline.com/predictive-analysis/
It can reduce the time needed to collect data from multiple sources, filter data according to unique preferences, and analyze information using various methodologies and algorithms. Data may also be formatted in different visualizations to present information with ease. Most predictive analysis systems even have centralized repositories to store data and robust API capabilities for hassle-free interface customization. This software will help to collect and analyze data collected over time on child's preferences and parents' purchasing behaviors.

Recurly www.recurly.com
Provides enterprise-class subscription management for thousands of businesses worldwide. Provides a sophisticated, secure subscription management platform with the flexibility to support constantly evolving billing models with consistently superior customer experiences. Recurly has an enterprise-class subscription management platform that cuts through the complexity of subscription management to optimize and automate revenue growth.

Online Rental Portal/Website Builder
Fatbit Technologies, Inc. www.fatbit.com/rental-business-portal-script.html

Customer Success Management
Gainsight www.gainsight.com
Its software helps businesses to strengthen ongoing relationships and achieve better member retention rates by offering a customer success solution with their members. It uses data science to enable businesses to make their customer experiences a priority.

Frontleaf www.frontleaf.com
It helps companies drive higher customer lifetime value by generating actionable insights from product usage and other indicators of customer health. Frontleaf operates across the

customer lifecycle, serving as the intelligence center for programs to increase trial or freemium conversions, reduce churn, and achieve revenue expansion. Acquired by Zuora.

Preact   www.preact.com

A cloud-based customer success service that helps subscription software companies maximize customer lifetime value by reducing churn, acquiring new paid customers, and increasing user revenues. Preact provides health metrics tailored to each user and account by tracking detailed session-level usage of web and mobile applications and server APIs. Preact predicts and informs which customers are likely to churn, renew, or upgrade by modeling usage and behavior patterns using big data analytics, behavioral science, and machine learning. In addition, Preact provides deep, real-time visibility into product usage to improve customer support and product quality. Preact integrates with Gmail, Salesforce, Stripe, Zendesk, Desk.com, Helpscout, Mixpanel, and Marketo, and other leading cloud-based apps. Acquired by Spotify in 2016.

Totango   www.totango.com

A leading enterprise customer success solution that enables companies to align around their customers to increase loyalty and customer lifetime value. Their solution connects all customer information so companies can proactively and intelligently engage with their customers to drive adoption, retention, expansion and referrals.

Marketing Automation Software

Marketo   www.marketo.com

Provides a complete marketing automation software solution that is powerful and easy to use for fast-growing small companies and global enterprises alike. Enables companies to create personalized connections with their members. It is designed to allow companies to launch their first campaign in days and scale to meet the needs of the most complex global enterprise. Their solution delivers everything a marketer needs to deliver more sales leads with less work, including inbound marketing, lead management, social marketing, event management, instant CRM integration, sales dashboards, and marketing ROI reporting and analytics. With proven technology, comprehensive services and expert guidance, Marketo helps thousands of companies around the world turn marketing from a cost center into a revenue driver. It has also established its own credentialing program.

Salesforce   www.salesforce.com/products/sales-cloud/features/marketing-automation-software/?d=7010M000001yBiM

Generates leads using email marketing, custom landing pages, smarter lead capture forms, and a central marketing dashboard, and helps to prioritize and nurture those leads.

Hubspot   www.hubspot.com

It develops cloud-based, inbound marketing software that allows businesses to transform the way that they market online. Its service portfolio includes social media publishing and monitoring, blogging, SEO, website content management, email marketing, marketing automation, and reporting and analytics. HubSpot's sales application enables sales and service teams to have effective conversations with leads and prospects. HubSpot is headquartered in Cambridge, Massachusetts with an office in Dublin, Ireland

Eloqua www.oracle.com/marketingcloud/products/marketing-automation/
A software as a service (SaaS) platform for marketing automation offered by Oracle that aims to help B2B marketers and organizations manage marketing campaigns and sales lead generation. ... Oracle's marketing solution is most often used in large enterprises that primarily market to other businesses.

Customer Relationship Management
Salesforce www.Salesforce.com
Over 150,000 companies use Salesforce CRM to grow their businesses by strengthening customer relationships. Customer Relationship Management helps companies understand their customers' needs and solve problems by better managing customer information and interactions — all on a single platform that's always accessible from any desktop or device. Salesforce also sells a complementary suite of enterprise applications focused on customer service, marketing automation, analytics and application development.

Optimizely www.optimizely.com
A leader in customer experience optimization, allowing businesses to dramatically drive up the value of their digital products, commerce and campaigns through its best in class experimentation software platform. By replacing digital guesswork with evidence-based results, Optimizely enables product and marketing professionals to accelerate innovation, lower the risk of new features, and drive up the return on investment from digital by up to 10X. Over 26 of the Fortune 100 companies choose Optimizely to power their global digital experiences. Optimizely's impressive customer list includes eBay, FOX, IBM, The New York Times and many more global enterprises.

RightNow Technologies, Inc. www.rightnow.com
Their customer experience suite helps organizations deliver exceptional customer experiences across the web, social networks and contact centers, all delivered via the cloud. With more than eight billion customer interactions delivered, RightNow is the customer experience fabric for nearly 2,000 organizations around the globe.

Janrain www.janrain.com
It is the creator of the first customer identity and access management (CIAM) cloud. Janrain is also the inventor of social login and a founding member of the OpenID Foundation—establishing many of the digital authentication protocols used globally today. Janrain continues to lead the CIAM market, with over half of the world's connected users within its Identity Cloud network. Janrain is based in Portland, Oregon. Janrain was acquired by Akamai Technologies in 2019.

InsideView www.insideview.com
It powers the world's business conversations, helping companies redefine their go-to-market strategies from a volume-based to more targeted approach. Its leading Targeting Intelligence platform helps sales and marketing teams quickly identify and qualify the best targets, engage with more relevancy, close more deals, and retain and expand accounts. InsideView's CRM partners include Microsoft, Marketo, andSalesforce.com.

Their content relationships include Facebook, Twitter, LinkedIn, Thomson Reuters, Capital IQ, Cortera, and NetProspex.

Community Building Software

Jive Software   www.jivesoftware.com

The largest independent vendor in the Social Business Software market. The company was founded in 2001, with its headquarters in Palo Alto, CA. Jive combines the power of community software, collaboration software, social networking software, and social media monitoring offerings into an integrated platform. The flagship product is Jive Engage. Previous products by Jive include Clearspace, Jive Forums, and the now open source Openfire & Spark. Jive makes it easy for groups to brainstorm, share ideas and see what everyone is working on. Recent versions include video, analytics, and social media monitoring. Jive also helps companies create highly-interactive online communities. They were acquired by Aurea Software in 2017.

Lithium   www.lithium.com

Lithium builds trusted relationships between the world's best brands and their customers, helping people get answers and share their experiences. Using that data and the company's software, Lithium customers boost sales, reduce service costs, spark innovation, and build long-term brand loyalty and advocacy.

Loyalty Programs

Punchcard   www.punchcard.com

A mobile engagement and loyalty network designed to give merchants an effective way to retain customers while rewarding shoppers for making frequent purchases at their favorite retailers. The Punchcard app is a mobile platform that uses an electronic "punchcard" system that is easy-to-implement and simple for shoppers and merchants alike. After scanning a receipt at any business, the shopper is entitled to a reward – in most cases it is cash back, but it can also be a free meal, free clothing, or a gift card. Merchants get real-time data about their customers' buying habits, as well as social and other demographic information that allows them to provide their loyal customers with targeted offers and rewards. Punchcard is part of the Idealab family of companies.

Belly Card   www.bellycard.com

Provides a loyalty program for merchants, using an in-store iPad for the merchant and an app for customers. It charges merchants $50 to $100 a month for the service, which includes an iPad, a case and lock for the iPad, marketing materials, plus data and analytics. Customers earn loyalty points by checking in at the store with a QR code technology to earn points that could be redeemed as a merchant chose.

Customer Support Services Software

Zendesk   www.zendesk.com

Example: https://www.zendesk.com/customer/le-tote/

Among the Support features that Le Tote appreciates are Zendesk Embeddables. By using the Mobile SDK, Web Widget, and the Zendesk API, Le Tote offers members the ability to engage with the Le Tote support team directly from the Le Tote mobile app or while they're browsing the site on a PC. Since members are guided to search Le Tote's knowledge base first, before initiating a live chat session or submitting a ticket via email, chat requests declined.

Service Cloud www.salesforce.com/products/service-cloud/overview/
It is built on the Salesforce Customer Success Platform, giving users a 360-degree view of their customers and enabling them to deliver smarter, faster, and more personalized service. With Service Cloud, users can automate service processes, streamline workflows, and surface key articles, topics, and experts to transform the agent experience. Enables connecting one-to-one with every customer, across multiple channels and on any device.

Parature www.parature.com
Provides on-demand customer service software, making it possible for any business to leverage the Internet to provide outstanding customer service and online support. Parature provides an efficient way to serve, support, retain, engage with and maximize the value of every customer.

Project Management Software
Wrike www.wrike.com
It provides a reliable step-by-step play to follow and keep everybody on the same page. In addition, Wrike's ability to provide transparency to stakeholders and prioritize tasks, helps management report on productivity levels.

General Rental Software Systems

Rental Software System	http://www.itwebexperts.com/
Sales Igniter Booking Software	http://www.rental-e-commerce-software.com/
Rental Booking Software	https://rentalbookingsoftware.com/toy-toy-purse-rental/
Rental E-commerce	www.rental-e-commerce-software.com/toy-purse-toy-rental-e-commerce-solution.php
Rental Software Directory	www.capterra.com/rental-software/

Hootsuite www.hootsuite.com
A media management program that supports social network integrations for Twitter, Facebook, Instagram, LinkedIn, Google+ and YouTube, and allows the user to schedule all social media posts in the morning and to go out throughout the day automatically.

Edited www.edited.com
Software used by brands and retailers to have the right product at the right price, at the right time. It's also become the single biggest source of real-time retail data in the world.

BBL Systems, Inc http://bblsystems.com/
This company has been designing software exclusively for members in the Bridal, Prom and Tuxedo Rental industry, assisting them with implementation and supporting their on-going needs for over 20 years.

3.8 Future Products and Services

_____ (company name) will continually expand our offering of subscription clothing rental services based on industry trends and changing client needs. We will not only solicit feedback via surveys and interviews from members on what they need in the future, but will also work to develop strong relationships with all our members, designers and vendors. We also plan to open ____ (#) additional locations in the ____ area starting in _____ (year).

Future Plans Timetable
In general, the product line, offerings, service, and pricing strategy will remain the same for the _____ (first/second?) year, with the following expectations:
1. After a year of doing business, some dresses will be old and no longer re-orderable. These items will be significantly discounted and sold off the rack as is.
2. All lines will be expanded to offer more choices, and slow-moving stock will be moved from the rental section to the quick sale rack.
3. The stock will be honed to increase profitability. Research will be conducted to determine what is selling best, most profitable price points, favored designers, popular sizes and colors, etc.

Pre-owned Dress Sales
As we build our inventory of rental dresses, we will start to feature our collection of pre-owned or pre-worn rental dresses for sale. This will enable our outlet store buyers to use our custom fitting and tailoring services.

Wedding Dress Consignment Sales
We will take pre-owned wedding dresses on a consignment basis to be rented or sold either in our outlet shop or online. In this manner, we will not tie up capital in our inventory of pre-owned wedding dresses. Online consignors will be able to upload images and descriptions of their previously worn wedding gowns.
Ex: http://www.preownedweddingdresses.com/sell-wedding-dress.html
http://www.therealreal.com/

Mobile Dress Rental Truck
We plan to remodel a used box truck and turn it into a mobile boutique sales/rental shop. We will use the truck to make home and remote fashion party sales presentations. We will stock the truck based on the measurements supplied by the prospective client or party giver. The truck will also have a fitting room and a beverage counter. We will also benefit from truck signage, which will act as a moveable billboard for our company. We will also provide incentives for hostesses to sign up to stage home sales parties. The truck will not only be used to sell apparel, accessories and jewelry, but to also acquaint visitors with our subscription clothing rental services. The truck will also have satellite WiFi access to our online website and fashion catalogue.
Example:
www.boutiquetruck.com
www.fashiontruck.com

Rent Temporary Pop-up Stores
This will help our company to meet our prospective members face-to-face, learn about their needs and concerns, and assess the potential of a new location before making a substantial investment in a fixed location. We will also use the direct contact opportunity to build subscriber profiles and solicit process and inventory feedback.
Resource: www.shopify.com/guides/ultimate-guide-to-pop-up-shops
Directories: www.thestorefront.com
www.popuprepublic.com
www.appearhere.us/

Develop Portable Kiosks
We will plan to develop conveniently located kiosks, in retail stores and shopping mall corridors, that will facilitate the subscription clothing rental registration and profiling processes, and the initiation of the first trial discounted clothing rental.
Example:
To make the in-store customer experience seamless, more efficient and rewarding, Rent the Runway is tapping iOS-based scanners and kiosks to foster a more personalized consumer interaction. RTR has deployed Aila Technologies' devices to rethink how consumers' closets should work and speed up returns and exchanges at its retail locations. It's also helping to better manage 450,000 pieces of designer fashions and collect data on users' interaction to make for a more efficient operation and a better customer experience. Using the Aila interactive kiosks, featuring TrueScan technology, customers can quickly pick up and drop off orders and exchange clothing on the spot at the companies' stores. Customers and associates can scan the tiny labels on RTR products quickly, easily and accurately. Aila's iOS-based kiosks and devices rely on proprietary technology that combines integrated scanning technology with sleek, store-ready design. Its devices can be used in a wide range of in-store operations, from price checking and custom ordering to point-of-sale transactions.
Source: www.retailcustomerexperience.com/articles/rent-the-runway-taps-kiosks-scanners-to-boost-in-store-digital-experience/
Resource: //info.ailatech.com/rtr-case-study

Specialty Travel Services
We will develop specialty services that will give us top-of-the-mind awareness in certain stressful situations. As an example, we will develop the expertise to develop a wraparound service for women business travelers, and ship rental clothing to their destination of choice. We will also teach them how to travel light, with a limited number of basic articles of clothing that can be combined in various ways to create very different looks. We will also establish an alliance with a luggage manufacturer or drop-shipper to become a one-stop travel service center. We will also create packing checklists to help our members to accessorize and dress appropriately for different business functions or special occasions, in different parts of the country/world. We will also ask for and process customer feedback, so that we can help to make the next trip even more rewarding, safer and/or hassle-free. We will give our subscribers access to unlimited clothing while traveling to different climates and attending special events. They will be no need to spend time packing, paying airline baggage fees or purchasing destination

climate appropriate clothing that will be rarely, if ever, worn again.
Resource:
https://sightdoing.net/rent-the-runway-travel-packing/
Examples:
Rent the Runway   www.renttherunway.com
They have a great selection of outerwear, so subscribers are able to avoid paying baggage fees and buying seasonal pieces that they only need a handful of days a year.

Dufl   www.dufl.com/
This app gives frequent business travelers the freedom to roam, untethered. Their secure platform delivers the user's bag where and when they need it. With each use, the clothing is cleaned the way they like it, stored in their virtual closet, and prepared for the next trip.

Special Event Priority Rentals
This will be our 'Rent by Occasion' service. We will create an optional, added-value plan that enables our subscribers to rush order clothing for special events. These shipments will be more time-critical and focus on high-quality designer goods. And because these items will be time-sensitive, we will ask members to make back-up or alternative selections in each garment category. This service will be for women planning to go to a prom, competing in a pageant or looking for a gorgeous evening gown, a designer cocktail dress or a short party dress for a wedding or other special formal occasion, and may never wear it again. Our plan is to partner with dress wholesalers from _____ (New York's?) Fashion District.
Examples:
www.poshare.com
www.armarium.com/occasions

Used Clothing Sales
We will create a separate website to sell used clothing that is no longer suitable for our rental business or involves fashions that have either become outdated or were never accepted in the marketplace. These items will be professionally repaired and dry-cleaned before listing them on our site. This site will also accept postings by subscribers or third parties, who may be interested in selling their used clothing, paying us a sales commission and directly shipping the items to the ultimate consumer. This service will also be good for our rental business, because it will help subscribers to free up valuable space in their closets, so they can create more storage space for our rental clothing.
Directory:
www.babble.com/latina/clean-out-your-closet-10-web-sites-to-sell-your-used-clothes/

Used Clothing Consignment Sales
We will also use our used clothing ecommerce website to sell the used clothing of third parties on a consignment basis.
Examples:
www.thredup.com/
www.swap.com

Standalone Mail Order Tailoring Service
We will offer a mail order tailoring service because of our ability to easily handle the shipment of garments through various carriers and our expertise with mending various types of garments by our trained seamstresses. We will list our fees for certain standard types of jobs, such as hemming, patch applications, seam repairs and button replacements. We will also encourage members to email us photos of the garments that need to be repaired so we can generate an accurate quote. To take advantage of this service, customers will be able to simply mail the items with a description of work requested and include their email address and contact information. We will email when we receive the items with an invoice payable through Pay Pal or to discuss the project or ask more questions. We will also incorporate this service into our mobile unit.
Example:
http://rapidsalterations.com/mail-order-alterations/http://rapidsalterations.com/mail-order-alterations/

Exclusive Fashion Designer Arrangements
We will contract with fashion designers that are popular with our subscriber base to create clothing lines that are exclusive to our company. This will serve to help reduce the subscriber churn rate, because we will be the only source for these original items.
Examples:
https://contracts.onecle.com/polo/jones.design.1995.10.18.shtml
https://www.docracy.com/3152/designer-sample-contract

Designer and Brand Manufacturer Consulting Services
We will use the data we collect from member feedback surveys to provide guidance to designers and brand and private label manufacturers. We will be able to use our collected data to inform these companies as to why certain products were purchased and why they were returned. Based on the feedback we receive, we will also be able to instruct or guide brands as to how to reconfigure their garments for the next season to improve fit, design and styling, and increase overall customer satisfaction to reduce returns. We will also use the customer feedback collected to guide the designer's creativity processes and help to create our own private-level products.
Resource: https://www.cnbc.com/2017/02/10/le-tote-puts-designer-fashions-within-reach.html

Special Events Focused Subscription Plan
We will ask members for a list of all the coming special events in their private and work lives and give them the ability to make continuous changes to this list of key occasion dates. We will also ask them to express their preferences for the types of garments they wish to wear for these planned special occasions. We will propose the following types of special event packages to our members:
1. Winter Ski Trip   Tropical Beach Trip
2. Birthday   Anniversary
3. Graduation   Pregnancy
4. Baptism   Christmas Party
5. Easter Celebration   Wedding Reception

6. Cruise Vacation   Honeymoon
7. Business Trip   Bachelorette Party
8. Funeral   Cocktail Party
9. Job Interview   Disney Vacation
10. European Sightseeing Vacation

Examples:
https://thefashionpass.com/collections/vacation
www.renttherunway.com/pdp/shop/unlimited_long_weekend_getaway/products#1545494551691

Cosmetics Sampling (Box Subscription) Program
We will maximize the return on our shipping charges, by including a limited line of free cosmetics samples in our shipments. We will ask the cosmetics manufacturers to help fund the costs of these trial size products because the products will function as a marketing channel for the selected cosmetics brands. We will ship the resulting full-sized product orders in subsequent clothing rental boxes. We will expand the member quiz to provide insights into preferred cosmetic products and list this product inventory on a separate webpage. We will also introduce auto-refill plans with a discounted pricing schedule.
Resource: www.birchbox.com

To improve the chances for customer acceptance of our subscription box program, we will do the following:
1. Charge very competitively for our products so the customer realizes a savings for their steady business.
2. Enable hassle-free, automatic monthly Credit Card payments.
3. Do not require a long-term contract or commitment from customers so they are free to terminate the subscription at any time without any hassles or penalties.
4. Use an upfront survey to determine what types of products are more highly desired by specific clients.

Resource:
http://www.digitalbusinessmodelguru.com/

VIP Membership Program
We will use the following tactics to encourage customers to join our VIP Membership Program:
1. Offer immediate special benefits, such as reduced pricing and exclusive offers.
2. Add customers to our database to receive free monthly e-newsletter with coupons.
3. Develop a quiz that uncovers customer style preferences.
4. Make membership joining easy via our website and mobile apps, and card sized application forms.
5. There will be various membership levels with different benefits based on costs and committed term of membership.

This program will produce the following benefits:
1. There will be less of a need to reacquire existing customers as more customers will remain in the active status.
2. There will be less need to experiment with inventory choices, because the quiz will help to develop a composite profile of customer needs and wants.

3. More customers will be motivated to make their first purchase, because the first purchase discount will reduce much of their perceived purchase risk.

Examples of Membership Plan Options:
Term: Monthly, Semi-annual (6 months), Annual (12 months)
Plan Cost: Tied to length of the committed membership.
Insurance: Amount of coverage.
Free: Amount of Gift Card to give to a friend.
Extras: Access to original premium podcasts.
Discounts: Additional __ % on all garment purchases.
Shipments: Priority carrier service.
Refunds: Exercise time limit.
Selection: Priority exposure to new designer offerings.
Other: Able to place hold on account or skip months at no extra cost.
Example:
https://chicmarie.com/en/concept/

Specialty Themed Rental Plans
We will set up specialty rental plans for the following types of hot-selling, luxury grade, designer garments and use the connection to sell related, lifestyle inspired products, such as water bottles, headbands, wristbands, specialty footwear, nutritional supplements, books, music, jewelry, towels, backpacks, etc.:
1. Yoga Athleticwear
2. Bicycling Suits
3. Tennis Outfits
4. Jogging Apparel
5. Mountain Climbing/Hiking Outfits
6. Skiing Apparel
7. Tropical Watersport Attire

Resource:
www.sectorsdonut.co.uk/sectors/consumer-services/clothes-hire/your-target-customers

Members of these rental plans will realize the following benefits:
1. Much smaller cash outlays (rent vs purchase).
2. Ability to try on garments in the comfort of own home.
3. Able to have the garments shipped to the recreation destination.
4. No laundering or mending services required.
5. Ability to stay current on fashion trends.
6. Guidance on the relevant wraparound lifestyle.
7. Fitness guarantees even through weight transition periods.
8. Ability to sample fabrics with different properties.
9. Able to rent only for the vacation or recreation period.

Resource: https://urbantastebud.com/best-yoga-subscription-boxes/

Personalized Gift Giving Program
To become more valuable to subscribers, we will help them to develop a database of

the people they want to regularly give our products as gifts to, and we will assist them in collecting feedback on the actual gift received, so future gift recommendations will more precisely match the recipient's needs and can be automatically shipped.

Holiday Gifting Program
We will develop a gift card that entitles the recipient to receive a three-month subscription to our clothing rental service at a discounted rate. This will become a secondary revenue source and encourage more consumers to try our service.
Example: www.armoire.style/holiday-gift/

Basic Gifting Program
We will develop a very low-risk, low-priced, monthly, starter club membership that basically gives the gift recipient a taste of the benefits our subscription business. We will make it extremely easy to give as a gift and we will match the funding provided by the gift giver to make it very affordable as a gift item. It will automatically expire in one year or less. We will use the customer touchpoint opportunities to convince the recipients to upgrade their basic membership plan. Other benefits to our company will be the ability to cross-sell other products and services to these temporary members, such as our _____ (style consulting?), tailoring and dry-cleaning services.

Gift Registry
We will add a gift registry service to our website to facilitate the gift giving of our subscription clothing rental service.

Tailoring and Alterations Services
We will promote our tailoring services for the following audiences:
> For hard-to-fit members, custom tailoring will be available, but may involve an additional per hour charge, depending on the scope of the work to be done and the requirement for a guaranteed extended rental period, committed to by the subscriber.

> For non-members, we will accept tailoring jobs via the internet. These alterations will be on a fee-for-service basis. Any potential extra charges will be discussed with and approved by the customer beforehand. Common alterations will include: adding or replacing covered buttons, changing a zipper back to a corset back, replacing a broken zipper, changing the length of a dress or hemming pantsuits, changing an A-line into a trumpet, adjusting the waistline measurements, changing the neckline or collar size, and cutting-off or adding a train.

Independent Style/Fashion/Image Consulting Service
We will offer a fee-based fashion consulting service to non-members. Our style/fashion consultants will offer the following range of services:
> Analyze suitable colors, cuts and designs for clients.
> Select clothing, makeup and hairstyle conforming to figure of client and occasion.
> Decide clothing during photo shoots, fashion shows or any other event.
> Develop and provide consultancy to customer for garment purchases.

Help client to achieve all fashion related goals, including suitable outfits for job interviews, business events, special occasions, etc.

Stay abreast of fashion trends and incorporate such knowledge into recommendations.

Determine the specific areas the client would like to change and enhance.

Evaluate current wardrobe, including shoes and accessories.

Help client move towards their new goals and image by eliminating outdated attire.

Create new outfits and styles from the client's existing wardrobe.

Create a customized shopping list to update the client's wardrobe.

Suggest brands and styles that best suit the client's lifestyle, style goals and body type.

Example: www.mabellestyle.ca/image-fashion-consultant/
Resource:
Association of Image Consultants Int'l   www.aici.org/page/Fashion_Stylist_Inst
Fashion Stylist Institute   https://www.fashionstylistinstitute.com/

Independent Closet Organizing Consulting Service

We will work with certified, independent, sales-commissioned closet organizers to help people with their closet organization and classification of clothing as per occasion. We will also help our clients to designate certain items for clear-out and charity clothing drives. We will help our clients to make room for a more organized closet that really works with client's style goals and lifestyle.

Example: www.stylechemistryconsulting.com/services/#closetdetox
Resource:
National Association of Productivity & Organizing Professionals   www.napo.net/

Mobile Dry-Cleaning/Laundering Service

We will offer fee-based mobile dry-cleaning and laundering services to non-members. We will use our very efficient dry-cleaning facilities and stain or spot removal expertise to create a secondary revenue stream. We will capitalize on the fact that our spotters already have a deep knowledge of fibers, materials, and chemicals. This frequently used mobile service will also allow us to use the mobile vehicles to more conveniently and cost-effectively deliver rental clothing and pick-up returns. We will also offer a journeyman program open to any employees who want to learn the spotting trade.

Resource:
www.fastcompany.com/3036876/inside-rent-the-runways-secret-dry-cleaning-empire
Example: http://mobile-dry-cleaners.com/ourservices.html

Style Consulting and Sip Parties

We will use these events as a secondary revenue stream and as a marketing tool. We will organize fee-based, fun, fashion parties, where the following practices will occur:

1. A mini-seminar will be conducted by our 'Style Consultant'.
2. The eco-friendly benefits of subscription clothing rentals will be discussed.
3. Attendees will learn how to describe, analyze and document their personal style.
4. Attendees will be given the opportunity to model designer clothing and post

photos of themselves to social media sites.
5. Trending fashions will be circulated and reviewed for attendee suitability.
6. Attendees will learn how to upcycle, refashion or redesign clothing.
7. Attendees will sip wine/champagne with artisan cheeses and breads, as they receive personalized tips tailored to their fashion needs.

Inspiration: www.armoire.style/1-1-style-appointments/

Develop Own Wardrobe and Outfit Planning App
To deepen the relationship with our subscribers, we will develop our own wardrobe and outfit planning app. As an added benefit, data for this app will be automatically supplied from the transactions that occur on our subscription rental software platform. The app will support our subscribers in the following ways: offer closet organization tips, make weather-based and occasion type outfit suggestions, provide "style stats", post articles about current fashion trends, enable free access to a network of fashion bloggers and paid access to contracted style consultants offering inspiration and ideas, access to videotaped fashion shows and online tutorials, and the ability to make packing and donation lists.
Examples:
https://insideoutstyleblog.com/2016/03/readers-favourite-style-and-wardrobe-apps.html
https://closetspace.com/women/shop

Organize Mobile Fashion Shows
We will customize a vehicle to offer mobile fashion shows, as a fee-based service, to new fashion designers to be able to showcase their new creations. We will take these shows to college campuses, libraries, community centers, country clubs, etc. These shows will generate a secondary revenue stream, improve our visibility and help us to establish our fashion expertise.
Resources:
http://mobfashionweek.com/
www.eventbrite.com/e/mobile-fashion-week-2019-tickets-46921676999
https://en.wikipedia.org/wiki/Fashion_show

Organize Fundraising Fashion Shows
Our services will be free, and we will organize all aspects of the show. The client will need to book the venue and sell their event tickets in advance. The client will raise funds primarily from ticket sales, and the selling of raffle tickets, drinks and snacks. In addition to providing a fantastic night of shopping and entertainment for clients at no cost, tickets and promotional posters will be sent free of charge. All we will require is a deposit. The deposit will be fully refundable subject to the minimum number of people attending the event. We will benefit from the exposure, closeout sales of unrentable garments and new subscription membership leads or actual sign-ups.
Resources: www.coloursfashionshows.com/charity

Mobile Clothing Boutiques
We will franchise our mobile clothing boutique business model. We will custom design the vehicle and stock it with a mix of our slow- and fast-moving rental items. Customers

will be able to purchase these items and/or sign-up for our subscription clothing rental service. The truck will also serve as a traveling billboard for our company and collect direct feedback and email addresses from prospects and customers. We will also charge designers to sponsor new item promotional campaigns in these vehicles. These vehicles will also service home party plan sales events, using hostesses and sales consultants.

Software Development Package
We will perfect the technology platform that we have developed to automate our subscription business and market the software package to retail businesses that want cloud access to systems that will facilitate the efficient operations of a subscription clothing rental business as a new sales channel. We will use our business to demonstrate the bug-free, plug-in software components, and the quality and reliability of our comprehensive technology platform. We will also work to structure the dialogue between the style consultant and the subscriber, by designing a questionnaire with a built-in decision tree and the offer the ability to include photos as a focal point of the discussions.
Example: www.caastle.com

Subscription Clothing Rental Business Contractor
The contracted package, with retail clothing boutiques, will include the use of our digital technology platform, plus the spotting, repairing, cleaning and warehousing support services needed to run a clothes-rental business. We will also build a consumer-facing, front-end suite in the retailer's name, and get paid on a per-customer basis every time a consumer signs-on with the retailer's designated ecommerce web address.
Source:
www.economist.com/business/2019/06/07/rent-the-runway-is-taking-clothes-sharing-mainstream
Example:
www.pymnts.com/news/retail/2019/gwynnie-bee-ecommerce-apparel-retail-subscription/

Standalone Subscription Rental /Sales Websites for Designer Handbags and Jewelry
We will set up separate websites for the subscription rental and sales of designer handbags and jewelry, because we expect significant demand for these items and we have the existing digital platform to handle the efficient processing of these items. We will also provide links to our primary subscription clothing rental website for those members who want to incorporate these items into their subscription clothing rental program.

Home Fashion Sales/Rental Hosted Parties
Our mobile fashion style truck will be used to acquaint attendees with our designer clothing subscriber rental service, present seminars on current fashion trends and how to dress for success, register new subscription members and possible hostess candidates, and to sell close-out stock at significantly discounted prices. This multi-purpose truck will support the following types of events:
- Home Sales Parties
- Events, such as art & craft festivals and fashion shows.
- Fundraisers for churches, schools, charities, etc.
- Customer and Employee Appreciation Days
- Employee Event Days

- Fashion Shows

Examples:
My Style Truck   https://mystyletruck.com/host-a-party/
Resource:
Home Party Sales Secrets   www.youtube.com/watch?v=ltdfx1J15KQ

Instructional Tutorials

We will teach people how to 'affordably dress for success' because it will organically reveal why they need to become members of our subscription clothing rental program. We will post video tutorials to YouTube, with embedded links to our website, that instruct viewers 'how-to affordably dress' to achieve the followings types of successes:
1. Romantic Match Success
2. Business Career Success
3. Holiday Party Event Appearance Success
4. Job Interview Success

Examples:
Party Appearance   www.youtube.com/watch?v=uOysedYPrOU
                        www.youtube.com/watch?v=46E6T4CcU7g
                        www.youtube.com/watch?v=n8PNdP7zTJg
Career Success   www.youtube.com/watch?v=raH9MfLYxKw
First Day of Work   www.youtube.com/watch?v=WZ2u2m3HOk8

Total Wardrobe Management Service

To play a vital role in the lifestyle of our members and to justify our mobile weekly home or office service plan, we plan to develop a total wardrobe management service that will include the following types of services:
1. Flexible Extra Luxury Wardrobe Storage Space.
2. Organizing and decluttering service.
3. Style and Image Consulting Services.
4. Online software access to wardrobe catalog app
5. Hanging, storing and protecting clothing supplies and guidance.
6. Pickup and Delivery Services for Tailoring, Dry-cleaning, Spotting, etc.
7. Pickup and Delivery Services for Subscription Clothing Rental Service.

Examples: www.totalwardrobestorage.com
Resources:
https://totalwardrobecare.co.uk/
www.artofmanliness.com/articles/how-to-build-a-manly-wardrobe-1/
https://insideoutstyleblog.com/2016/03/readers-favourite-style-and-wardrobe-apps.html

Localization

Localization (also referred to as "l10n") is the process of adapting a product or content to a specific locale or market. This is also known as the "Theory of Local Relevance", which means that we need to get grounded in and familiar with the communities we operate within. The aim of localization is to give a product the look and feel of having been created specifically for a target market, no matter their language, culture, or location. As a subscription clothing rental company, we will customize our offerings to local markets or consumer communities that are growing more focused in terms of ethnicity, wealth, lifestyle, and values. We will roll out different fashion designers, product lines, and alternative approaches to pricing, marketing, staffing, and customer service based on the demographics of certain zip codes. Localization and the resulting customization will encourage local experimentation, which will be difficult for competitors to track, let alone replicate. When well executed, localization strategies will provide a durable competitive edge. As an example, in known heavily Italian communities, we will highlight with banners the display of fashions and accessories favored by this ethnic group.

Resources:
Globalization and Localization Association   www.gala-global.org
GALA is comprised of members worldwide who specialize in localization, translation, internationalization, and globalization. Every day they help companies, non-profit organizations, and governments communicate effectively to global audiences. They do this by making sure the content of their clients' communications is culturally sensitive and presented in languages that their audiences understand.

4.0 Market Analysis Summary

Our Market Analysis will serve to accomplish the following goals:
1. Define the characteristics and needs and wants of the target market.
2. Serve as a basis for developing sales, marketing and promotional strategies.
3. Influence the e-commerce website design.

According to _____ County population projections, the number of females here will increase by about _____ (three?) percent over the next five years. It is safe to conclude from these facts that there is a solid customer-base for our Subscription Clothing Rental Company that will increase slightly in the years to come.

Each of our targeted market segment consists of people who either live, work, or vacation in the ___ area. Our target market will be seeking a Subscription Clothing Rental Company that will meet their desire for responsive and knowledgeable service, cash savings, convenient access hours, a broad selection of business casual wear, innovative stylist support services, all provided from an easy to shop Subscription Clothing Rental Company.

Our Subscription Clothing Rental Company will be located on the main road through town and is used daily by thousands of commuters between the two local _____ (towns/cities?). The closest Subscription Clothing Rental Company in either direction is over ____ (#) miles away.

Forces and trends in the market environment will affect _____ (company name), like all businesses. These include economic, competitive, legal/political, technology, and recordkeeping issues.

- **Economic Environment**—It is believed that the Subscription Clothing Rental Company is basically recession proof because we help professional people to reduce their clothing expenditures. We will offer significant cash savings over the traditional outright dress purchase. Positive forces include the generally stable local economy that is searching for a way to return, declining unemployment, stable wages and low inflation.
- **Legal/Political Environment**—Town of _____ supports the opening of this needed business venture and has issued and approved building permits and licenses to support use of the commercial property.
- **Technology and Recordkeeping Environment**—Use of computerized databases will capture and generate accounting/inventory detail. Computer programs will greatly simplify the inventory management, subscriber profiling, rental tracking, dress purchasing from trending designers, financial recordkeeping and tax preparation functions. We will outsource the accounting tax functions but will maintain the daily financial records in-house.

_____ (company name) has a defined target market of middle and upper-middle class consumers that will be the basis of this business. Effective marketing combined with an optimal subscription clothing rental execution plan will be critical to our success. The owner possesses solid information about the market and knows a great deal about the common attributes of those that are expected to be loyal members. This information will be leveraged to better understand who we will serve, their specific needs, and how to better communicate with them. The owner strongly believes that as more and more products become commodities that require highly competitive pricing, it will be increasingly important to focus on the development of innovative, fashion-based rental services, that can be structured and leveraged to help members conserve their limited cash assets.

4.1 Secondary Market Research

We will research demographic information for the following reasons:
1. To determine which segments of the population, such as Hispanics and the elderly, have been growing and may now be underserved.
2. To determine if there is a sufficient population base in the designated service area to realize the company's business objectives.
3. To consider what products and services to add in the future, given the changing demographic profile and needs of our service area.

We will pay special attention to the following general demographic trends:
1. Population growth has reached a plateau and market share will most likely be increased through innovation and excellent customer service.
2. Because incomes are not growing, process efficiencies and sourcing advantages must be developed to keep prices competitive.
3. The rise of non-traditional households, such as single working mothers, means developing more innovative, efficient and personalized programs.
4. As the population shifts toward more, young to middle aged adults, ages 30 to 44, and the elderly, aged 65 and older, there will be a greater need for child-rearing and geriatric mobile support services.
5. Because of the aging population and increasing pollution levels, new 'green' ways of dealing with the resulting challenges will need to be developed.

We will collect the demographic statistics for the following zip code(s):
_____

Snapshots of consumer data by zip code are also available online:
http://factfinder.census.gov/home/saff/main.html?_lang=en
http://www.esri.com/data/esri_data/tapestry.html
http://www.claritas.com/MyBestSegments/Default.jsp?ID=20

1. **Total Population** _____
2. **Number of Households** _____
3. **Population by Race:** White ____% Black ____%
   Asian Pacific Islander ____% Other ____%
4. **Population by Gender** Male ____% Female ____%

5. **Income Figures:** Median Household Income $_____
Household Income Under $50K ____%
Household Income $50K-$100K ____%
Household Income Over $100K ____%

6. **Housing Figures** Average Home Value - $_____
Average Rent $_____

7. **Homeownership:** Homeowners % _____
Renters % _____

8. **Education Achievement** High School Diploma % _____
College Degree % _____
Graduate Degree % _____

9. **Stability/Newcomers** Longer than 5 years % _____

10. **Marital Status** ___% Married ___% Divorced ___% Single
__% Never Married __% Widowed __% Separated

11. **Occupations** ___%Service ___% Sales ___% Management
___% Construction ___% Production
___% Unemployed ___% Below Poverty Level

12. **Age Distribution** ___%Under 5 years ___%5-9 yrs ___%10-12 yrs
___% 13-17 yrs ___%18-years
___% 20-29 ___% 30-39 ___% 40-49 __% 50-59
___% 60-69 ___% 70-79 ___% 80+ years

13. **Prior Growth Rate** _____% from _____ (year)

14. **Projected Population Growth Rate** _____%

15. **Employment Trend** _____

16. **Business Failure Rate** _____

Secondary Market Research Conclusions:
This area will be demographically favorable for our business for the following reasons:
_____
_____

Resources:
www.allbusiness.com/marketing/segmentation-targeting/848-1.html
http://www.sbdcnet.org/industry-links/demographics-links
http://factfinder2.census.gov/faces/nav/jsf/pages/index.xhtml

4.1.1 Primary Market Research

We plan to develop a survey for primary research purposes and mail it to a list of fashion magazine subscribers, purchased from the publishers by zip code. We will also post a copy of the survey on our website and encourage visitors to take the survey.

We will use the following survey questions to develop an Ideal Customer Profile of our potential client base, so that we can better target our marketing communications. To improve the response rate, we will include an attention-grabbing _____ (discount coupon/ dollar?) as a thank you for taking the time to return the questionnaire.

1. What is your zip-code?
2. Are you single, divorced, separated, widowed or married?
3. Are you male or female?
4. What is your age?
5. What is your approximate household income?
6. What is your educational level?
7. What is your profession?
8. Are you a dual income household?
9. Do you have children? If Yes, what are their ages?
10. What are your favorite magazines?
11. What is your favorite local newspaper?
12. What is your favorite radio station?
13. What are your favorite television programs?
14. What organizations are you a member of?
15. Does our community have an adequate number of clothing rental businesses? Yes / No
16. Does your family currently patronize a local Subscription Clothing Rental Company? Y/N
17. Are you satisfied with your current Subscription Clothing Rental Company? Yes / No
18. How many times on average per year do you visit your wedding dress rental business? _____
19. What subscription services do you typically purchase?
20. What products do you typically rent?
21. On average, how much do you spend on Subscription Clothing Rental purchases per year? ____
22. What is the name of your currently patronized Subscription Clothing Rental Company?
23. What are their strengths as service providers?
24. What are their weaknesses or shortcomings?
25. What would it take for us to earn your subscription clothing rental business?
26. What is the best way for us to market our subscription clothing rental company?
27. Do you live in _____ community?
28. Do you work or study in _____ community?
29. Do you think you will be in need of clothing rentals in the near future?
30. Would you be interested in joining a Subscription Clothing Rental Company Club that would offer special Membership benefits?
31. Describe your experience with other Dress Rental Companies.
32. Please rank (1 to 17) the importance of the following factors when choosing a Subscription Clothing Rental Company:
    ___ Quality of Product   ___ Garment Selection

    ___ Reputation   ___ Staff Courtesy/Friendliness
    ___ Waiting time before service   ___ Staff Professionalism
    ___ Convenient location   ___ Value Proposition
    ___ Referral/References   ___ Complaint Handling
    ___ Rental Agreement   ___ Convenient Layout
    ___ Garment Cleaning/Sanitation   ___ In-stock availability
    ___ Styling Consultant Knowledge   ___ Price
    ___ Returns Policies   ___ Other _____

33. Please prioritize the importance of the following:
    ___ Free Fabric Swatches   ___ Fashion Shows
    ___ Gift Cards   ___ Accessories Availability
    ___ Style Consultants   ___ Jewelry Sales/Rentals

34. What information would you like to see in our Subscription Clothing Rental Company newsletter?

35. Which online social groups have you joined? Choose the ones you access.
    ___ Facebook   ___ Periscope
    ___ Twitter   ___ LinkedIn
    ___ Ryze   ___ Ning

36. What types of Subscription Clothing Rental Company services would most interest you?

37. When do you plan to get married? Date: _____

38. When will you attend your first job interview? Date: _____

39. What are your suggestions for realizing a better Subscription Clothing Rental Company experience?

40. Are you on our mailing list? Yes/No   If No, can we add you? Yes / No

41. Would you be interested in attending a free seminar on designer fashion trends?
42. Would you be interested in making an appointment with a stylist consultant?
43. Can you supply the name and contact info of person who might be interested in our clothing rental services?

Please note any comments or concerns about subscription clothing rental services in general.

We very much appreciate your participation in this survey. If you provide your name, address and email address, we will sign you up for our e-newsletter, inform you of our survey results, advise you of any new clothing rental business openings in your community, and enter you into our monthly drawing for a free _____.

Name   Address   Email   Phone

4.1.2   Voice of the Customer

To develop a better understanding of the needs and wants of our subscription clothing rental members, we will institute the following ongoing listening practices:
1. Focus Groups
2. Individual Interviews
3. Customer Panels
4. Customer Tours
5. Visit Members
6. Trade Show Meetings
7. Toll-free Numbers
8. Customer Surveys
9. Mystery Shoppers
10. Salesperson Debriefing
11. Customer Contact Logs
12. Customer Serviceperson's Hotline
13. Discussions with competitors.
14. Installation of suggestion boxes to encourage constructive feedback.

We will work hard to implement reasonable suggestions in order to improve our service offerings as well as show our commitment to the customer that their suggestions are valued.

4.1.3   Marketing Research

____ (company name) will conduct several focus groups to gain valuable insight into customer style preferences and rental decisions. A total of ____ (#) focus groups will be held. One with each of the two target markets and a third with members of both target markets present.

The focus groups will present the participants with the general business proposition of subscription clothing rentals and feedback will be collected. In addition to an open discussion, there will be a list of specific questions to be asked of all three focus groups. The results of the focus groups will be invaluable, with many of their suggestions eventually incorporated into the business model.

4.2 Market Segmentation

Market segmentation is a technique that recognizes that the potential universe of users may be divided into definable sub-groups with different characteristics. Segmentation will enable our organizations to target messages to the needs and concerns of these well-defined subgroups. We will segment the market based on the fashion needs and rental requirements of select customer groups. We will develop a composite customer profile and a value proposition for each of these segments. The purpose for segmenting the market will be to allow our marketing/sales program to focus on the subset of prospects that are "most likely" to purchase our subscription clothing rental services. If done properly this will help to ensure the highest return for our marketing/sales expenditures.

After we have decided upon our target audience of _____, we will determine the designers and brands we wish to carry, including _____. And then the choice of designers will determine the rental amount that will ultimately suit our target consumer.

There following major market segments will be served by _____ (company name):
1. Professional Women
2. Pregnant Women
3. Business Men
4. Millennials
5. Children

Prime Target Markets:
- Working Women: ages 25-48
- Baby Boomers with surplus income
- Mostly in urban areas.
- Likely online shopper.
- Household Income >100K

- Millennial Men: ages 18 - 34
- College Educated
- Predominantly single.
- Individual Income – 78K

Table: Market Analysis

Potential Members	Growth	Number of Potential Members		
		2019	2020	2021
Professional Women	10%			
Business Men	10%			

Pregnant Women	10%	_____
Millennials	10%	_____
Children	10%	_____
Other	10%	_____
Totals:	10%	_____

4.3 Target Market Segment Strategy

Our target marketing strategy will involve identifying a group of members to which to direct our wedding dress rental services. Our strategy will be the result of intently listening to and understanding customer needs, representing members' needs to those responsible for product production and service delivery, and giving them what they want. In developing our targeted customer messages, we will strive to understand things like: where they work, worship, party and play, where they shop and go to school, what designer brands they prefer, how they prefer to shop and pay for clothing, how they spend their leisure time, what magazines they read and organizations they belong to, and where they volunteer their time. We will use research, surveys and observation to uncover this wealth of information to get our subscription rental plan details and brand name in front of our prospective members when they are most receptive to receiving our messaging.

_____ (company name) will start by primarily targeting middle to high-income business professionals and millennials. Additionally, _____ (company name) will give the "other items" or accessories their own significance. In our Subscription Clothing Rental Company, "other items" will no longer be an afterthought, but rather a packaged focus. Our marketing strategy will create awareness, interest and demand from our target markets for our rental services. We will focus on the following well-defined target market segments and emphasize our good value, high quality, unique and varied designer selections, minimal cash outlays and great service.

Target Professional Women
We will target this group because research shows that the women end user segment accounts for the highest market share, accounting for nearly 58 percent. This segment is comprised of women in the age range of 25 to 50. They are married, have a household income >$100,000, own at least one home, and are socially active. They are members of at least one club or organization. They have high disposable or discretionary income and are considered the family decision-makers. Some these professional women have jobs that involve some traveling. We will help these women to learn the art of having rental clothing shipped directly to the travel destination and renting multi-faceted pieces that can be worn multiple times, in multiple ways, as there will often be no time to wait for luggage to be deplaned. What this group also likes about clothing rentals is that renting requires less of a commitment, and when they rent, women tend to go for a more directional style and are able to step out of their comfort zone and rent more daring and luxury items. In this, they are also encouraged by social media, where the name of the

game is constant make-over. We plan to amass many professional women subscribers by promising to solve the problem of what to wear to work, and to satisfy the expectation to appear poised, professional and trend conscious on a daily basis, for everyone from new hires to C-suite executives.
Source:
www.manifestyourself.com/how-to-dress-for-your-dream-job/
http://alltheweigh.com/2013/03/does-anyone-here-use-gwynniebee/

Target Executive Headhunters
We will target executive headhunters and recruiters and executive search firms, because they often coach their job candidates on how to 'dress for success' or at least for a successful job interview. We will create a separate sales brochure for this market and include helpful business attire insights and a checklist of dress for success apparel requirements.
Resources:
Association of Executive Search Consultants   www.aesc.org
Blue Steps   www.bluesteps.com/executive-search-firms.aspx
Online Recruiters Directory   www.onlinerecruitersdirectory.com/

Target Subscribers of Fashion Magazines
We will make a direct mailing to local subscribers of fashion magazines because they may appreciate the ability to rent trendy fashions with low cash outlays.
Resources:
Directory of Fashion Magazines
         www.fashiontrendsetter.com/content/directory/magazines.html
Lucire   http://lucire.com/shopping/d.shtml#JUGvR8MP7VB5U5SH.97

Target College Campuses/University Students
We will target the students of local colleges and universities, because this group has very limited cash reserves and needs to pursue rental arrangements. We plan to market to college-age women, an envisioned core customer base, by deploying hundreds of trained sales reps at campuses and sororities. On college campuses, we will benefit from the network effect, which typically starts when one woman has a subscription, becomes a walking billboard and praises the money-saving benefits of the service.

Target Millennials
Research indicates that Millennials are driving the growth of the apparel rental segment, and three key millennial lifestyle trends are underpinning the segment's development:
The "Instagram effect"—or the desire to be perceived on social media as living a fun, interesting, experience-rich life—combined with celebrity culture and the selfie phenomenon necessitate that millennials have an ever-changing, on-trend wardrobe.
Millennials value experiences over acquiring products and apparel rentals allow millennials to wear high-end brands at lower cost, and so funnel more of their spending toward services and leisure experiences.

Millennials are considered budget conscious, so renting items makes sense for them, especially when it comes to high-worth and expensive designer items that are used only occasionally.

Millennials are active socially and prefer not to be seen wearing the same clothes or outfits at commonly attended events.

Source:

https://coresight.com/research/deep-dive-millennial-lifestyles-drive-growth-apparel-rental/

https://www.latimes.com/business/la-fi-retail-rentals-20171220-story.html

Target Millennial Men

We will target this group because budget conscious end-users in the millennials age group are very ecommerce and social media savvy, and a great target market for the online clothing rental industry.

Target Millennial Women

Millennials are leading a migration away from ownership to subscribing and sharing to conserve money and natural resources. Our service will appeal to millennial women because they are less inclined to use their disposable income on luxury investments. We will benefit from the fact that we will enable them to reduce the financial investment that fashion consumers are often required to make for limited use garments.

Target Pregnant Women

We will create a subscription clothing rental plan that only features maternity clothing and nursing tops. This customer base will be comprised of women who are going through temporary stages of rapid size change. This service will be ideal for pregnant women who do not want to make a big investment in specialty clothing that will be worn for fewer than nine months. We also plan to develop strategic referral alliances with companies that service the needs of babies, including baby boutiques, toy stores and studio photographers. We will promote this service through medical doctors, hospital maternity wards and Lamaze classes. Research indicated that there are over 4 million pregnant mothers in the U.S., who spend an estimated $1.5 billion on maternity clothing each year. We will provide the alternative solution for women searching for maternity formal wear and we will offer hassle-free exchanges if an item does not fit.

Resource: www.whatsupfagans.com/le-tote-maternity-review/

Target Aging Baby Boomers

Since people age 50 and older have more discretionary money, they are more prone to take advantage of the new money-saving rental services.

Target Vintage Clothing Buyers

We will target vintage clothing buyers because they are comfortable wearing previously owned clothing, which is a growing consumption trend. Its aficionados, people who aren't put off by the idea that vintage clothes have been worn before, will be our primary target market for apparel rental, as well as for subscription services, a solution which the market seems increasingly ready to embrace.

Target Budget Conscious Fashion Lovers

This will be a great target market for our online clothing rental business. These people are typically subscribers to fashion magazines, such as Glamour, InStyle and Marie Claire.

Target Bargain Hunters
We will create a separate website to sell designer clothing that is no longer suitable for rental purposes.

Target Weight Loss Centers
Target Bariatric Surgery Centers
We will target these businesses because they service members/patients who may experience wide swings in body weight and may need the flexibility to rent and return clothing for short periods of time during this transitional period. These members will appreciate the ability to wear the clothes as many times as they want, and then exchange them for others as they continue to lose weight.
Source: www.bmioftexas.com/blog/revamp-your-post-weight-loss-wardrobe-with-these-money-saving-tips/

Target Job Seekers and New Job Hires
These are women that need to dress a certain way during the job interviewing process and then must conform to what is office appropriate. Women making the transition to the workforce will temporarily need the right clothing to make a good first impression, and then they need the flexibility to adjust to the dress code at their new place of employment.

Target Film, TV and Theater Production Companies
We will target these companies because they often need to cost-effectively assemble large wardrobes for the involved actors, background actors or extras and stunt doubles, for a relatively short period of time. We will seek to establish referral relationships with 'Wardrobe and Fashion Stylists' and 'Costume Supervisors'.
Resource:
www.productionhub.com/directory/profiles/wardrobe-stylists

Target Bridal Shows or Expos
Bridal shows are conventions for local vendors to display their products and services to brides and grooms. We will display our most popular rental wedding dresses as well as a sample of all the different accessories we carry. It will be important that we talk to brides and grooms to listen to their needs and show them how our shop can meet all those needs. We will also provide a special discount for bridal show attendees only or a coupon if the bride provides her bridal party contact information. This way a few days after the bridal show we can touch base with them and hopefully schedule an appointment for them to see what we have to offer. If the bride needs more time to think about it or isn't ready to make an appointment, we will let her know that we will touch base with her another time that is more convenient for her.
Resources:
Bridal Show Producers   https://bspibridalshows.com/directory.php
Wedding Wire   www.weddingwire.com/wedding-vendors

Target Parents of Young/Small Children

We will target this group with a line of designer children's clothing for special events, because they sometimes need to acquire clothing for their child's special occasion, and clothing becomes rapidly obsolete due to the growth stages that children rapidly progress through. Rather than paying full price for clothing that won't fit in just a few months, these consumers want to simply rent items today in their current correct size. We ask permission to circulate our marketing materials in preschools and child daycare centers. We will also realize a lot of attention by reaching out to parenting bloggers, who tried and loved the service and promoted it on their websites. These blogger will also help us to build trust in the mommy community.

Resource:

Preschool Directory	www.preschool.directory/
Mom Blogger Directory	www.cision.com/us/2014/05/top-50-u-s-mom-bloggers/
	http://mommybloggerdirectory.com/view-all

Target Ethnic Groups

Ongoing demographic trends suggest that, in the coming decades, programs will be serving a population of people which is increasingly diverse in economic resources, racial and ethnic background, and family structure. Our plan is to reach out to consumers of various ethnic backgrounds, especially Hispanics, who comprise nearly 13 percent of the country's total population. Overall, the Ethnic wear segment possesses higher market share and is expected to witness a considerable growth, owing to their frequent use in festivals, higher cost of rental, and greater maintenance costs. In addition to embarking on an aggressive media campaign of advertising with ethnic newspapers and radio stations, we will set up programs to actively recruit bilingual employees and make our shop more accessible via signage printed in various languages based on the store's community. We will accurately translate our marketing materials into other languages. We will enlist the support of our bilingual employees to assist in reaching the ethnic people in our surrounding area through a referral program. We will join the nearest _____ (predominate ethnic group) Chamber of Commerce and partner with _____ (Hispanic/Chinese/Other?) Advocacy Agencies. We will also develop programs that reflect cultural influences and brand preferences, and network via ethnic festivals.

Target Plus-size Women

We will target this market because 75 percent of adult women wear a size 10 and above, and two thirds wear 14 and above. Yet, they only spend about 17 percent of the apparel dollars, or about $17 billion in an apparel market estimated at $110 billion, according to NPD Group. We will target plus-size women because it is often more difficult and expensive for them to locate fashion forward garments that fit well. It will give this niche market the opportunity to more easily experiment with fashion and have fun while doing it. They will be able to try different pieces and trends that they normally wouldn't think about wearing, without making the upfront time and financial commitments. Also, because sizing for plus brands tend to be inconsistent, we will allow these women to try on a variety of brands, so they can figure out the right size for them in each brand. We will also offer to form cross-marketing alliances with 'plus-size designers.'

Directory of Plus Size Magazines
https://thecurvyfashionista.com/plus-size-fashion-resources/plus-size-magazines-communities/
Directory of Plus Size Designers
https://thecurvyfashionista.com/plus-size-fashion-resources/curvy-designers/
Source:
www.marketwatch.com/story/is-american-fashion-finally-embracing-the-plus-size-woman-2015-09-21

Target Travelers
We will target travelers because our systems will enable them to travel light. Customer who travel with their return envelopes, and take their return slip along, can conveniently drop it off in the mailbox at the end of their trip. Members will also be able to edit their shipping address to get their garments shipped to their travel destination anywhere within the US. There will also be no need to hire the services of a dry-cleaning company. We will promote this service via airline newsletters and travel magazines.

Target Travel Bureaus and Agencies
Target Travel Clubs
We will target adventure travel agencies that book trips to places with extreme warm or cold weather conditions, where it will not make sense to assemble a suitable wardrobe for a relatively short period of time. As an example, a customer taking an upcoming vacation to a tropical area, will not need to purchase cute tropical pieces for one-time usage, when they can easily rent the same. It will be especially great because our members will be able to have the garments shipped directly to the vacation location, to save both luggage space, and airline luggage fees.
Resource: www.affordabletravelclub.net/directory.html

Target Image and Style Consultants
We will target these consultants because our service will be ideal for people who are experimenting with the creation of a new image and/or want to maintain a 'no repeat' reputation.
Resources:

Association of Image Consultants International   www.aici.org

Target Financial Planners
We will target financial planners because they should be interested in helping their clients to engage in better wardrobe management techniques, for the benefit of career advancement, mental well-being and cost savings.

Target Catering Halls
We will target catering halls and other entertainment venues for special events, because online clothing rental is mainly suitable for people who do not want to purchase an expensive dress for a one-time event or borrow items every time from a friend. Designer gowns and accessory rentals, that were once the exclusive territory of celebrities, are

becoming a norm common to all. Women prefer variations in new designer brands and decide about the investment. With our online rental platform, consumers can now easily experiment with fashion or try new designer brands for special occasions.

Target Costume Party Goers
We will carry the following lines of themed clothing for costume party attendees: Western Garb, Vintage Roaring 20s Clothing and Ethnic Clothing for family reunions. We will advertise this service in Country Western Dance Halls and Party Supply Stores.

Target Celebrities
We will target celebrities because they have a branded image to maintain and will appreciate the ability to always appear fashion-forward when in the public eye. We will also benefit from the visibility or exposure that these celebrities will naturally generate. We will also make certain to carry some of the specific garment styles that celebrities have worn to special red-carpet events.

Target Fashion Trendsetters or Influencers
We will carefully curate a group of high-value clients who are considered to be trend-setters. Whenever we get new clothes, we will do exclusive previews for them in the hopes of them wanting to rent them and helping to set a new trend, which will directly affect demand in that type of clothing. In fact, Deloitte reports that customers who discover a brand on social media are 129 percent more likely to convert, so we will search for rising YouTube stars or Instagram users and try to form relationships that are mutually beneficial.

Target Hair and Make-up Artists
We will target these service professionals because they are sometimes asked to make wardrobe or fashion sourcing recommendations.

4.3.1 Market Needs

_____ (company name) will be providing its members with reasonable, practical, alternatives to purchasing clothing. Tradition is the only thing that demands the purchase of clothing. Economic realities are forcing people to reconsider this blindly accepted premise. The escalating cost of clothing, the increasing demand for high-end designer labels, and the trend toward staying more fashion current are making designer clothing rental more appealing.

Other drivers of the sharing economy or collaborative consumption include: an increase in peer-to-peer social networks and real-time technologies that fundamentally change the way we behave; the ability to collect and analyze big data patterns, pressing unresolved environmental concerns; and a global recession that fundamentally shocked consumer behaviors and spending habits.

Research indicates that all women, tend to leave 70 to 80 percent of their clothing hanging in the closet, unworn, for more than a year. It's estimated that the average person only wears about 20% of the clothes in their closet on a regular basis. Our company will be the solution to this waste-generating problem. We will be offering fashionable "clothing as a service" to choose, try and send back when finished.

Our members will be women who typically buy clothing or accessories and wear it once or twice. We will educate them as to why it makes no sense to own that item, and why it's just smarter to rotate that item in and out. On the emotional side, our members will be able to wear a much more interesting assortment of clothing.

_____ (company name) will seek to fulfill the following benefits that are important to members.
1. Selection- A wide choice of dresses and accessories will be offered.
2. Affordability- The rental pricing structure will provide high quality merchandise at reasonable fees.
3. Customer Service- We will hold the customer's hand as they proceed through the selection, wearing and returning processes.
4. Experience – We will provide a pleasant, hassle-free shopping experience that allows them to learn about fashion trends, select items, try on assortments, rent and return or purchase the items they want from the comfort of their own homes.

4.4 Buying Patterns

A Buying Pattern is the typical manner in which /buyers consumers purchase goods or services or firms place their purchase orders in terms of amount, frequency, timing, etc. In determining buying patterns, we will need to understand the following:
- Why consumers make the purchases that they make?
- What factors influence consumer purchases?
- The changing factors in our society.

Research indicates that our subscribers will rent clothes for the following reasons:
1. To stay abreast of or explore new fashion trends.
2. To be able to afford new designer fashions.
3. To reduce total cash outlays for clothing and increase expenditures on experiences.
4. To be able to try clothes on in the comfort of their own homes.

According to award-winning financial planner Pete Dunn, a person's clothing budget should be 5% of their Take-Home Pay. As an example, if take home pay is $3500 per month after taxes, spend no more than $175 each month on clothes, or $2100 a year.
Source:
www.whowhatwear.com/monthly-shopping-clothing-budget-guide-2014/slide2
https://financialbestlife.com/how-much-should-i-spend-on-clothing/

The average adult aged 25-34 spends $161 per month on clothing. Adults aged 35-44, however, spend slightly more, at $209 per month. This makes sense since the mean income for adults aged 35-44 is 26% higher than adults aged 25-34. The average adult aged 25-34 spends $161 per month on clothing. Adults aged 35-44, however, spend slightly more, at $209 per month. This makes sense since the mean income for adults aged 35-44 is 26% higher than adults aged 25-34.

On average, women aged 16 and over spend 76% more than men of the same age. Women spend around $571 per year. Women aged 45-54 also spend the most, though, at $793 per year.

Women have an average of $1,000 to $2,500 of clothing sitting in their wardrobe. Even though this seems high, 9% of women have more than $10,000 sitting in their closet.

More than 50% of women claim 25% of their wardrobe sits in the closet collecting dust. This equates to around $600 thrown out the window.

A whopping 73% of women update 25% of their closet every 3 months. Just over 15% of women don't have any clothes older than 5 years in their wardrobe.

On average, women pay 8% more than men for their clothing. The highest difference is in shirts. Women's tops cost 15% more than men's shirts. Jeans were a close second, costing 10% more for women than men's jeans.

Men aged 16 and over spend an average of $323 per year on clothing. Surprisingly, the men spending the most are between 45-54 years old. They spend $121 more per year than men aged 35-44.
Source:
https://www.creditdonkey.com/average-cost-clothing-per-month.html

Research indicates that on average, the American woman buys 64 new pieces of clothing a year, and half of which she will wear only once. Social media sites, like Facebook and Instagram, are also making things worse by putting pressure on women not to be seen wearing the same outfit repeatedly.

Research indicates that women purchase clothing for the following top 10 reasons (in order of importance):
1. Use the thrill of shopping to cheer themselves up.
2. To treat others
3. To feel they are looking good.
4. Because they are feeling a bit low.
5. Because they are feeling happy and joyful.
6. To impress others.
7. To remedy the feeling of being unhappy.
8. Things are not going well with their partner.
9. Because of feeling unattractive.
10. Because of feeling worried or depressed.

Source: www.prisonerofclass.com/how-much-women-actually-spend-on-clothing-accessories/

In most cases, members make the purchase decision on the basis of the following criteria:
1. Referrals and relationship with other members.
2. Personality and expected relationship with the style consultant personnel.
3. Internet-based information gathering.

____ (company name) will gear its offerings, marketing, and pricing policies to establish a loyal client base. Our value-based rental pricing, easy online access, preferred membership programs, home-based services and basic quality designer selection will be welcomed in _____ (city) and contribute to our success.

4.5 Market Growth

We will assess the following general factors that affect market growth:

Current Assessment
1. Interest Rates   _____
2. Government Regulations   _____
3. Perceived Environment Impact   _____
4. Consumer Confidence Level   _____
5. Population Growth Rate   _____
6. Unemployment Rate   _____
7. Political Stability   _____
8. Currency Exchange Rate   _____
9. Innovation Rate   _____
10. Home Sales   _____
11. Gasoline Prices   _____
12. Trend Linkage   _____
13. Overall Economic Health   _____

The subscription clothing rental market is relatively new. Currently, there are only ___ (#) different companies that rent clothing on the ____ (east/west?) coast. The clothing rental business started with formal attire for special occasions, such as weddings. These companies have grown quickly within recent years. But, additionally, almost all business people utilize formal or causal business attire, so the demand is there. All that is required is the willingness to be guided by practicality and break away from tradition.

The current pioneers have seen 35% increases in sales per month. The only thing that has been holding them back is awareness. When the right demographic hears about the idea of renting designer clothing at affordable prices, they are usually very enthusiastic about this low-cost alternative
.

_____ (company name) has forecasted significant growth within the industry. Granted there will be a learning or awareness curve as people become familiar with the subscription clothing rental industry, but once awareness has been generated, growth is expected to be exponential.

We believe there is a market for our clothing rental services in ___ (city) and that the market has potential for a ___ % growth rate. _____ County's population in the year 2010 was ____ and is expected to grow at a rate of ___ (5)% over the next ten years. ____ (city) is dedicated to remaining a travel destination "hot spot" without losing its "small town" feel. Because of its unique appeal it is likely to attract many vacationers and settlers for years to come. Our business will grow as members become familiar with our unrivaled designer selection and money saving, low-cost rental services.

The general industry analysis shows that _____ (city) is expected to experience _____ (double digit?) population, housing and commercial business growth. This suggests that as more families continue to move into the ____ area, there will be an increasing demand for quality subscription rental services, and this makes it a prime location for a Subscription Clothing Rental Company that is willing to think outside-of-the-box.

4.6.0 Service Business Analysis

Online clothing rental portals offer a wide range of clothes, which can be characterized based on occasions, size, color, fabric types, type of outfits, designer brands, and prices.

The online clothing rental market is segmented based on end-users, clothing styles, and geography. Based on end-users, it is classified into women, pregnant women, men, and kids. For clothing styles, it is categorized into ethnic, western, and others. Geographically, it is analyzed into, North America (U.S., Canada, and Mexico), Europe (UK, Germany, France, and Rest of Europe), Asia-Pacific (India, China, Japan, and Rest of Asia-Pacific), and LAMEA (Latin America, Middle East, and Africa). With regards to the market competition, online renting and e-commerce companies are expanding the pre-owned clothing and jewelry markets with pioneering solutions to big data analysis, personalization, efficient returns handling, feedback pattern analysis, eco-friendly laundering, and hassle-free, one-stop renting with no shipping charges, to cater to distinctively different segments. Additionally, As, broadband internet increases, so will the demand for online shopping and online rental services. Additionally, a steady significant increase in the use of mobile technology is further expected to boost the market.

The impact of social network sites, such as Facebook, Instagram, and online communities is also expected to have a great impact on the expansion and growth of the market as these social network sites and online communities help to spread the knowledge about companies and startups in the online clothing rental market. The rapid growth in urbanization has also spawned consumers with more expenditure capabilities in the market and an urge to stay either fashion current or fashion-forward, to establish one's own identity or branded image.

Source: www.alliedmarketresearch.com/online-clothing-rental-market

It will be important to set up the systems to accomplish the following:

1. Track the location of each item.
2. Select the best shipping methods.
3. Set rental prices based on demand.
4. Control inventory by creating algorithms to analyze customer reviews to forecast which garments are renting for which uses or occasions.
5. Evaluate the purchase of all new garments, based on a list of data points, such as fabric, zippers, color fading, stitching and shape to determine whether it will hold up to the demands of the rental market.

The demand for Subscription Clothing Rental Companies is increasing for the following reasons:
1. Members appreciate the knowledgeable and attentive service provided by the style consultants.
2. Time-starved members appreciate the convenience of one-stop shopping.
3. Members want to free up cash for other living expenses.

Successful Subscription Clothing Rental Companies offer convenience, substantial cash savings and have a staff that is friendly and approachable. They understand that they are the originating point for important business, social and family times and are very supportive of members who require help with clothing selection recommendations, fitting services, budgeting advice, returns processing and eco-friendly fabric recycling, or garment mending and reselling.

4.7 Barriers to Entry

_____ (company name) will benefit from the following combination of barriers to entry, which cumulatively present a moderate degree of entry difficulty or obstacles in the path of other subscription clothing rental businesses wanting to enter our market.

1.	Business Experience.	2.	Community Networking
3.	Referral Program	4.	People Skills
5.	Marketing Skills	6.	Supplier Relationships
7.	Operations Management	8.	Cash Flow Management
9.	Website Design	10.	Capital Investment
11.	Stylist Consulting Skills	12.	Organizational Skills
13.	Software Development	14.	Big Data Analysis

4.7.1 Porter's Five Forces Analysis

We will use Porter's five forces analysis as a framework for the industry analysis and business strategy development. It will be used to derive the five forces which determine the competitive intensity and therefore attractiveness of our market. Attractiveness in this context refers to the overall industry profitability.

Competitors The degree of rivalry is high in this segment, but less when compared to the overall category. There are _____ (#) major competitors in the

_____ area and they include: _____

Threat of Substitutes
> Substitutes are high for this industry. These include other garment rental companies, 'fast fashion' chains, clothing boutiques, resale shops, etc.

Bargaining Power of Buyers
> Buyer power is moderate in the business. Buyers are sensitive to quality and pricing as the segment attempts to capitalize on the pricing and quality advantage.

Bargaining Power of Suppliers
> Supplier power is moderate in the industry. Inventory can be obtained from a number of distributors and designers. A high level of operational efficiency for managing supplies can be achieved.

Threat of New Entrants
> Relatively moderate in this segment. The business model can be copied after a sizeable investment in inventory and specialty software development.

Conclusions: _____ (company name) is in a competitive field and has to move fast to retain its competitive advantage. The key success factors are to develop operational efficiencies, innovative rental program options, cost-effective marketing and customer service excellence.

4.8 Competitive Analysis

Competitor analysis in marketing and strategic management is an assessment of the strengths and weaknesses of current and potential competitors. This analysis will provide both an offensive and defensive strategic context through which to identify our business opportunities and threats. We will carry out continual competitive analysis to ensure our market is not being eroded by developments in other firms. This analysis will be matched with the target segment needs to ensure that our subscription clothing rental services continue to provide better value than the competitors. The competitive analysis will show very clearly why our products and services are preferred in some market segments to other offerings and to be able to offer reasonable proof of that assertion.

Competitor	**What We Can Do and They Can't**	**What They Can Do and We Can't**

There are currently about ___ (#) Subscription Clothing Rental Companies in _____ County; however, the primary focus of all of those shops is just formal attire, so they have a very limited selection casual attire and accessories. _____ (company name) is unique in ____ County in focusing on all the rental needs of the entire ____ community.

Other competitive factors include breadth and depth of available stock, product knowledge, customer service, expense management, marketing programs, employee training and productivity, management of detailed customer information in databases, extended hours of operation, incoming and outgoing delivery efficiencies, packaging, customer loyalty programs, out-of-area competition, rental program pricing options, and branded reputation.

Competitors:
There are other direct marketers and major advertisers that can deliver into our territory, But we expect our local delivery service will be faster and more responsive than these bigger players. Internet storefronts are emerging competitors and may be more of a longer-term issue, since the industry is in the process of testing and adapting to changing conditions in search of an online subscription business model that works best. We intend to develop our own website and grow with website economics that make this a self-funding outlet for sales and service. We are also aware of the importance of cultivating personal relationships with our members, so we can develop a long-term loyal customer base.

We will conduct good market intelligence for the following reasons:
1. To forecast competitors' strategies.
2. To predict competitor likely reactions to our own strategies.
3. To consider how competitors' behavior can be influenced in our own favor.

Overall competition in the area is _____ (weak/moderate/strong).
But, as people's finances become overextended, women are making critical decisions on how they spend their money. As disposable income becomes a scarce resource, they are, now more than ever, willing to sacrifice someone else's uninformed opinions, and embrace the idea of wearing a rental garment in return for freeing up their cash for other purposes.

Competitive analysis conducted by the company owners has shown that there are _____ (# or no other?) Subscription Clothing Rental Companies currently offering the same combination of dress rental services in the _____ (city) area. However, the existing competitors offer only a limited range of traditional purchase arrangements. In fact, of these, _____ (# or none) of the competitors offered a range of clothing rental services comparable with what _____ (company name) plans to offer to its members.

Self-assessment
Competitive Rating Assessment: 1 = Weak .... 5 = Strong

	Our Company	Prime Competitor	Compare
Our Location	_____	_____	_____
Our Facilities	_____	_____	_____
Our Products	_____	_____	_____
Our Services and Amenities	_____	_____	_____
Our Management Skills	_____	_____	_____
Our Training Programs	_____	_____	_____
Our Research & Development	_____	_____	_____
Our Company Culture	_____	_____	_____

Our Business Model   _____   _____   _____
Our Distribution System   _____   _____   _____
Overall Rating   _____   _____   _____
Rationale: _____

The following Subscription Clothing Rental Companies are considered direct competitors in _____ (city):

Competitor	Address	Market Share	Primary Focus	Secondary Prod/Svcs	Strengths	Weaknesses

Indirect Competitors include the following:
_____
_____

Alternative Competitive Matrix

Competitor Name: Us   _____   _____   _____
Location: _____   _____   _____
Location Distance (miles)   _____   _____   _____

Comparison Items:
Sales Revenue   _____
Buying Power   _____
Product Focus   _____
Inventory Type   _____
Inventory Size   _____
Membership Programs   _____
Membership Benefits   _____
Profitability   _____
Market Share   _____
Brand Names   _____
Specialty   _____
Services   _____
Returns Policies   _____
Shipping Policies   _____
Capitalization   _____
Target Markets   _____
Service Area   _____
Open Days   _____
Operating Hours   _____
Operating Policies   _____
Payment Options   _____
Other Financing   _____
Membership Pricing   _____
Price Level L/M/H   _____
Discounts   _____
Yrs in Business   _____

Reputation _____
Reliability _____
Quality _____
Marketing Strategy _____
Methods of Promotion _____
Alliances _____
Brochure/Catalog _____
Website _____
Sales Revenues _____
No. of Staff _____
Competitive Advantage _____
Credit Cards Accepted Y/N _____
Comments _____

Competitor Profile Matrix

	Our	Competitor 1	Competitor 2	Competitor 3
Critical Success Factors	Score	Rating Score	Rating Score	Rating Score
Advertising				
Product Quality				
Service Quality				
Price Competition				
Management				
Financial Position				
Customer Loyalty				
Brand Identity				
Market Share				
Total				

We will use the following sources of information to conduct our competition analysis:

1. Competitor company websites.
2. Mystery shopper visits.
3. Annual Reports (www.annual reports.com)
4. Thomas Net (www.thomasnet.com)
5. Trade Journals
6. Trade Associations
7. Sales representative interviews
8. Research & Development may come across new patents.
9. Market research can give feedback on the customer's perspective
10. Monitoring services will track a company or industry you select for news.
    Resources: www.portfolionews.com   www.Office.com
11. Hoover's   www.hoovers.com
12. www.zapdata.com   (Dun and Bradstreet) You can buy one-off lists here.
13. www.infousa.com   (The largest, and they resell to many other vendors)
14. www.onesource.com (By subscription, they pull information from many sources)

15. www.capitaliq.com   (Standard and Poors).
16. Obtain industry specific information from First Research (www.firstresearch.com) or IBISWorld, although both are by subscription only, although you may be able to buy just one report.
17. Get industry financial ratios and industry norms from RMA (www.rmahq.com) or by using ProfitCents.com software.
18. Company newsletters
19. Industry Consultants
20. Local Suppliers and Distributors
21. Customer interviews regarding competitors.
22. Analyze competitors' ads for their target audience, market position, product features, benefits, prices, etc.
23. Attend speeches or presentations made by representatives of your competitors.
24. View competitor's trade show display from a potential customer's point of view.
25. Search computer databases (available at many public libraries).
26. Review competitor Yellow Book Ads.
27. www.bls.gov/cex/   (site provides information on consumer expenditures nationally, regionally, and by selected metropolitan areas).
28. www.sizeup.com

4.9 Market Revenue Projection

For each of our chosen target markets, we will estimate our market share in number of members, and based on consumer behavior, how often do they buy per year? What is the average dollar amount of each purchase? We will then multiply these three numbers to project sales volume for each target market.

Target Market	Number of Members	No. of Rentals per Year	Average Dollar Fee per Rental	Total Sales Volume
	A x	B x	C =	D

Using the target market number identified in this section, and the local demographics, we have made the following assessments regarding market opportunity and revenue potential in our area: **Potential Revenue Opportunity** =

         _____ Local No. of Households (>60k Income)
(x)   _____ Expected ___% Market Share
(=)   _____ Number of likely local members
(x) $ _____ Average annual fee dollar amount
(=) $ _____ Annual Revenue Opportunity.

Or

                      No. of Members   (x)   Avg. Sale   (=)   Daily Income
                      Per Day
Services   _____   _____   _____
Product Sales _____   _____   _____

Other
Total:
Annualized: (x)   300
Annual Revenue Potential:
Recap
Month   Jan Feb Mar Apr May Jun Jul Aug Sep Oct Nov Dec   Total
Products

___

Services

___

Gross Sales:
(-) Returns
Net Sales

Revenue Assumptions:
1. The sources of information for our revenue projection are:

2. If the total market demand for our product/service = 100%, our projected sales volume represents ____% of this total market.
3. The following factors might lower our revenue projections:

5.0   Industry Analysis

North America is expected to contribute significantly towards the online clothing rental market, due to the increase in fashion consciousness and huge adoption of the 'No Ownership' trend towards clothes. It is anticipated to dominate the market throughout the analysis period. However, Asia-Pacific is expected to witness the highest growth rate, owing to the presence of emerging countries, such as China.

This industry comprises establishments primarily engaged in renting clothing, such as casual and formal wear, costumes (e.g., theatrical), or other clothing (except laundered uniforms and work apparel).

Renters of clothing can now relax in the comfort of their own home, while they peruse through the thousands of available ready-to-wear fashions and accessories available for rent via the Internet. Not only will most online clothing rental sites match the rental to suit the subscriber's unique size, shape and style, many will deliver the outfit, together with any requested matching accessories, right to the customer's front door, and make arrangement for the return and dry cleaning of the garment.

5.1 Industry Leaders

We plan to study the best practices of industry leaders and adapt certain selected practices to our business model concept. Best practices are those methods or techniques resulting in increased customer satisfaction when incorporated into the operation.

The best known of the industry leaders is US-based Rent the Runway, which launched in 2009 and today has over 5.5 million members. However, the swath of start-ups in the field includes Girl Meets Dress in the UK, Chic by Choice in Europe and Glam Corner in Australia, as well as more niche ventures, such as Gwynnie Bee (plus-size fashion rental) and Borrow for Your Bump (maternity wear rental). Other key companies operating in the global online clothing rental market are Poshmark, Elanic Services Pvt Ltd., Dress & Go, Envoged, Etashee, Secoo Holdings Ltd, and Secret Worldwide.
Source:
www.businessoffashion.com/articles/fashion-tech/will-the-sharing-economy-work-for-fashion-rent-the-runway-rental
www.futuremarketinsights.com/reports/online-clothing-rental-market

Start-ups in the subscription fashion rental space include Golden Tote (which sends members a monthly selection of clothing, costing upwards of $49), Elizabeth & Clarke (quarterly deliveries of white shirts, costing $60), Adore Me (a monthly lingerie selection for $39.95) and Avenue A, Adidas' subscription service for women's sportswear, costs $150 a quarter.

Source:
www.businessoffashion.com/articles/intelligence/can-subscription-services-work-for-fashion

The key players include Bag Borrow Steal (U.S.), Dress & Go (Brazil), Glam Corner Pty Ltd (Australia), Gwynnie Bee (U.S.), Le Tote (U.S.), Lending Luxury (U.S.), Rent the Runway (U.S.), Secoo Holdings Limited (China), Secret Wardrobe (India), and Share Wardrobe (India). Share Wardrobe, Stylish Play, FlyRobe, Walkin Closet, and Secret Wardrobe are other major players operating in the global online clothing rental market
Source: www.alliedmarketresearch.com/press-release/online-clothing-rental-market.html

The major players in France are Dressing Avenue and Les Cachotières (renting among private consumers), Le Closet (clothes-box renting), L'Habibliothèque (targeting the young), Sac de Luxe (for leather goods) and 1 Robe pour 1 Soir (event-based).
Source:
https://us.fashionnetwork.com/news/Is-renting-the-future-for-fashion-and-luxury-,962147.html#.XBAl0uJOmUk

Gwynnie Bee   https://closet.gwynniebee.com/

This subscription service is often called the 'Netflix of Fashion' and 'Netflix for Clothes' due to the similarities in their service models. The owner was attracted to Netflix's approach of all access for one price rather than the transactional nature of 'Rent the Runway's' business model. In the GB business model, a member creates a virtual 'closet' queue of 25 desired items, prioritizes items of special interest, receives and keeps the shipment at home, according to the number of garments permitted in the selected plan (1 to 10 items) for any length of time. The customer then either sends the item(s) back in a pre-paid envelope for new items, when they are ready, or purchases, at a significant discount, any of the items they want to permanently add to their home wardrobe collection. As items are added to the virtual closet, the company uses this information to help them learn about the subscriber's style preferences, which allows them to predict and suggest the right, personalized items to be included in future shipments.

Since its 2012 launch, the Long Island City, NY based company has shipped more than four million boxes, established 150-plus brand partners and has more than 3,000 styles in rotation. Gwynnie Bee started for women sized 10 to 32 and is adding sized 0 to 8. The number of items that can be rented at any one time is determined by the subscription level chosen. There are six different subscription boxes from $49 for one rented item at a time, to $199 per month for 10 items at a time.

Membership Benefits:
They offer a 30-day free trial to new accounts. Members are initially asked to put 25 items in their virtual closets and flag eight "priorities." When available, GB promises to send the customer at least one of their priority picks. Members can also choose to purchase rented items but are not allowed to buy pieces before trying them on. The site also claims that items are retired once light wear and tear begins to show and are then donated to a local charity. There is no limit to how many times a month the customer can swap items. Shipping is always free, and to facilitate the return of the clothing, there are postage prepaid bags included in each box of clothing. Also, laundering items before returning is not necessary. GB asks that if clothing needs to be washed between usage occasions that their clothing either be washed on the gentle cycle in cold water or dry-cleaned. They also do not hold members responsible for normal wear and tear to their clothing. But they do ask that the customer email or call customer service to give them a heads up that the item will need repair or replacement.

Returns Processes:
The company takes the pledge of garment sanitary cleanliness very seriously. At its 250-person warehouse in Ohio, each garment is washed or dry cleaned after every return. It's then inspected for stains, damage, or odor by three different employees before it can be re-boxed and shipped out again to the next customer. When a garment no longer looks new, it's taken out of circulation and donated to a worthy cause.

GB Mission:
Their mission is to create a service that helps women discover, experience, and enjoy great fitting clothing without the following types of limitations: how often will each garment be worn, whether it will match other items in the wardrobe or go out of style, and the stress of finding the right fit when the customer has a size change. Their objectives are to deliver all the great, self-confidence building feelings that fashion has to offer, without all the stress.

Successful Strategies:
Part of their success can be attributed to the fact that the company adds new styles to its website every other day. To maintain subscriber interest, they constantly bring the customer newness and freshness and provide them with things that they feel they need to try. They also developed the expertise to upsize standard-sized patterns for plus-size women. They basically offered to complete full, plus-size patterns for designers to be used in the manufacturing process. Gwynnie Bee presents brand partners with opportunities to plug into their growing membership and the unique feedback loop of consumer insights. Gwynnie Bee has not only helped straight-size brands to expand their size range but has also worked with international brands to launch their collections in the United States. Their recent co-branded launches with Rachel Antonoff, Hemant & Nandita and Tocca have all been very successful. These co-branded launches have enabled GB to bring exclusive, unique product to their members. They have also been successful in building a supportive and welcoming community around the common interests and needs of plus-size women. GB also enjoys the buying power afforded to the largest buyer of plus-sized garments in the market. GB also does a good job of encouraging members to use their website, Instagram page, and even creating their own fan pages on Facebook, to share photos, styling tips, reviews, and more.

GB Apps
Equipped with BeKitzur made apps Gwynnie Bee clients can browse all the cloth selection, track shipping, scan products and communicate to personal stylists and GB customer support.
Resource: https://bekitzur.com/project/gwynniebee-netflix-for-clothes/

Source:
www.inc.com/magazine/201607/zoe-henry/christine-hunsicker-gwynnie-bee-plus-size-clothing.html
www.thenativesociety.com/tnspeak/christine-hunsicker-ceo-founder-gwynnie-bee.html

Their partnership with Amazon allows customers to leverage 'Alexa' to manage the subscription process and provide insight and details that may otherwise be missed. Gwynnie Bee launched a voice-activated unboxing experience through Amazon Alexa. The feature lets shoppers interact with and learn about the retailer's size-inclusive subscription service as they open their delivered box of products and try on their items in real time. Gwynnie Bee's voice-activated experience is a fun way for members to imagine themselves wearing newly arrived clothing while Alexa guides them through a customizable story as they unbox their products.
Source:
www.amazon.com/Gwynnie-Bee/dp/B07DX3TDHD
www.mobilemarketer.com/news/gwynnie-bee-calls-on-alexa-for-voice-powered-unboxing/529513/

Financing Sources:

According to CrunchBase, the privately held company has raised about $8 million in financing so far from venture capital firms, including Cava Capital and Grace Beauty Capital, and claims that sales are growing 15 percent month-over-month.

Resources:
www.crunchbase.com/organization/gwynnie-bee#section-funding-rounds
https://pitchbook.com/profiles/company/85425-76
www.bloomberg.com/research/stocks/private/snapshot.asp?privcapId=231901468
https://craft.co/gwynniebee
www.cnbc.com/2016/03/23/how-swapping-clothes-sparked-a-billion-dollar-biz-idea.html

DressVault   http://dressvault.ning.com/

This "online closet service" facilitates the lending and borrowing of dresses to and by site members. It is a fashion social network of virtual closets with over 900 current members. The selection is, at present, somewhat limited, but rapid expansion of membership and available clothing is possible in the coming months. This site provides easy access to reasonably priced off the rack designs, but they need to add a search by size function to make things simpler. The idea that lending and borrowing clothing is "environmentally friendly," and with their detailed instructions, the customer will know just what to expect in terms of price, repairs, cleaning, deposits, and so on.

Wantable   www.wantable.com

An online lifestyle service that promises to help take the legwork out of shopping by delivering handpicked clothing and accessories straight to the customer's doorstep. Members need to choose a category and take a short style quiz, after which they will receive five to seven items tailored by their personal stylist to their individual tastes, needs, and wants. After receiving the goods, members can buy the ones they want and return the rest. And at any time, members can visit their online Stream to view quiz matches, request those they like with a click, and decline those they don't.

Wantable offers three product categories from premium brands such as Hudson, Cupcakes & Cashmere, Kensie, Seven7, Kut From the Kloth, Glyder, Wear it to Heart, Rhone, and Alternative Apparel. Their categories include 'Style', which is clothing, such as jeans and pants, jackets, shirts, dresses, blouses, and fitness wear, as well as accessories such as scarves, jewelry, and clutches/wallets, and 'Women's Fitness' and 'Men's Fitness' which include training, performance, and loungewear apparel such as pullovers, jackets, shirts, bottoms (including compression pants and shorts), socks, and undergarments. Women's Style and Fitness options are available in sizes XS-3X (0-24W), while Men's Fitness items are sized between S and XL.

After choosing a category, members take a quick quiz to assess their personal preferences. In the end, members can add notes for their stylist, and then sign up for an account. Based on customer responses, one of the company's stylists will send out seven premium, handpicked pieces. Once received, the customer has five days to try everything before deciding which options to keep and buy, and which options to send back.

They offer shipping plans on an ongoing basis (back-to-back), monthly, every two months, or every three months. Members can manually skip a shipment by logging in to their 'Plan Manager'. What members pay depends on their preferences and how many 'Edit' items they choose to keep. Members will also have to pay an upfront $20 styling fee per Edit (seven total pieces), which will be applied to their purchase. While this fee is nonrefundable if you don't select any items, Wantable offers free shipping on all U.S. orders, along with a prepaid return envelope for any items the customer chooses not to keep. In order to avoid being charged, members will need to have this envelope postmarked by 4:00 pm CST within five days of receiving their package. Apparel and accessories must be unworn with the tags still attached in order to qualify.

Fabletics

It is free to become a VIP Member, however, by signing up, the customer agrees to be charged $49.95 every month. The cost is applied to their monthly outfit purchase. Standard shipping is always free for Fabletics members. Members can also select express shipping for $8.95. Additionally, the first purchase as a member is discounted to only $25.00. Fabletics offers a 30-day return policy for all new, unworn items with original tags. However, the return will be subject to a $5.95 restocking fee.

The first step in signing up for a Fabletics membership is taking a quiz. Members can browse Fabletics for new outfits each month, or also receive personalized suggestions based on their style and workout preferences at the beginning of each month. Fabletics clothing is available in a wide range of sizes. Between the 1st and 5th of each month, Fabletics notifies members of a new personalized selection, based on quiz responses, awaiting their approval. Members can choose what's been suggested or shop the Fabletics collection, instead. Members can skip a month of Fabletics as many times as they like but must log in during the same date range to select "skip a month" to avoid charges. Suggested outfits won't ever ship without customer approval. However, if the customer forgets to log in to either shop around or skip the month, they will still be charged the $49.95 and the funds will be credited to their account to be used for a future purchase. Cancelling a Fabletics membership can be done at any time by calling customer service.

Source: https://www.highya.com/fabletics-reviews

Rent the Runway   www.renttherunway.com

This company was launched in 2009 and now claims six million members in the USA. By the end of 2019, Rent the Runway will offer fifteen thousand styles by more than five hundred designers, with a total inventory of eight hundred thousand units. This inventory is kept in a three-hundred-thousand-square-foot warehouse and dry-cleaning complex in Secaucus, New Jersey. It began by renting out dresses for all occasions, and then launched a wedding boutique in 2016, where bridesmaids can rent designer frocks for between $40 and $150 from designers such as Calvin Klein, Vera Wang, Badgley Mischka and Nicole Miller. Rent the Runway recently introduced plus-size styles to its line-up, so now all bridesmaids can rent their dresses (including identical dresses) from this service. The company is presently averaging 30 turns per dress, which means some get worn many more times and great care is taken to mend and clean returning garments to improve profitability.

The company also just launched a new subscription service called 'Unlimited' that lets members borrow up to three accessories (sunglasses, bags, jackets) for as long as they want for $75 a month. The company has also been plowing resources into data science, pricing models and a mobile platform, which now accounts for 40% of traffic. The company's plan is to be a marketplace for retailers and brands to rent unsold inventory instead of shipping it off to discount outlets, and/or become a high-end consignment store. The company believes that their subscribers spend nineteen hundred dollars a year, and the average subscriber gets forty thousand dollars' worth of value in return.

The company receives wholesale pricing, quantity discounts and full-size runs of each season's trendiest dresses. The company also partners with young, unknown designers for exclusive collections only available through Rent the Runway. In 2016, Neiman Marcus partnered with Rent the Runway to attract more millennials to its San Francisco store.

Rent the Runway has launched a feature where real members model the website's designs. The feature, called "Our Runway," shows women of all shapes and sizes describing their experience wearing the dress they rented from the e-commerce site. Women also include information like their weight, body type, dress size and height. On the revamped Rent the Runway site, users can also ask questions of the real-life wearers. To enrich the hassle-free experience, Rent the Runway offers options like in-store kiosks with product label scanning capabilities, live chats with stylists and the ability to order a free back-up size. They continually tweak their algorithms to identify pieces that customers might like and highlight them on the app's home screen, similar to recommendations offered by Amazon. They are creating one-to-one style personas for every subscriber they have, which is helping them to create an individual home page for each customer, where they can recommend clothing that the customer might like. Essentially, they are using data to bring a greater degree of satisfaction to the clothing acquiring and wearing experiences. It also shares its findings with the designers whose clothing it stocks, so they can produce a better quality, more in-demand garment with a longer lifecycle.

Rent the Runway has invested heavily in logistics, to ensure products that are returned to the company in the morning can be ready to ship to a new customer that evening. They are planning to build multiple fulfillment centers across the country to reduce dress 'in transit' downtime. It is also currently the US's biggest dry cleaner, operating a 160,000 square foot fulfillment center that dry cleans 2,000 dresses every hour. With its own in-house dry-cleaning plant, RTR can continue to meet the high demand for items: 60% of dresses depart the same day they arrive back to the warehouse. Due to the high-quality in-house operations, RTR averages 30 uses per garment, with every save by the highly skilled 'spotters' allowing more revenue per piece. They have dedicated a 2,500 square foot shop in the warehouse where coveted items are sold at up to 90% off retail, after their days being shipped across the U.S. have ended.

Source:
https://rctom.hbs.org/submission/rent-the-runway-a-successful-fashion-forward-business/

In 2014, they officially started renting everyday apparel for work and play as part of its 'Unlimited' offering. Rent the Runway 'Unlimited' members can rent three designer dresses, tops, skirts, or accessories at a time and keep them for as long as they want. RTR Unlimited: Members get the first month for $99, after it is $159/month and customers can keep up to four items at a time, rotating out any piece as often as she likes. They have also opened a retail store, with a limited inventory, as a kind of testing ground in which to observe users' behavior and adapt accordingly.

In 2019, the co-founders of Chinese web giant Alibaba, Jack Ma and Joe Tsai, invested $20 million in the designer dress and accessory rental service Rent the Runway. Conde Nast is also an investor.

Resources:
htttps://qz.com/1104344/can-rent-the-runway-ever-become-the-spotify-of-fashion/
www.nytimes.com/2019/10/12/business/rent-the-runway-office-clothes.html
www.usatoday.com/story/tech/reviewedcom/2019/03/23/used-rent-runway-unlimited-
	year-actually-worth-money/33214461/
www.forbes.com/sites/sashagalbraith/2013/12/03/the-secret-behind-rent-the-
	runways-success/
www.newyorker.com/magazine/2019/10/22/rent-the-runway-wants-to-lend-you-your-look

Stitch Fix

Offers clothing for men (28-42W) and women (0-24W). Sends five pieces of clothing to the customer's door, and they keep and pay for the ones they want. No rentals are available, and no subscription is required. Includes maternity. Items range in price between $20 and $600 (average $55 each). $20 per-box styling fee. Members cannot wear, damage, and then return these items. Members can either keep them and wear them, or don't try them at all and simply send them back.

Stitch Fix hires stylists to devote their attention to individual subscribers. This personal shopping service StitchFix lets members schedule how often they want to receive its boxes of clothing, the contents of which are selected through a combination of human stylists and an algorithm. The algorithm was developed to suggest styles for individual members, which stylists can make a selection from, based on data and conversations they have had with the customer. The algorithm is able to say probabilistically what is most like to be kept.

Stitch Fix costs a flat fee of $20 for every styled shipment received. Each shipment includes five items. The $20 fee covers the services of the personal stylist. Any clothes that the customer decides to keep are extra. Stitch Fix states that their average price point is $55 per item. However, that they do their best to stick to the prices that the customer indicated in their answers to the style quiz and budget questions. Additionally, Stitch Fix makes that fee a little easier to handle by applying it as a credit, if the customer chooses to keep any of the items in their shipment.

Stitch Fix shipments can come as often as the customer likes. That can be every 2-3 weeks, every month, every other month, or every three months. The $20 billings depend on how frequently the customer decides to receive deliveries. Members can also choose to use Stitch Fix on a shipment-by-shipment basis, with no required subscription memberships. Members not interested in receiving ongoing shipments, can indicate this preference when they sign up. Members can also change their upcoming shipment frequency or cancel at any time without penalty.

Stitch Fix gives members three business days to try on their clothing and make sure it really works for them. If a customer needs more time, they can extend their return window by contacting customer service. But if they don't request an extension or ship things back within three days, the customer will be charged for the entire shipment, and that charge is final. Each shipment comes with a prepaid return mail envelope, to help with returning items by the third business day. Stitch Fix also sends a sheet of Style Cards, which shows the subscriber how to wear and accessorize their new items.

Le Tote   www.letote.com
This company is led by Rakesh Tondon, who is their Co-Founder & CEO. Allows members to rent unlimited apparel and accessories over the internet for one low, monthly price. All items are sent directly to the customer's door within 2-3 business days in boxes (or totes). Allows their members to receive clothing, add items to 'Closets' that are sent out on a regular basis, return clothing using pre-paid labels, provide coverage for light damage, and the ability to purchase clothing at a less-than-retail discount. Unlimited totes per month. Thousands of brands and styles, including maternity and Kate Spade jewelry. Charges $59 - $79/mo. The company offers free two-day shipping both ways. Members can enjoy their rented pieces as long as they like before sending their tote back and picking out a new one. In addition, all the items are purchasable in case the customer falls in love with something.

Members can skip their questionnaire and immediately begin browsing the Le Tote website by section, such as New Arrivals, Collections, Clothing (categories like dresses, tops, skirts, etc.), and Accessories (bracelets, earrings, scarves, and the like), and adding items to their closet. Then, when they have enough items in their closet, one of Le Tote's stylists will hand pick a total of 5 (three garments and two accessories) and send them to the customer's door. Members can try these items for as long as they like, whether it's a week or a month. If the customer likes some of the pieces received, they can keep them and send the rest back using the included prepaid envelope, for a possible 30%-50% savings off retail. Le Tote offers monthly membership plans starting at $69/month for Classic and $79/month for Maternity.

Le Tote offers the following plan options:
Le Tote Classic: Flat monthly fee, unlimited "totes" and all clothes that you hand select.
Le Tote Select: A stylist selects new clothing items (no accessories or shoes) and
         members get to pick which items they want to purchase.
Le Tote Maternity: Just like Le Tote Classic but with all maternity for pregnant women.

As soon as Le Tote receives the return shipment, they will charge the customer's card on file for any items they decided to keep. Returned items are dry-cleaned, machine-washed, and/or disinfected and reviewed by Le Tote's Quality Control Department. They will also immediately send a new tote with 5 more items, and the process begins anew. There is no limit to the number of totes the customer can receive each month.

Style Personalization Strategies:
Members can customize what they receive in each tote by logging in to 'Your Style Profile' and opt out of receiving certain prints, colors, or items (i.e. earrings). Customer can also rate all the items in their 'virtual closet', which can further help them to receive products suited to their preferences. They will also text the subscriber with a link to their tote before it is shipped, and the subscriber can view it and swap out unwanted items, as a way to add to the personalization factor. Le Tote also works closely with vendors to offer consumers correct measurements. Vendors and brands are also given information about a product's purchase rate, number of units sold, popularity of colors, etc. to improve their offerings. And conversely, the e-commerce site uses consumer reviews to help other members decide which size will actually fit their measurements correctly, since each brand's measurements vary. In addition, customer reviews are a huge part of data collection at Le Tote. Products are rated at 80%, which is a much higher engagement than on other apparel sites. Le Tote's personal styling is done not by humans but through a proprietary, in-house fit algorithm that collects all the data about a member, including quiz responses, transaction histories, member box selection overrides, and feedback and rating surveys. And, because Le Tote wants members to wear the products immediately after they open their box, they don't sell for seasons ahead. Rather, they look at the weather 10 days out and based on the zip code, they put that weather information into the algorithm.
Source: www.fierceretail.com/technology/le-tote-s-data-keeps-members-vendors-happy

Differentiation Strategies:
Le Tote has been developing their own designer clothing lines, such as Hayes, which can only be rented or purchased through their company.

Extreme personalization has led to retention rates of 94% and year-over-year growth of 500%, and this success relies on the retailer's ability to collect, analyze, and make actionable, large reams of customer data.

Their personalization algorithm is named 'Chloe' and it processes large reams of data produced by each customer, as they interact with Le Tote online and on mobile. Analyzing everything from sizing to order history to favorited items, Chloe is able to predict which products members are most likely to be interested in each month. Chloe even manages to solve the sorts of sizing problems that can often occur when shopping across different brands.

Personalization is not only the result of the analysis of customer feedback, order transaction history and stated style preferences that goes into producing customized tote recommendations, but a whole host of external factors, such as geography and what is popular in the subscriber's city and region. It also takes into account the local weather forecast. The shipping zip code is used to help recommend products, based on forecasted weather conditions for the next 10 to 12 days.

Source: https://etaileast.wbresearch.com/how-le-tote-uses-data-to-deliver-personalized-fashion-rental-experiences-ty-u

Most of Le Tote's inventory is provided by top fashion brands including Nine West, Vince Camuto and French Connection, and they all slash their prices for Le Tote members in exchange for the vast amounts of customer insights the company is able to extract for them, using their software platform. Le Tote also utilizes machine learning to garner insight from comments left by members on the company's website, as well as direct feedback gained from surveying members with specific questions about style, service, and fit.

Growth Strategies:
Le Tote is constantly adding new designer collections to their inventory. Le Tote carries name brands like Nike, Free People Movement, Calvin Klein, Kenneth Cole, French Connection, Free People, MPG, KUT from the Kloth, Vine Camuto, Kate Spade, House of Harlow, Cashmere and Cupcakes, Scotch and Soda, Juicy Couture and others.

Le Tote teamed up with actress, model, and TV presenter Olivia Culpo to introduce the retailer's first ever influencer collection – Olivia Culpo x Le Tote, and issued the appropriate press releases to raise awareness of the company and this alliance. Additionally, for the first time, Le Tote has ungated its site for the Olivia Culpo x Le Tote Collection, enabling everyone to shop these items, even those without a membership commitment. But, although the Culpo collection is available to all, Le Tote members receive a significant discount: member prices range from $58 to $128, whereas prices for non-members range from $78 to $178.
Source: www.letote.com/olivia
https://etaileast.wbresearch.com/le-tote-influencer-collection-with-customer-data-ty-u

Le Tote is the first US subscription service to enter the highly competitive Chinese market. Le Tote China is launching in partnership with seasoned retailer and executive, Clement Tang.
Source:
https://finance.yahoo.com/news/le-tote-announces-international-expansion-131500376.html
www.businesswire.com/news/home/20190130005254/en/Le-Tote-Announces-International-Expansion-Debut-Le

Le Tote continues to add new specialty services, such as 'Le Tote Select'. With 'Le Tote Select' the stylist curates the customer's clothing and accessory tote, but everything is brand new, so the customer does not get to wear it, and they have to decide within five days what, if anything they would like to keep. LeTote Select is $20 a month, which is a stylist fee and the customer can use that as a credit toward anything that they buy in that tote. Source: https://planblogrepeat.com/2019/02/25/letote-review/

Pricing Strategies
A monthly Le Tote membership costs $49, which is billed on a recurring basis. Members can also add insurance for an extra $5 (covers all damage) per month. Each tote will contain items worth $250+, and members receive their first one within 1-2 business days

of signing up. All Le Tote's totes include free USPS Priority shipping each way, and after the company receives the tote, another will immediately be sent out. Le Tote provides a 100% satisfaction guarantee on all the items they sell through a 14-day refund policy. There aren't any contracts or commitments of any kind and their shipments can be paused at any time.

Le Tote Unlimited Monthly Maternity Box Subscription Options:
- $69 – 3 Garments, 2 Accessories
- $79 – 5 Garments
- $89 – 5 Garments, 3 Accessories
- $99 – 8 Garments
- $109 – 7 Garments, 3 Accessories
- $119 – 10 Garments
- $129 – 10 Garments, 5 Accessories

Newscast Video Marketing
www.youtube.com/watch?v=_xBCo_xTTAY
https://www.youtube.com/watch?v=bqyzz8FYI4U
https://www.youtube.com/watch?v=ov_Ko2CzBK8

Blogging:
Employee Profiles
https://blog.letote.com/2019/03/06/behind-le-tote-9-5-with-kavita-sharma-dmm-of-apparel/

Financing Sources:
The Y Combinator backed company has raised venture funding from Andreessen Horowitz, Google Ventures, Azure Capital Partners, Lerer Hippeau Ventures, Simon Venture Group, AITV, Epic Ventures, Arsenal Venture Partners and Funders Club.
Source: http://fortune.com/2015/11/19/le-tote-15-million-funding/

Resources:
www.yahoo.com/lifestyle/women-apos-clothing-subscription-boxes-150500022.html
https://legosinmylouis.com/5-le-tote-tips-real-le-tote-customer-reviews/
www.whatsupfagans.com/what-is-le-tote-reviews/
www.subaholic.com/2015/02/19/get-le-tote-subscription/
https://thegritandgraceproject.org/health-and-beauty/everything-you-need-to-know-about-le-tote-fashion-rental
http://julieverse.com/2015/10/02/heres-why-we-arent-sure-le-tote-is-a-worthwhile-investment/
www.businessinsider.com/le-tote-clothing-subscription-service-review-2019-6?r=UK&IR=T
www.nasdaq.com/article/faces-of-entrepreneurship-rakesh-tondon-ceo-and-founder-of-le-tote-cm984244

Luxury Lending   https://lendingluxury.com/

Located in Tampa, FL, it is a provider of apparel rental services for weddings, charity events and birthday parties. Each rental is either 5 or 10 days and prices start at only $50 for a dress that would comparably cost hundreds at the retail shops. Dry-Cleaning, return shipping and insurance are all included. Members can reserve a dress up to a year in advance. They are continuously updating their looks to keep pace with the latest fashion trends throughout the world. Not only do they provide rentals of high-quality brands, they also offer the option to purchase these chic items at extremely affordable prices.

Bag Borrow or Steak www.Bagborroworsteal.com

Operates an online boutique where women and men borrow, collect, and share luxury accessories. It offers luggage and vintage handbags, as well as accessories, such as watches, jewelry, and sunglasses. The company provides pre-owned designer handbags, shoes, and accessories; enables customers to sell their handbags; and provides hand bag cleaning, repair, and refurbishment services. Some luxury merchandise is available for purchase—excluding rental pieces—and shoppers receive a 25% discount by using the promotional code on the retailer's website. Consumers also can sell gently used designer pieces on consignment through or directly to Bag Borrow or Steal by filling out a form online and submitting photos. Bag Borrow or Steal accepts certain brands of designer handbags, shoes, jewelry, sunglasses and accessories for resale. Sellers receive 70% of the purchase price of consigned items within a week of sale. This Seattle, WA ecommerce vendor was launched in 2004 as Avelle.
Source:
www.digitalcommerce360.com/company/bag-borrow-or-steal-inc/
www.bloomberg.com/research/stocks/private/snapshot.asp?privcapId=26285843
www.crunchbase.com/organization/avelle#section-overview
www.businessnewsdaily.com/544-avelle-clothing-rental-business.html

Fly Robe www.flyrobe.com

Provider of an on-demand apparel rental platform created to rent branded & designer clothing for Men & Women online in India. Its present in 10 major Indian cities and also has offline stores in Mumbai and Delhi. The company operates a fashion rental platform where users can browse and temporarily rent from a collection of premium designer wear. It offers dresses, tops, jumpsuits and playsuits, gowns, jackets, maxi dresses, skirts, shorts and trousers, and more for various occasions, which include club night, cocktail, date, day out, formal and holiday. The Company also provides accessories, such as jewelry and bags.
Source: https://craft.co/flyrobe
https://www.crunchbase.com/organization/flyrobe

Frank and Oak www.frankandoak.com/

Their shoppers can opt into a subscription box service, but can also buy items à la carte, the way they would shop any other e-commerce site. Subscribers receive exclusive pieces made in limited editions, personally selected for them by their expert stylists. The style team will choose 3 new styles for the subscriber every month based on their stated style and size preferences. Subscribers are able to preview and personalize their box if they want. Subscribers can only keep what they love, return the rest for free. Subscribers can skip a month or cancel at any time. There is no monthly fee. Items range in price from $29 to $149. Each box shipped has a $25 styling fee, which is credited toward any items kept. As long as the subscriber keeps at least one item from their monthly Style Plan box, the styling fee will be waived. Subscribers are charged when the box is shipped, but returns are shipped free and are refunded or credited back to the account immediately.

They offer free regular shipping on all Style Plan orders and their packages ship via Canada Post, USPS or UPS depending on the location. Subscribers have 30 days from the date of purchase to return any unwanted items and get their money back. They even provide a return label, which can be requested online through the subscriber's order history page. Products such as underwear, grooming products and swimwear are non-refundable.
Resource:
www.subaholic.com/2019/10/31/frank-and-oak-style-plan-oct-2019-review/
www.glamour.com/story/womens-work-clothing-subscription-box-reviews

### Tulerie	www.tulerie.com
A peer-to-peer, invitation-only fashion rental company. Provides a mobile platform for women to lend and borrow high-end clothing and accessories. Allows users to rent clothing, shoes, and accessories to one another, with the app acting as a medium for borrowers and lenders. The company comes from Merri Smith and Violet Gross, two women who worked in fashion and finance, respectively, and believe there's a huge opportunity in the fashion rental industry. The Lender is responsible for cleaning the item after it has been returned by the Borrower. The cleaning fee is determined by the Lender and included in the rental price. The Borrower is charged $9.95 on top of the rental fee which covers round trip 2-day shipping. A return shipping label is provided by the Lender in the parcel for easy return delivery. Once the Lender accepts the Borrower's request, the Borrower's payment method will be charged for the entire amount. Whether the request is two days or two months away, Tulerie holds the payment to give both parties time to make sure that everything is as expected. Around the 15th of every month Tulerie releases payments to Lenders and/or Borrowers (e.g. refunds). Tulerie provides a suggested rental price based on the retail value of the item, at which point the Lender can accept or amend the rental price for each period of rental days. The Lender can choose if they want to loan their pieces for 4, 10 or 20 days. Each piece will be noted with the allowed loan time.

### Five Four Group	www.fivefourgroup.com/
This company has created an online platform of vertically-integrated brands focused on men's fashion and style. Founded by Andres Izquieta and Dee Murthy in Los Angeles, Five Four Group is changing the way men shop. Through their e-commerce site Menlo House, membership service Menlo Club, and lifestyle brands; Five Four, New Republic by Mark McNairy, Grand Athletic Club, Oshenta, and Mercer & Clay; Five Four Group's vision is to become the global, online leader in men's fashion. It charges $60 a month for an individually curated package of up to three items from their seasonal collection until the customer pauses or cancels. On average, they receive 2 items per month and every month is different. Plus, they receive easy size exchanges, free shipping, and pause or cancel anytime.   Source: www.themenlohouse.com/club?redirect=true

### MM.LaFleur	https://mmlafleur.com/
An independent clothing line that carries offerings for the formal workplace. Their pieces are timeless, and subscribers are often selected to be brand ambassadors. They have a reputation for excellent customer service was excellent and enable subscribers to

communicate with an actual stylist. An MM.LaFleur stylist will send the customer a box (bento) of their current favorites, based on responses to their quiz questions. There's no commitment, and they are not a subscription service. The first Bento Box of dresses, separates and accessories for a week at the office is completely free. Subsequent boxes are charged a $25 styling fee, which is credited towards future purchases. Prices range from $110 (for tops) to $595 (for dresses), but the quality is excellent. They are known for their more formal and classic selections. Members have four days to decide what to keep.
Source:
www.marketwatch.com/story/heres-what-happened-when-i-tried-4-clothing-subscription-services-to-adult-my-work-wardrobe-2019-01-08

Dia & Co. www.dia.com
Provides a dedicated personal stylist. Offers 25% off when the customer buys everything in their Style Box. Charges a $20 per-box styling fee, which is credited toward any items the customer decides to keep. Members cannot wear, damage, and then return these items. Members can either keep them and wear them, or don't try them at all and simply send them back.

Amazon's Prime Wardrobe www.amazon.com/b?node=16122413011
This service lets Amazon Prime members select clothing and accessory items to fill a box. Once the Prime Member selects at least three Prime Wardrobe-eligible pieces from over a million clothing options, Amazon will ship their selections to them in a resealable return box with a prepaid shipping label. Members will have seven calendar days to try on their items at home, starting on the day the Prime Wardrobe order is delivered. Any items they don't wish to keep can be returned within seven days for no charge. Prime Wardrobe also comes with free scheduled pickups from UPS. If the member decides to keep at least three items, they will get a 10 percent discount off their purchase, and if they keep five or more pieces the discount rises to 20 percent. With Prime Wardrobe, Amazon can apply its trove of consumer data and logistics network to increase its convenience proposition as well as the offerings tied to its $119-a-year Prime membership.
Resource:
www.retaildive.com/news/5-retailers-making-moves-in-subscription-services-in-2019/532784/
Source:
www.amazon.com/gp/help/customer/display.html/ref=hp_left_v4_sib?ie=UTF8&nodeId=202159370

Trunk Club www.trunkclub.com
After five years of serving only men, Trunk Club added a clothing service for women in the summer of 2015. Trunk Club has operated as a wholly owned subsidiary of the fashion retailer, Nordstrom, since the retailer acquired it in August 2014. It ships high-end, premium, customized, hand-selected men's clothing directly to the customer's door. As such, Trunk Club claims to feature items from more than 50 premium manufacturers, and to help men to achieve a great look without all the work. Trunk Club is primarily a discovery commerce website. Members receive a box (known as a "trunk") containing up

to 8 pieces of clothing that are based on their specifications. Ultimately, Trunk Club claims that this helps members to discover awesome clothes without all the hassle of visiting a store or shopping online. Members are assigned to a personal stylist based on their preferences, who will hand-select items that better meet their body type, preferences, and lifestyle. On top of this, Trunk Club doesn't require any kind of subscription membership, and only sends boxes whenever requested. Customer can get a box when they request one with the option to set up a regular schedule, like a monthly delivery, if specifically requested. There is a $25 styling fee for every Trunk, but it is waived if a Nordstrom credit or debit card is used. Members can also make an appointment for a fitting at their Clubhouses in Boston, Chicago, Dallas, Washington D.C., Los Angeles or New York City. The stylist will show a selection of clothes that fits the customer's size, style, and spending preferences. They can try everything on and take favorites home the same day. Trunk Club works by first completing a style survey. Then their extensively trained personal stylists will hand-select the clothing, and can be contacted directly via phone, email, text message, or through the Trunk Club iPhone app or website. The box is then sent directly to the customer's home. Members can try them on and leave feedback for their stylist, which can then be used to dial in their preferences for future trunks. After receiving the trunk, members have 10 days to decide which items to keep. Trunk Club includes a prepaid return shipping label, which means they simply have to email the company and then send any unwanted items back, all at no cost to them. Once 10 days have passed, the credit card will be charged for any items not returned. The are no membership fees or commitments associated with Trunk Club, and the enrollment can be cancelled at any time. Trunk orders include free shipping and a prepaid return shipping label.
Source: https://www.highya.com/trunk-club-reviews
www.investopedia.com/articles/personal-finance/021316/trunk-club-review-it-worth-it.asp

The Mr. and Ms. Collection   www.themrcollection.com/

The Mr. & Ms. Collection, also known as The Mr. Collection and The Ms. Collection, is a personal styling subscription service that will connect members with brands they can rent, without the fear of commitment. Their Style Team will hand-select looks, using the member's Style Profile, sizing, preferences and feedback as their guide. Members can also purchase items they love with their exclusive member discount. Their stylists will hand-select casual or professional looks that members can rent, with the option to buy. Once the box is received, the recipient can enjoy those items for the month, and so long as the box is returned to The Mr. Collection by the specified date, he will receive another box of clothing the following month. Men interested in purchasing any of the items that he really likes will be offered a discount. Three different style options are available: Casual clothing for $39 per month, business clothing for $45 per month or men's accessories for $25 per month.
Source: https://money.usnews.com/money/the-frugal-shopper/2014/08/20/8-clothing-subscription-services-for-men
Resource: https://themrmscollection.zendesk.com/hc/en-us/articles/115000630507-How-does-a-membership-to-The-Mr-Ms-Collection-work-

Armoire   www.armoire.style/

This clothing rental service recommends ensembles based on the customer's preferences and, for a flat monthly fee, sends four pieces at a time. The company emerged from the MIT Accelerator Program, an entrepreneurship program designed to aid startups. The newly-formed company recently relocated to Seattle, headed by CEO Ambika Singh, Using a combination of algorithms, current fashion trends and input from customers, Armoire offers personalized, curated closet sets for women based on their individual style preferences. Without the hassle of closet clutter and time-consuming shopping trips, Armoire offers customers access to high-end items (an average retail of $300), including shipping and maintenance costs, for the beta subscription price of $149 a month.
Source: www.seattlemag.com/shopping/whos-boss-armoire-new-clothing-subscription-service-you-are

Glam Corner   www.glamcorner.com.au

A Sydney-based dress rental service began in 2012 and has since become one of the leading websites for Australian women to shop for designer dress and gown rentals. A Certified B Corporation, the company is passionate about offering women the experience of wearing high-end garments while also reducing the impact clothing production has on the environment, and the subscriber's wallet. Glam Corner offers inclusive sizing for all body types, including bump-friendly dresses and plus-size gown rentals.

Little Borrowed Dress   www.littleborroweddress.com

The first online wedding boutique to offer bridesmaid dresses for rent – which means that the days of that once-worn frock gathering dust in the back of your closet will soon be nothing more than a distant memory. Prices start at just $50, which gives brides the opportunity to choose a style they love that they can be sure all of their bridesmaids can afford. The entire collection of bridesmaid dresses will also be for sale, too, starting at just $150. Members can place their rental reservation online and the dresses will arrive two weeks before the wedding ready-to-wear. After the big day, members can pop them back in the mail, in the pre-paid packaging, and Little Borrowed Dress will handle even the cleaning. A free back up size is sent with every rental, so members are guaranteed to look awesome and feel comfortable in their gown. Fabric swatches will be free to ensure a perfect color match. Trunk Shows will be hosted in San Francisco, Chicago, Los Angeles, Houston and DC. Little Borrowed Dress makes crinkle chiffon dresses in 12 styles and 18 colors. The rental costs between $50 and $75 depending on the style, and bridesmaids receive two sizes in the mail two weeks before the wedding. After the wedding, dresses are returned in prepaid envelopes. Little Borrowed Dress stocks 3,000 dresses. Each dress features touches like sashes, adjustable straps or hidden elastic waistbands. They run from size 0 to 18. Bridesmaids can also convert the rental into a purchase, if alterations are an absolute must. In the winter of 2014, Little Borrowed Dress announced a seed round of $1.25 million, which included investors such as Andreessen Horowitz, Index Ventures, Launch Capital and angel investor Joanne Wilson. The funding will be used to redesign the website, expand the dress style options available, and build up the team, which now numbers five. This company is good at redesigning the style lineup after taking a close look at customer satisfaction rates with various dresses. The company is projecting 400% growth in 2014. In addition to rental dresses, the company has also started offering matching men's ties and bowties for sale.

Express Inc.   www.expstyletrial.com

This retailer has launched a clothing rental subscription service called 'Express Style Trial'. Shoppers can rent three items at a time for $69.95 per month with unlimited exchanges. Shoppers can keep the items as long as they want before shipping all three items back for free. When Express receives the three rented items, it sends three more garments. It requires the shopper to send all three items back before it sends the next shipment. Express Style Trial ships new items in about two to three days from the time it receives the returned items. Shoppers also can purchase items they find through the service at a discount. Shoppers can cancel their subscription at any time. Currently, the service does not rent shoes or accessories, and shoppers cannot return their items or rent items from Express stores. When subscribing to the service, a shopper creates an account on Expstyletrial.com and populates her "closet" with eight items. Once a shopper has eight items in her closet, she can rent her first box. Shoppers prioritize items in their closet, so the service knows which items she would rather get first. Express donates rental items that begin to show too much wear to charity. Express built its subscription rental service through technology company 'Caastle', which also provides clothing rental services to Ann Taylor and New York & Co. Inc., two women's apparel chains that have launched rental services.
Source:
www.retaildive.com/news/express-launches-apparel-subscription-service/538870/

Boon + Gable   www.boonandgable.com/

It has developed an app that enables members to explain a little about themselves, their favorite styles and clothing brands. Once a customer has entered their measurements, budget, personal information, and favorite brands, they book an appointment for a time convenient to them. The Boon + Gable's bespoke recommendation engine, called 'Clark', then uses the customer's information to browse the clothing available at local stores and whittle it down to a few hundred items which fit the parameters. These items are then sent to the mobile devices of Boon + Gable's style experts, who select 20 items they think are the most suitable. The style experts then arrive at the customer's homes at the arranged time, and spend an hour helping them try the items on. The style experts will also look at the customer's existing wardrobe and offer suggestions on outfit combinations which will go well with the new items. Boon + Gable's style experts are paid a wage regardless of whether any items are purchased so members never experience the hard sell. The idea is, as stylists make more visits to a customer, their recommendations will get better. Boon + Gable will continue to develop and upgrade the software which allows it to make its recommendations, but the company is equally committed to keep building rapport and relationships with members.
Source:
https://etailwest.wbresearch.com/boon-gable-personal-shopper-strategy-to-join-digital-age-ty-u
Resource:
www.crunchbase.com/organization/boon-and-gable

Daily Look   www.dailylook.com

This L.A. based service is for a more fashion-conscious person who wants access to the latest trends, seasonal fashions, and a hipper, more "LA" vibe. DAILYLOOK the premium personal styling experience that provides on-trend looks tailored to the member's lifestyle, while saving them time and effort. They make shopping simple, by curating looks based on the subscriber's body shape and lifestyle. Their experienced Stylists mix/match their collection to style beautiful outfits for them to try on in the convenience of their own home. Subscriber's buy what they love and return the rest. Free shipping both ways.

Armarium — www.armarium.com/occasions

Armarium was officially launched in April 2016 through an invite-only mobile app, e-commerce platform and a New York City showroom. The program includes not only the ability to borrow pieces from their expertly curated lineup of couture, ready-to-wear, and accessories, but also, the option of hiring one of a number of professional stylists to assist with day-of dressing needs. Their goal is to find statement pieces from the runways to wear to events or even to dinner with friends. Their clients do not have to be concerned about dry-cleaning, storage or wearing the garment a second time.

Allume — www.allume.co/

Offers the services of a style consultant for a $20 styling fee that gets credited back if the member buys something. This service is good for anyone who wants to know what it feels like to have a personal shopper. Offers an actual one-to-one personal shopping service. Members sign up online, take a detailed style quiz, then get paired with an experienced stylist who curates the look or proposed selection. The pair then arrange a time to text with one another, a sort of initial consultation that takes about 20 minutes via text.

Couture Collective — https://couturecollective.com/

Offers a luxe selection of high-end ready-to-wear looks from designers like Valentino, Dior, and Stella McCartney, that subscribers can rent for the season if they are a member. Members pay 20 percent of the retail price and choose up to five dates to wear the piece. There are also rental options for one night only and they pay 10 percent of the retail price for a single wearing.

FashionPass — www.thefashionpass.com

Their mission is to give members access to their dream closet, so they always have something new to wear.

Subscription Services for Men:

Bombfell — www.Bombfell.com

With a subscription to Bombfell, men can set a spending limit for the month and also specifically indicate what it is that he is searching for in any given month, such as a pair of jeans and a dress shirt. Men fill out a style profile and then a personal stylist will be assigned that will help pick out new styles to send each month. He will only pay for the styles he decides to keep.

Curator and Mule   www.(curatorandmule.com
This is the site for men who are always on the lookout for the newest accessories. Each season he will receive an assortment of new items, such as sunglasses, bags, socks and more for $60. Each box will ship with four to five of that season's must-have accessories.

Hall&Madden   www.hallmadden.com
This company caters to men who need business shirts. Men will receive three shirts for $150 and shirts can be delivered every three, four or six months. Shirts are tailored to fit different body types and are available in slim cut, athletic cut or classic cut.

Manpacks   www.manpacks.com
Offers the finishing touches that every man needs, including underwear and socks. Men choose what they want to receive and then every three months he will receive a reminder that it is time to reorder (he can also reorder sooner if necessary).

Root Bizzle   www.rootbizzle.com
This is a tie delivery service. A subscription costs $25 per month and men will receive one new silk tie per month in their choice of three overall styles: business, skinny or whimsical.

Fresh Neck   www.freshneck.com
Rents from casual to formal, ties and accessories for any occasion. Offers selections from emerging designers and 'Made for FreshNeck' exclusives. It has supplier relationships with over 300 of the best designers, from Hermes and Gucci, to Rag & Bone and Charvet Memberships starting at $29.99/month. Free Shipping and Free Dry Cleaning
The 'Try-before-you-buy' concept keeps items costing for 20-60% off retail. Subscribers can also sample accessories, such as bow ties, lapel pins, tie bars, suspenders, and more.

Maternity Clothing Subscription Services:
Belly Bump Boutique   www.bellybumpboutique.com
It debuted in 2008, and rents out elegant, special-occasion dresses for women in all stages of pregnancy. Belly Bump offers hassle-free exchanges if an item does not fit.

Borrow For Your Bump   https://borrowforyourbump.com/
Provides the option of either borrowing a dress for a special event or renting a box of clothing with four items. With 'select a dress for a special occasion', the user can borrow it for only 1 week or up to 4 weeks. The user can select the delivery date for a few days before the event. With 'rent a box', the member must first fill out their style profile. They will then receive 4 items to keep as long as they want or exchange anytime.

Children's Clothing Subscription Services:
Mac & Mia
This service delivers hand-picked goods for children, aged newborn to six-years-old. Mac

& Mia has an in-house team of style experts ready to help busy parents to find quality unique pieces that fit the child's personality. Each box is conveniently delivered to the home and curated to fit the customer's needs. They focus on finding the best emerging and established brands and work with clients one-on-one to deliver a personalized experience to busy families across the country. *Pricing:* $20 Stylist Fee + Price of items you keep. 15% off full box purchases.
Source: www.forbes.com/sites/sboyd/2016/10/31/the-year-of-the-subscription-box/#28521e7ae778

Fitted Tot www.Fittedtot.com
An online baby and toddler clothing subscription company based in Spring Lake, Michigan which helps new parents all over the country. For just $65.99 a month, parents can take care of all their kids' clothing needs, and not have to worry about what to do with stained, damaged or outgrown clothes. Upon registration, Fittedtot.com members complete a short survey to explain their style and preference of clothing for their kids. They will then receive a combination of clothes (including pajamas and playwear) every month. Members are allowed to exchange their kids' clothing at any time for more clothes at no extra charge. There is no extra charge for stained or damaged clothes sent. Their system allows parents to have an unlimited amount of cute outfits for their kids without spending lots of money, and without the clutter.

Borrow Mini Couture
This company rents children's formal outfits for special occasions, because children typically quickly outgrow their clothing and these expensive items are never worn again. This company has gained a lot of attention by reaching out to parenting bloggers, who tried and loved the service and promoted it on their websites.

Garment Rental Apps:
Style Lend www.stylelend.com
This company allows users to browse through thousands of unique designer items that have been hand selected from New York's most stylish closets. They can have a special occasion piece delivered in 2-3 days (or within hours in NYC!) They can then keep the piece for 7 days, and if the dress isn't perfect, they can submit a 'Fit Return' and they will swap it in time for the event or issue a refund. They suggest pricing rental items at 5-10% of the retail price depending on when the item was purchased. There is a $5 insurance fee on every rental that covers minor rips, stains, and tears (up to $50 in repairs). If an item is beyond repair and needs to be replaced (or over $50 in damages), StyleLend will replace the item or compensate the lender for the current market value of the dress and bill the renter accordingly. Lenders can print out both shipping labels and use the envelopes provided. Lenders are responsible for cleaning items before renting them out again.

Garment Exchange http://garment-exchange.com/
This site is positioning itself as "the Airbnb of clothing," meaning that users can rent from someone else's closet. Features include browsing by clothing style (both formal and casual that can be filtered by style and color) or by owners' wardrobes. User have the option to be the renter *and* the owner. To rent, users make their selection, allow four to

five business days for shipping, save the shipping label and bag, and return the piece (flip the label and reuse the bag), and drop it off at a UPS location by the return date.

Date My Wardrobe
This digital consignment app splits the difference between Rent the Runway and Le Tote, dealing in high-end fashion but at relatively affordable prices. This Boston-based company does not own any of the clothing it offers and therefore does not have to pay for real estate that would be required to house it. Date My Wardrobe seeks to be the Airbnb of clothing.

5.2 Key Industry Statistics

1. As PricewaterhouseCoopers predicts in its 2015 report, companies that adhere to the sharing economy's business model of access over ownership have the potential to increase global revenues from roughly $15 billion today to about $335 billion by 2025.
2. According to industry analyst firm Plunkett Research, Ltd., 67 percent of American women are plus size. But, plus size fashion makes up less than 20 percent of the women's apparel market.
3. The $120 billion women's apparel industry is ripe for digital innovation.
4. One-third of U.S. women wear plus-size clothing, but they represent under a fifth of women's apparel spending.
5. According to a 2015 report by PwC, just 2 percent of the US population have engaged in a sharing transaction in the retail sector, compared to 6 percent for hospitality and 8 percent for transport.
6. A North Dakota State University study from 2010 found that the average American household spends about 3.8 percent of their income on clothing. The Census Bureau states that the average household income is about $50,000 per year, so that means roughly $2,000 per year, per household.
7. In terms of value, the global online clothing rental market is anticipated to expand at a CAGR of 9.8% during the forecast period and is expected to be valued at US$ 1,952.4 Mn by the end of 2026.
8. Amongst all demographic segments in the global online clothing rental market, revenue from the men and kids' segment is projected to be the highest, with a CAGR of 10.3% and 10.4% respectively over the forecast period 2016–2026.
9. Nearly 40% of subscribers of any service type cancel, according to a report from McKinsey and Co., and more than a third cancel in less than three months, and over half cancel within six.
10. The thriving sharing economy is estimated to hit $40.2 billion by 2022.
11. In the month of April 2017, subscription company websites had about 37 million visitors. Since 2014, that number has grown by over 800%
12. Seventy-five million professional women in this country spend three thousand dollars a year or more on clothing for work.
13. The women segment is expected to remain dominant and is projected to account for 61.0% value share over the forecast period.
    Source: www.futuremarketinsights.com/reports/online-clothing-rental-market

5.3 Industry Trends

We will determine the trends that are impacting our consumers and indicate ways in which our members' needs are changing and any relevant social, technical or other changes that will impact our target market. Keeping up with trends and reports will help management to carve a niche for our business, stay ahead of the competition and deliver products that our members need and want.

Research indicates that because consumers know they will keep the rental clothes only temporarily and only as long as they choose to hold them, they choose clothes that are riskier, more fashion-forward and less basic, with more design content.

Subscription companies are facing a big threat from existing retailers, especially online direct-to-consumer retailers who have the inventory to do it themselves.

More retailers are considering acquiring the software platform to rent out their inventory because it opens up a new channel for the distribution of product and helps to get some of the unsold merchandise off the store floor. This solves a real estate space problem and gives retailers and brands a new way to profit from their clothes inventory that doesn't interfere with their mainstream businesses.

While renting a wedding dress was not popular a couple years ago, this trend has taken off due to the recession. Before women saw the few hundred-dollar difference between renting and buying as a minor decision but now days every dollar counts.

Renting shows exactly how the concept of 'possession' is disappearing, in favor of the focus on 'usage'. Renting by on-going, long-term subscribers is becoming a powerful tool to promote brand loyalty.

According to the 2017 Retail Trends Report by Strategy&, the global consulting team at PwC, physical fashion apparel stores experienced a return rate of about 3%, compared with about 25% for online sales. By sending curated selections and incorporating feedback, subscription clothing rental retailers may be able to significantly cut the return rate.

5.4 Industry Key Terms

We will use the following term definitions to help our company to understand and speak the common language of our industry, and aid efficient communication.

A/B Testing
A way to compare two versions of something to figure out which performs better. It is now used to evaluate everything from website design to online offers to headlines to product descriptions.   Source: https://hbr.org/2017/06/a-refresher-on-ab-testing
Activation Rate

The rate at which acquired customers become active customers by initiating an activation event. The overall activation rate can also be monitored by marketing channel, such as via social media marketing or PPC advertising. A useful spin-off metric is "time to activate", which is how long it takes for a customer to initiate an activation event once he or she has initially engaged with our marketing content or signed up for a trial account.
Source: https://effinamazing.com/blog/everything-need-know-activation-metrics
            www.intercom.com/blog/mention-increased-activation-rate-50/

Active Churn
Results when a member makes the decision to cancel a membership.

Adoption Activities
All the activities involved in making sure the customer is successfully adopting or deploying and expanding their use of the solution. The payback is in customer expansion and higher renewal rates, leading to increased profitability.

Algorithm
A detailed series of instructions for carrying out an operation or solving a problem. Computers use algorithms to list the detailed instructions for carrying out an operation. In terms of efficiency, various algorithms are data-driven and able to accomplish big data analysis, operations or problem solving easily and quickly. In fact, Harvard studies suggest that people are often comfortable accepting guidance from algorithms, and sometimes even trust them more than other people.
Source: https://hbr.org/2019 /10/customers-trust-algorithms-more-than-companies-
            realize

Annuity Services Revenue
The customer pays for ongoing premium services wrapped around the basic subscription, usually in an annual or multi-year contract.
Premium support or success services, information services and managed services fall into this revenue category.

Annual Contract Value (ACV)
New revenue brought in by new customers or customers upgrading or renewing their existing contract. Businesses invest in sales and marketing to drive new revenue, because ultimately this increases ARR.

Annual Recurring Revenue (ARR)
The amount of revenue expected to repeat. This does not include one-time revenue. It only includes revenues that recur. ARR is a forward-looking number.
Source: https://www.zuora.com/guides/subscription-finance-basics/

Behavioral Loyalty
The consumer's tendency to repurchase a brand. This is easy to measure given the access to purchase information, but it is not necessarily a good indicator of loyalty as repeat business could simply be a result of lack of alternatives or the switching costs required to change suppliers.

Behavioral Therapy
An umbrella term for types of therapy that treat mental health disorders. This form of therapy seeks to identify and help change potentially self-destructive or unhealthy behaviors. It functions on the idea that all behaviors are learned and that unhealthy behaviors can be changed. The focus of treatment is often on current problems and how to change them.

Bounce Rate
The objective measure of product stickiness. It represents the percentage of visitors who enter the site and then leave rather than continuing to view other pages within the same site.

Business Casual Attire
A style of clothing that is less formal than traditional business wear but is still intended to give a professional and businesslike impression. It is typically defined as a professional yet relaxed style.
Source: www.businessinsider.com/what-business-casual-really-means-2014-8

Churn Rate
The percentage of subscribers to a service who discontinue their subscriptions to the service within a given time period. The inverse of the retention rate. For a company to expand its clientele, its growth rate, as measured by the number of new members, must exceed its churn rate. This rate is generally expressed as a percentage. The causes of customer churn include a bad customer experience, poor onboarding process, a lack of ongoing customer success, poor customer service, natural causes that occur for all businesses from time to time, a lack of value, low-quality communications, and a lack of brand loyalty. Strategies to reduce the churn rate include; improving customer service, building customer loyalty through relevant experiences, surveying members to collect improvement suggestions, and personalized service.
Source: www.ngdata.com/what-is-customer-churn/

Collaborative Consumption
It is considered part of the sharing economy because it means that individuals rent out their underused assets. It is most likely to be used when both the price of a particular asset, such as a car, is high and the asset is not utilized at all times by one person. By renting out an asset when it is not being used, its owner turns the asset into a sort of commodity. This creates a scenario where physical objects are treated as services.
Resource: https://en.wikipedia.org/wiki/Collaborative_consumption

Contract Value Renewal Rate
A measure of whether renewing customers are spending more or less with the company as the result of negative churn or discounts, or positive expanded service purchases.

Circular Economy
A regenerative economic system in which resource input and waste, emission, landfill dumping, and energy leakage are minimized by slowing, closing, and narrowing energy and material loops. This can be achieved through long-lasting design, maintenance, repair, reuse, remanufacturing, refurbishing, renting, recycling, and upcycling. The goal of a circular economy is to decouple economic growth from resource consumption by focusing on value retention.
Resources:
www.ellenmacarthurfoundation.org/circular-economy/concept
https://kenniskaarten.hetgroenebrein.nl/en/knowledge-map-circular-economy/what-is-the-definition-a-circular-economy/

Client Onboarding System
The process of welcoming new clients into the business, addressing their questions and concerns, and ensuring they understand the services and privileges available to them. It begins when the contract is signed, and the deposit is paid and ends when the work of

servicing the account begins. An onboarding system with clear, simple communication is the key to quickly establishing the common ground and interface mechanisms with the client, providing the client with the knowledge to help them feel more comfortable, empowered, and excited about the formation of a potentially long-term relationship, and recapping the scope of the offerings, the solution servicing and complaint filing processes, and what comes next in this new journey.
Source: https://jenniferbourn.com/what-is-client-onboarding/

Cloud Computing
A kind of outsourcing of computer programs. Using cloud computing, users can access software and applications from wherever they are; the computer programs are being hosted by an outside party and reside in the cloud. This means that users do not have to worry about things such as storage and power.

Cohort
A subset of users grouped by shared characteristics. In the context of business analytics, a cohort usually refers to a subset of users specifically segmented by acquisition date (i.e. the first time a user visits your website).

Cohort Analysis
Uses data from a web application and separates it into related groups of people, rather than just looking at all customers as a whole. Enables users to compare the behavior and metrics of different cohorts over time. Users can then find the highest-performing (or lowest-performing) cohorts, and what factors are driving this performance. Used by marketers to run a time-bound campaign with certain characteristics to be tested, such as ad content, marketing channel, target audience, landing page design, etc. The marketer can then compare metrics for reach, engagement, and conversion for these different marketing campaigns, to see which factors of the campaign actually added value to the business, and which didn't.
Source: https://medium.com/analytics-for-humans/a-beginners-guide-to-cohort-analysis-the-most-actionable-and-underrated-report-on-google-c0797d826bf4

Collaborative Consumption
It is considered part of the sharing economy because it means that individuals rent out their underused assets. It is most likely to be used when both the price of a particular asset, such as a car, is high and the asset is not utilized at all times by one person. By renting out an asset when it is not being used, its owner turns the asset into a sort of commodity. This creates a scenario where physical objects are treated as services.
Resource: https://en.wikipedia.org/wiki/Collaborative_consumption

Committed Monthly Recurring Revenue (CMRR)
A forward-looking metric that combines actual monthly recurring revenue (MRR) data with known bookings and churn data. It begins with existing MRR (last month's recognized MRR), adds known new bookings, and subtracts known cancellations and downgrades. For businesses who sell annual contracts, you will calculate this as a CARR number, or committed annual recurring revenue.
Source: www.thesaascfo.com/committed-monthly-recurring-revenue/

Commoditization
Removes the individual, unique characteristics and brand identity so that the product becomes interchangeable with other products of the same type. Making commodities

interchangeable allows competition with a basis of price only and not on different characteristics.
Source: www.investopedia.com/terms/c/commoditization.asp

Consumption Data
Used to describe what customers are actually doing with the product and then to predict possible customer renewal and expansion patterns.

Conversion Rate
The number of people who perform a desired action divided by the number of people who see the product or visit the site.

Cost of Goods Sold (COGS)
The costs associated with making, installing and warranting the specific offer that is driving the revenue stream. Hosting costs and basic customer support costs are typically the major components of COGS.

Cross-selling
Means adding complimentary items to a purchase. A strategy designed to sell additional services with new features and improved functionality to provide a more comprehensive solution or get more value out of the service.

Curation-based Subscriptions
The dominance of this type of subscription reflects the online customers' demand for a continued series of personalized, high-quality experiences. Generally, these subscriptions are based on a theme and they contain a different selection of items, usually delivered every month or quarter. It's this surprise element that is part of the appeal. Customers never know exactly what their box will contain when it arrives. The best boxes are known for being curated well, with a unique and interesting variety of items that are a good value for the price. The most popular categories are beauty, food and apparel.

Customer Acquisition Costs
This cost equals sales and marketing costs tied specifically to landing new customers and acquiring new revenues.

Customer Advisory Board (CAB)
A form of market research whereby a group of existing customers is convened on a regular basis to advise company management on industry trends, business priorities, and strategic direction.

Customer Experience
The phrase used to describe the relationship a customer has with a business. Customer experience refers to the total of all experiences the customer has with the business, based on all touchpoints, interactions and thoughts about the business across the customer's lifetime. It is usually measured by survey results.

Customer Health Score
A value that indicates the long-term prospect for a customer to drop off or, conversely, to become a high-value, repeat customer through renewal or cross-selling or up-selling strategies. Key performance indicators (KPIs) for customer health scores include the churn rate, which identifies customers who don't return and renewal rates for customers who continue to make purchases.
Source: https://searchcrm.techtarget.com/definition/customer-health-score
Resource: http://customerthink.com/what-is-customer-health-score-and-how-can-your-business-build-one/

Customer Success Management
The business methodology of ensuring customers achieve their desired value outcomes, while using the product or service to drive loyalty. Customer Success is relationship-focused client management, that aligns client and vendor goals for mutually beneficial outcomes. Effective Customer Success strategy typically results in decreased customer churn, faster and better adoption, increased upsell opportunities and better customer satisfaction scores. Responsible for building the customer monitor and optimize plans. Uses data to proactively predict and avoid customer challenges and will usually be measured by retention rates and upsells.
Source: www.gainsight.com/guides/the-essential-guide-to-customer-success/

Experience Economy
Describes the fact that American society is yielding to a society focused on dreams, adventure, spirituality, and feelings where the story that shapes feelings about a product will become a large part of what people buy when they buy the product and serve to create a memorable event. Sometimes described as the commercialization of emotions or the buying of stories, legends, emotion, and lifestyle. Customer participation or interactivity or the role the consumer plays will be key in creating the event or interaction that generates the experience.
Source: www.forbes.com/sites/danielnewman/2015/11/24/what-is-the-experience-economy-should-your-business-care/#6ee8067d1d0c

Fast Fashion
A term used by fashion retailers to describe inexpensive designs that move quickly from the design phase to stores to meet new trends. As a result of this trend, the tradition of introducing new fashion lines on a seasonal basis is being challenged. Today, fast-fashion retailers are introducing new products multiple times in a single week to stay on-trend. Its goal is to quickly produce an item that is both cost-efficient and responds to fast-shifting consumer demands. The assumption is that consumers want high-fashion styled garments at a low affordable price. Fast fashion more closely links the manufacturer with the consumer in a mutually beneficial relationship. The speed at which fast fashion happens requires such collaboration and the ability to refine and accelerate supply chain processes. There is also considerable pressure to keep costs as low as possible. Spanish chain Zara (owned by Inditex) is all but synonymous with fast fashion, serving as an exemplar of how to cut the time between design, production and delivery.
Source: www.investopedia.com/terms/f/fast-fashion.asp

Fast Fashion Chains
Chains known for copying designer looks and selling inexpensive versions of them for less.

Free Trial Period
The opportunity for prospects to sample the full benefits of a product or service for a fixed period of time without paying.

Freemium
Refers to products or services that a company gives away free of charge, on an ongoing basis, to initiate a relationship, then charges customers for additional optional features, increased volumes or expanded use. Used when members have the ability to request fee-based upgrade options from upselling campaigns, build awareness via viral marketing and/or create a value-adding network effect.

Gamification
The idea of applying game thinking and mechanics to nongame settings, usually as an early stage, extrinsic involvement or participation motivator. Usually involves tracking points and status levels and providing prizes for achieving certain levels of participation or milestone achievements or skill set mastery.

Gross Revenue Retention
Eliminates the impact of cross-selling, up-selling, price-increases, and organic customer growth within the installed customer base. It is a better indicator of how the company is really doing in retaining revenue from its customers over time. Gross revenue retention is always equal to, or lower than, net revenue retention and cannot be greater than 100%. The basic calculation is the same as net revenue retention, however, the MRR for each individual customer in the current month cannot exceed the MRR for that customer from one year ago. This approach eliminates the impact of all the factors mentioned above.
Source: www.saas-capital.com/blog/essential-saas-metrics-revenue-retention-fundamentals/

Growth Efficiency Index
GEI is the sales and marketing costs to get $1 in additional Annual Recurring Revenue. GEI equals the cost of revenue acquisition divided by annual recurring income. The lower the Growth Efficiency Index the better, but the GEI is determined by the profits from new revenue.
Source: http://cloudstrategies.biz/saas-sales-and-marketing-roi/

Implicit Personalization
The business learns about the member through customer profile quizzes, transaction database analytics, and/or feedback surveys, and then adjusts the membership experience or offerings based on that information.

Infrastructure as a Service (IaaS)
A third-party hosts elements of the infrastructure, such as hardware, software, servers, and storage, also providing backup, security, and maintenance.

Landing Activities
All the sales and marketing activities required to land or close the first sale of a solution to a new customer and the initial implementation of that solution.

Managed Services
These services offer the following value propositions: monitoring customer performance, operating the supporting environment for the product or delivered service, reducing and/or making more predictable operational costs, accelerating adoption, optimizing the Return on Investment (ROI) or educational benefits of the product or service, and helping the customer to integrate a new set of capabilities by reducing operational complexity. They help to differentiate the offerings of the subscription company by forcing the development of new unique capabilities that can unlock the full potential of the provided solution.

Minimum Viable Product
The early, basic version of a product that enables entrepreneurs to quickly, easily and inexpensively collect meaningful data about their customer needs and wants. This is the baseline product that will be improved with customer feedback.

Net Promoter Score
An index ranging from -100 to 100 that measures the willingness of customers to

recommend a company's products or services to others. It is used as a proxy for gauging the customer's overall satisfaction with a company's product or service and the customer's loyalty to the brand. To calculate the score, customers are surveyed on one single question. They are asked to rate on an 11-point scale (0 to 10) the likelihood of recommending the company or brand to a friend or colleague. Based on their rating, customers are then classified in 3 categories: detractors, passives and promoters.
Source: https://www.medallia.com/net-promoter-score/

Network Effect
A situation in which each additional member drives added value for all existing members just by joining and expanding the network membership. The number of users required for significant network effects is often referred to as critical mass. After critical mass is attained, the product or service should be able to attract many new users because its network offers utility.
Source: www.investopedia.com/terms/n/network-effect.asp

Onboarding Process
The process of effectively starting the adoption and value journey with the customer. Involves customizing the customer's startup experience to fit their needs and expectations and starting a relationship to build long-term trust and show value.
Resources: https://blog.hubspot.com/service/onboarding-best-practices
             www.tallyfy.com/definition-customer-onboarding/

Optimization
The interventions that maximize the outcome for the customer. May include correcting technical or adoption problems. It also includes identifying what is working well and taking steps to expand upon that success.

Paid Subscription Business
A business model where a customer must pay a subscription price periodically (monthly, yearly or seasonal) to gain access (partial or fully) to a product or service.

Passive Churn
Results when a subscription business loses members because of a problem with member payments.

Pay-as-you go
A subscription where you subscribe to purchase a product periodically. This is also known as the convenience model because it is a convenience for the customer to not have to remember to go find their product and buy it periodically. This model has been popularized by companies like Dollar Shave Club, and Birchbox.

Paywall
An online feature that prevents (freemium) users from accessing specific options, content or features without paying a higher price. They encourage users to upgrade their membership to gain access to the greater value proposition.
Resource: www.techopedia.com/definition/23653/paywall

Platform as a Service (PaaS)
The branch of cloud computing that allows users to develop, run, and manage applications without having to get caught up in code, storage, infrastructure and so on.

Predictive Analytics
The practice of extracting information from existing data sets in order to determine patterns and predict future outcomes and trends. It encompasses a variety of statistical

techniques from data mining, predictive modelling, and machine learning, that analyze current and historical facts to make predictions about future or otherwise unknown events.

Pricing Tiers

A strategy employed to define a price per unit within a range. Also involves creating multiple payment options for a subscription service. As the value increases through added features, volume, customization, integration and service levels, the subscription rate rises into another pricing tier.

Ex: https://labs.openviewpartners.com/tiered-pricing-optimization/#.XFBqqs1OmUk

Product Market Fit

The attained state in which a product and its customers are in perfect harmony with one another, because the product fulfills a real and compelling need for a real and defined group of people.

Project Services Revenue

The customer pays for specific deliverables, such as implementation or user training.

Queue (file list)

Subscribers or users of a rental service can select the items they would like to rent, today and into the future, and place them in a file list, or queue, on the company's website. The subscriber can then use the 'queue management' tools to prioritize the order in which items from the queue will be rented. The subscriber presses the "Add" button to put the item in his or her queue at the bottom of the list. The subscriber can also press the "Move to Position #1" button to place that item at the top of the list instead.

Queue Management

Subscribers can reorganize their subscription service queues by pressing the "Top" button next to an item, which moves it to the #1 position, or by typing a number into the space next to an item to change its numerical order. The subscriber can also click on an item title and drag it to the desired position in the list. The "X" button can remove an item from the queue. After making queue changes, the user presses the "Update Queue" button to activate the change.

Retention Rate

The percent of activated users who remain customers over a period of time. The ratio of the number of retained customers to the number at risk.

Resource: https://postfunnel.com/analyzing-retention-rate-subscription-based-businesses/

Sharing Economy

An economic system in which assets or services are shared between private individuals, either free or for a fee, typically by means of the Internet. Sharing economies allow individuals and groups to make money from underused assets. In this way, physical assets are shared as services.

Source: www.investopedia.com/terms/s/sharing-economy.asp

Stickiness

An indication of how likely someone is to buy a product or service repeatedly or recommend it to others. Sticky products tend to be simple, credible, unexpected, and emotionally connecting with a memorable story line. It is a critical element in member retention.

Subscription

Customers pay a periodic fee for access to services, content or physical products.

Subscription-based Pricing Model
A payment structure that allows a customer or organization to purchase or subscribe to a vendor's services for a specific period of time for a set price. Subscribers typically commit to the services on a monthly or annual basis. In a subscription-based model, customers typically pay upfront, prior to receiving access to the service. Prices are often based on the subscription's length and a longer subscription often translates to a lower cost. Subscription-based pricing is increasingly being used for cloud computing.

Subscription Economy
Companies are seeing the value in renting their assets and collecting steady revenues via the subscription business model, rather than depending on sporadic individual sales and bad debt write-offs.

Subscription Gross Profits
The company's profit margin after deducting the cost of subscriptions – the Recurring Revenue minus the Cost of Service. The Cost of SaaS Service includes the hosting, personnel, and support costs of providing the SaaS subscription to the client.
Source: http://cloudstrategies.biz/saas-sales-and-marketing-roi/

Subscription Profiles
These profiles contain the following types of information: subscription plan type, start and renewal dates, subscription referral source, destination address, delivery preferences, product preferences, preferred payment and contact methods, usage patterns, relevant interests, etc.

Success Science
Involves studying the best practices of high-performing customers with successful outcomes and finding ways to replicate those practices and teach them to other customers.

Sustainable Production
The creation of goods and services using processes and systems that are: Non-polluting, conserving of energy and natural resources, economically viable, Safe and healthful for workers, communities, and consumers, and socially and creatively rewarding for all working people.
Source: www.uml.edu/research/lowell-center/about/sustainable-production-defined.aspx

Switching Costs
The costs incurred by customers when they change from one solution provider to a substitute business. Although most prevalent switching costs are monetary in nature, there are also psychological, effort- and time-based switching costs. Companies that create unique products that have few substitutes and require significant effort to master their use enjoy significant switching costs.
Source: www.investopedia.com/terms/s/switchingcosts.asp

Time-to-Value (TTV)
The amount of time it takes a new customer to realize value from a product. The objective is to decrease TTV so new customers find value faster.

Trunk Show
Designer, manufacturer, or designer's representative takes the newest sample line to a store to show members and take orders. Test newest styles and colors for acceptability. Clothing Rental Companies take advantage of trunk shows to improve their local visibility.

Unbilled Deferred Revenue
Represents subscription service business that is contracted but unbilled and off the balance sheet. Results from giving customers price incentives to sign multi-year contracts.

Unit Renewal Rate
The percentage of customers that are renewing their subscriptions.

Upselling
Means upgrading the customer from one item to a higher-priced item. A strategy designed to sell a more feature-rich or expensive service edition. Requires developing insights from the subscriber's usage patterns to identify upsell opportunities. Sometimes involves offering a product bundle instead of a different product. These customers not only renew, but they also spend more for the same offer.

Wardrobe Stylist (also Fashion Stylist)
A consultant who selects the clothing for published editorial features, print or television advertising campaigns, music videos, concert performances, and any public appearances made by celebrities, models or other public figures.

Resources:
https://www.fatbit.com/glossary/

6.0 Strategy and Implementation Summary

Our marketing and sales strategies will emphasize our unique advantages for the consumers of high-quality designer garments. Our marketing strategy will begin with standard print and online listings in the fashion media and continue through networks of style consultants.

Our sales strategy is based on serving our niche markets better than the competition and leveraging our competitive advantages. These advantages include superior attention to understanding and satisfying changing customer styling needs and wants, creating a one-stop fashion solution, and value-driven rental fee pricing.

The objectives of our marketing strategy will be to recruit new members, retain existing members, get good members to spend more and return more frequently. Establishing a loyal customer base will be very important, because such core members will not only generate the most lifetime sales, but also provide valuable referrals.

We will generate word-of-mouth buzz through direct-mail campaigns, exceeding customer expectations, developing a Web site, getting involved in community cross-marketing events with local businesses, and donating our services at charity functions, in exchange for press release coverage. Our sales strategy will seek to convert potential and first-time members into long-term relationships and referral agents. The combination of our competitive advantages, targeted marketing campaign and networking activities, will enable _____ (company name) to continue increasing our market share.

6.1.0   Promotion Strategy

Promotion strategies will be focused to the target market segment. Given the importance of word-of-mouth/referrals among the area residents, we shall strive to efficiently service all our members to gain their business regularly, which is the recipe for our long-term success. We shall focus on direct resident marketing, publicity, seminars, and advertising as proposed. Our promotion strategy will focus on generating referrals from existing members and professionals, community involvement and direct mail campaigns.

Our promotional strategies will also make use of the following tools:
- **Advertising**
    - Yearly anniversary parties to celebrate the success of each year.
    - Yellow Pages ads in the book and online.
    - Flyers promoting special promotion events.
    - Doorknob hangers, if not prohibited by neighborhood associations.
    - Storefront banners to promote a themed promotional event.
    - Bags and shipping boxes with company name, logo and website.

- **Local Marketing / Public Relations**
    - Client raffle for gift certificates or discount coupons
    - Participation in local civic groups.
    - Press release coverage of our sponsoring of events at the local community center for families and residents.
    - Article submissions to magazines describing the benefits of clothing rentals.
    - Sales Brochure to convey our subscription benefits to prospective members.
    - Seminar presentations to local civic groups, explaining how to personalize the contents of clothing shipments and save substantial money with rentals.
    - Giveaway of free clothes closet planning booklets with company contact information.

- **Local Media**
    - Newsletter - We will send quarterly postcards and annual direct mailings to members. It will contain an explanation of new product and service introductions.

- o Radio Campaign - We will make "live on the air" presentations of our trial service coupons to the disk jockeys, hoping to get the promotions broadcasted to the listening audience. We will also make our formalwear rental expertise available for talk radio programs.
- o Newspaper Campaign - Placing several ads in local community newspapers to launch our initial campaign. We will include a trial coupon.
- o Website – We will collect email addresses for the monthly newsletter.
- o Cable TV advertising on local community-based shows focused on style, fashion and entertaining.

6.1.1 Grand Opening

An impressive 'Grand Opening' will be a must for our Subscription Clothing Rental Company. We will make an impressive and attractive start by spending freely on advertising. As far as our budget allows, we will give importance to the initial advertising campaign. We will place creatively phrased advertisements of considerable size in local newspapers and magazines. This is how we will get to be known in the fashion world.

Our Grand Opening celebration will be a very important promotion opportunity to create word-of-mouth advertising results. We will advertise the date of our grand opening in local newspapers and on local radio. We will provide the community with a reason to visit our Subscription Clothing Rental Company by offering free beverage and cheese samples.

We will do the following things to make the open house a successful event:
1. Enlist local business support to contribute a large number of door prizes.
2. Use a sign-in sheet to create an email/mailing list.
3. Sponsor a clothing design or dance competition.
4. Schedule appearance by local celebrities.
5. Create a festive atmosphere with balloons, beverages and music.
6. Get the local radio station to broadcast live from the event and handout fun gifts.
7. Offer an application fee waiver.
8. Giveaway our logo imprinted T-shirts as a contest prize.
9. Allow potential members to view your facility and ask questions.
10. Print promotional flyers and pay a few kids to distribute them locally.
11. Arrange for face contests, storytelling, models, and snacks for everyone.
12. Arrange for local politician to do the official opening ceremony so all the local newspapers came to take pictures and do a feature story.
13. Arrange that people can tour our facility on the open day in order to see our facilities, collect sales brochures and find out more about our services.
14. Allocate staff members to perform specific duties, handout business cards and sales brochures and instruct them to deal with any questions or queries.
16. Organize a drawing with everyone writing their name and phone numbers on the back of business cards and give a voucher as a prize to start a marketing list.
17. Hand out free samples of products and coupons.

6.1.2 Value Proposition

Our value proposition will summarize why a consumer should use our subscription clothing rental services. We will enable private access to our broad line of quality designers and innovative services that are affordably priced. Our value proposition will convince prospects that our subscription plans will add more value and better solve their need for a convenient, one-stop clothing rental company that understands the needs of the modern day _____ (career-driven/plus-size/professional?) women. We will use this value proposition statement to target members who will benefit most from using our clothing rental services. These are professional women with a forward fashion sense and the desire to have all their apparel needs satisfied in the privacy of their own homes. Our value proposition will be concise and appeal to the customer's strongest decision-making drivers, which are significant cash outlay savings, convenience, a time-efficient and well-managed rental experience, garment quality and selection, personalized selections, and quality of personal relationships with our virtual style consultants.

Recap of Our Value Proposition:

Trust – We are known as a trusted business partner with strong customer and vendor endorsements. We have earned a reputation for quality, integrity, and delivery of successful clothing rental solutions.

Quality – We offer _____ experience and extensive professional backgrounds in _____ at competitive rates.

Experience – Our ability to bring people with ___ (#) years of _____ (fashion?) experience with deep technical knowledge of _____ (software platforms?) is at the core of our success.

True Vendor Partnerships – Our true vendor partnerships with _____ and _____ enable us to offer the resources of much larger organizations with greater flexibility.

Customer Satisfaction and Commitment to Success – Through partnering with our members and delivering quality solutions, we have been able to achieve an impressive degree of repeat and referral business. Since ____ (year), more than ____% of our business activity is generated by existing members. Our philosophy is that "our customer's satisfaction is our success." Our success will be measured in terms of our customer's satisfaction survey scores and testimonials.

6.1.3 Positioning Statement

Our positioning strategy will be the result of conducting in-depth consumer market research to find out what benefits consumers want and how our subscription rental services can meet those needs. Due to the increase in female employment, many service-oriented professions are leaning toward differentiating themselves on the basis of convenience, societal givebacks and money saving benefits. This is also what we intend to do. For instance, we plan to have extended, "people" hours on various days of the week with our style consultants, and a hassle-free online home shopping service. We will also offer the highest level of customer service to ensure a steady stream of referrals and an innovative rental business model concept that will free up customer cash for a possible home down payment.

We also plan to develop specialized services that will enable us to pursue a niche focus on specific interest-based programs, such as wedding gown and formalwear online rentals. These objectives will position us at the _____ (mid-level/high-end) of the market and will allow the company to realize a healthy profit margin in relation to its low-end, discount rivals and achieve long-term growth. _____ (company name) plans to develop a reputation for personalized service, fair value-pricing, and turnaround reliability.

Market Positioning Recap
Price: The strategy is to offer competitive rental prices that are lower that the market leader yet set to indicate the value and worth of our subscription services.
Quality: The garment quality will have to be very good as the finished rental service results will be showcased in highly visible situations.
Service: On-time and customized service, based on customer selection specifications, will be the key to success in this type of business. Personal attention to the fashion and fit sensibilities of members will result in higher sales and word of mouth advertising.

6.1.4   Unique Selling Proposition (USP)

Our unique selling proposition will answer the question why a customer should choose to do business with our company versus any and every other option available to them in the marketplace. Our USP will be a description of a unique important benefit that our Subscription Clothing Rental Company offers to members, so that price is no longer the key to our sales growth.

Our USP will include the following:
Who our target audience is: _____
What we will do for them: _____
What qualities, skills, talents, traits do we possess that others do not: _____
What are the benefits we provide that no one else offers: _____
Why that is different from what others are offering: _____
Why that solutions matter most to our target audience: _____

6.1.5   Distribution Strategy

Members can contact the _____ (company name) by telephone, fax, internet and by dropping in. Our nearest competitors are ___ (#) miles away in either direction. The facility will also source and stock special request items for area residents.

We plan to pursue the following distribution channels: (select)
		Number	Reason Chosen	Sales Costs
1.	Our own retail outlets			
2.	Independent retail outlets			

3. Chain store retail outlets _____
4. Wholesale outlets _____
5. Independent distributors _____
6. Independent commissioned sales reps _____
7. In-house sales reps _____
8. Direct mail using own catalog or flyers _____
9. Catalog broker agreement _____
10. In-house telemarketing _____
11. Contracted telemarketing call center _____
12. Cybermarketing via own website _____
13. Online sales via amazon, eBay, etc. _____
14. TV and Cable Direct Marketing _____
15. TV Home Shopping Channels _____
16. Mobile Units _____
17. Franchised Business Units _____
18. Trade Shows _____
19. High-end Flea Markets _____
20. Consignment Shops _____
21. Home Party Sales Plans _____
22. Trunk Sales _____
23. Fundraisers _____
24. Farmer's Markets _____
26. Kiosks _____
27. Sublet Retail Boutique Space _____
28. In-home Boutique _____

6.1.6 Sales Rep Plan

We will use sales reps to market our rental services at home sales parties.

1. In-house or Independent _____
2. Salaried or Commissioned _____
3. Salary or Commission Rate _____
4. Salary Plus Commission Rate _____
5. Special Performance Incentives _____
6. Negotiating Parameters — Price Breaks/Added Services/_____
7. Performance Evaluation Criteria — No. of New Members/Sales Volume/_____
8. Number of Reps _____
9. Sales Territory Determinants — Geography/Demographics/_____
10. Sales Territories Covered _____
11. Training Program Overview _____
12. Training Program Cost _____
13. Sales Kit Contents _____
14. Primary Target Market _____
15. Secondary Target Market _____

Rep Name	Compensation Plan	Assigned Territory

6.2 Competitive Advantages

A **competitive advantage** is the thing that differentiates a business from its competitors. It is what separates our business from everyone else. It answers the questions: "Why do members buy from us versus a competitor?", and "What do we offer members that is unique?". We will use the following competitive advantages to set us apart from our competitors. The distinctive competitive advantages which _____ (company name) brings to the marketplace are as follows: (Note: Select only those you can support)

1. We will be able to handle special orders for the client in a timely manner by establishing and maintaining good terms with all suppliers.
2. Our stock will be fresh and new, because as stock ages, it will be discounted and sold off. If still not sold, it will be taken off the rack and stored, until closeout sales events, and then the price will be drastically slashed. Anything left after that will be donated to charity.
3. We will offer our members better designer dress rental choices and an increasing number of up-scale assortments.
4. Our inventory management software will reduce out-of-stock situations.
5. We will run seasonal promotions.

6. We closely monitor consumption trends to determine which items to list and de-list.
7. We will initiate a Supplier Scorecard Program to provide suppliers with objective and timely feedback to realize continuous improvement in supplier related activities.
8. Easy access to customer records, purchasing history and other information will help our sales force to provide members with the personalized information they need to shop with confidence.
9. Our business operations will be backed by a full team of managers and owners that will each devote their time and efforts into one specialized area of the business. This specialization will increase the effectiveness of each of the aspects of our business through cost-effective micro-management.
10. By having owners of the company being the principle managers of the company we will reduce employee costs and will ensure the honesty and reliability of our staff.
11. Our owners/managers we will be able to maintain a direct relationship with our members.
12. Our involvement with the community and our presence and availability within the outlet store on a regular basis will give our members the opportunity to give direct feedback, which will create a unique and appealing consumer environment.
13. We will enable our members to have online access to our total rental inventory via our website.
14. Focusing on high quality gowns and formal wear will draw members from the competition, as well as create a local market that has not existed before.
15. We will train our staff to answer most members questions, so that their time is valued.
16. Our website will enable online ordering and pre-ordering, and the issuance of reminder notices for automatic re-purchases.
17. We will utilize a software package that provides document management services and advanced management tools, such as basic and intermediate reporting functions, cost-benefit analysis, inventory management and audit functionality, in addition to electronic records storage and retrieval.
18. We will accommodate the members who like the idea of one-stop shopping.
19. We will offer discounts and other incentives for referrals.
20. We have the technological and professional staffing capabilities to provide our members with the highest possible level of personalized service.
21. We have an ethnically diverse and multilingual staff, which is critical for a service-oriented business.
22. We have formed alliances that enable us to provide one-stop shopping or an array of rental services through a single access point.
23. We developed a specialized training program for the staff, so they will be proficient at administering our service programs.
24. Our superior customer service, delivered through our trained staff, sets us apart and provides our competitive advantage
25. We guarantee minimal waiting to be serviced.
26. We have an inventory management system that reduces out-of-stock situations

and assures that needed items are in stock.
27. We regularly conduct focus groups to understand changing customer fashion and turnaround expectations.
28. We will develop a reputation for using our expertise to maintain a 'well-edited selection' that embodies the concept of reasonable rental value.
29. Our Collection includes an impressive group of designers, including Vera Wang and Melissa Sweet.

6.2.1 Branding Strategy

Our branding strategy involves what we do to shape what the customer immediately thinks our business offers and stands for. The purpose of our branding strategy is to reduce customer perceived purchase risk and improve our profit margins by allowing us to charge a premium for our subscription clothing rental services.

We will invest $____ every year in maintaining our personal brand name image, which will differentiate our rental business from other companies. The amount of money spent on creating and maintaining a brand name will not convey any specific information about our products, but it will convey, indirectly, that we are in this market for the long haul, that we have a reputation to protect, and that we will interact repeatedly with our customers. In this sense, the amount of money spent on maintaining our brand name will signal to consumers that we will provide subscription rental services of consistent quality.

We will use the following ways to build trust and establish our personal brand:
1. Build a consistently published blog and e-newsletter with informational content.
2. Create comprehensive social media profiles.
3. Contribute articles to related online publications.
4. Earn Career Certifications.
5. Remain readily accessible.
6. Find our voice and use it to be relatable on the human level.
7. Create a persona that combines who we are and who we want to be.
8. Stick with the niche in which we can offer the greatest value.

Resources:
https://www.abetterlemonadestand.com/branding-guide/

Our key to marketing success will be to effectively manage the building of our brand platform in the marketplace, which will consist of the following elements:
- **Brand Vision** - our envisioned future of the brand is to be the local source for subscription clothing rental solutions to manage the complications of wardrobe planning.
- **Brand Attributes** - Partners, problem solvers, responsive, wide designer clothing selection, fitting experts, comprehensive, reliable, flexible, big data trend analysts, expert style consultants and easy to work with.
- **Brand Essence** - the shared soul of the brand, the spark of which is present in every experience a customer has with our products, will be "Problem Solving" and

"Responsive" This will be the core of our organization, driving the type of people we hire and the type of behavior we expect.

Brand Image - the outside world's overall perception of our organization will be that we are the 'subscription clothing rental' pros who are alleviating the complications of selecting the right outfit for the right occasion.

Brand Promise - our concise statement of what we do, why we do it, and why members should do business with us will be, "To realize solid values with the help of our knowledgeable staff"

We will use the following methodologies to implement our branding strategy:

1. Develop processes, systems and quality assurance procedures to assure the consistent adherence to our quality standards and mission statement objectives.
2. Develop business processes to consistently deliver upon our value proposition.
3. Develop training programs to assure the consistent professionalism and responsiveness of our employees.
4. Develop marketing communications with consistent, reinforcing message content.
5. Incorporate testimonials into our marketing materials that support our promises.
6. Develop marketing communications with a consistent presentation style. (Logo design, company colors, slogan, labels, packaging, stationery, etc.)
7. Exceed our brand promises to achieve consistent customer loyalty.
8. Use surveys, focus groups and interviews to consistently monitor what our brand means to our members.
9. Consistently match our brand values or performance benchmarks to our customer requirements.
10. Focus on the maintenance of a consistent number of key brand values that are tied to our company strengths.
11. Continuously research industry trends in our markets to stay relevant to customer needs and wants.
12. Attach a logo-imprinted product label and business card to all products, marketing communications and invoices.
13. Develop a memorable and meaningful tagline that captures the essence of our brand.
14. Prepare a one-page company overview and make it a key component of our sales presentation folder.
15. Hire and train employees to put the interests of members first.
16. Develop a professional website that is updated with fresh fashion trend content on a regular basis.
17. Use our blog to circulate knowledge enriching content that establishes our niche fashion expertise and opens a two-way dialogue with our members.
18. Attach our logo to all shipping packages and policy statements.
19. Create an effective slogan with the following attributes:
    a. Appeals to customers' emotions.
    b. Shows off how our service benefits customers by highlighting our customer service or care.
    c. Has 8 words or less and is memorable
    d. Can be grasped quickly by our audience.

  e. Reflects our business' personality and character.
  f. Shows sign of originality.
20. Create a Proof Book that contains before and after photos, testimonial letters, our mission statement, copies of industry certifications and our code of ethics.
21. Make effective use of trade show exhibitions and fashion shows, and email newsletters to help brand our image.
22. Tell the unique story behind our company that touches on our history, our mission, our values, and our dedication to members so they feel a connection with our subscription business and embrace the beginning of what is hopefully a long relationship with our brand.

The communications strategy we will use to build our brand platform will include the following items:

- Website - featuring product line information, research, testimonials, cost benefit analysis, frequently asked questions, and policy information. This website will be used as a tool for both our sales team and our members.
- Presentations, brochures and mailers geared to the consumer, explaining the benefits of our clothing rental line as part of a comprehensive business casual styling servicing plan.
- Presentations and brochures geared to the family decision maker explaining the benefits of our club programs in terms of positive outcomes, reduced cost from complications, and reduced risk of lawsuits or negative survey events.
- A presentation and recruiting brochure geared to prospective sales people that emphasizes the benefits of joining our organization.
- Training materials that help every employee deliver our brand message in a consistent manner.

6.2.2 Brand Positioning Statement

We will use the following brand positioning statement to summarize what our brand means to our targeted market:

To _____ (target market) _____ (company name) is the brand of _____ (product/service frame of reference) that enables the customer to _____ (primary performance benefit) because _____ (company name) _____ (products/services) _____ (are made with/offer/provide) the best _____ (key attributes)

6.3 Business SWOT Analysis

Definition: SWOT Analysis is a powerful technique for understanding our Strengths and Weaknesses, and for looking at the Opportunities and Threats faced.

Strategy: We will use this SWOT Analysis to uncover exploitable opportunities and carve a sustainable niche in our market. And by understanding the weaknesses of our business, we can manage and eliminate threats that would otherwise catch us by surprise. By using the SWOT framework, we will be able to craft a strategy that distinguishes our business from our competitors, so that we can compete successfully in the market.

Strengths (select)

What Subscription Clothing Rental Company services are we best at providing? What unique resources can we draw upon?

1. Our location is in the heart of an upscale neighborhood and is in close proximity to a popular _____ with ample parking facilities.
2. The facility has been established as a _____ business for _ years.
3. The nearest competition is __ miles and has a minimal inventory of fashion-forward goods.
4. Our facility has been extensively renovated, with many conveyor system upgrades.
5. Our facility can easily change inventory focus based on special occasion and seasonal requirements.
6. Seasoned executive management professionals, sophisticated in business knowledge, experienced in the designer garment trade.
7. Strong networking relationships with many different organizations, including _____.
8. Excellent staff are experienced, highly trained and customer attentive.
9. Wide diversity of membership program options.
10. High customer loyalty and referral rates among members.
11. The proven ability to establish excellent personalized client service.
12. Strong relationships with suppliers, that offer flexibility and respond to special customer requirements and trending patterns.
13. Good referral relationships.
14. Client loyalty developed through a solid reputation with repeat members.
15. Our business has a focused target market of ____ (professional women?).
16. Sales staff has impressive style consulting credentials.
17. First to market in _____ (city).
18. A practical, efficient way to have a fashion-forward wardrobe, while minimizing sunk costs.
19. On staff dry-cleaning professionals, seamstresses and spotters continually make garments look like new and extend their rentable lifespans.
20. Offer a popular mix of couture lines and a ready-to-wear-lines.
21. _____

Weaknesses

In what areas could we improve?
Where do we have fewer resources than others?

1. Lack of developmental capital to complete Phase I start-up.
2. New comer to the area.
3. Lack of marketing experience.
4. The struggle to build brand equity.
5. A limited marketing budget to develop brand awareness.

6. Finding dependable and member-oriented staff.
7. Need to develop the information systems that will improve our match to customer fashion needs, productivity and inventory management.
8. Don't know the needs and wants of _____ (millennials?).
9. The owner must deal with the rental experience learning curve.
10. Challenges caused by the seasonal and fad natures of the business.
11. The company lacks visibility.
12. The whole industry is so cutting edge it lacks consumer awareness.
13. The requirement to generate awareness, not only about the company, but for the industry as a whole.
14. _____

Opportunities

What opportunities are there for new and/or improved services?
What trends could we take advantage of?
1. Seasonal changes in inventory.
2. Could take market share away from existing competitors.
3. Greater need for mobile rental services by time starved professional women.
4. Growing market with a significant percentage of the target market still not aware that _____ (company name) exists.
5. The ability to develop many long-term customer relationships.
6. Expanding the range of product/service packaged offerings.
7. Greater use of direct advertising to promote our services.
8. Establish referral relationships with local businesses serving the same target market segment.
9. Networking with non-profit organizations.
10. The aging population will need and expect a greater range of __ services.
11. Increased public awareness of the importance of 'green' matters and the eco-friendly implications of garment recycling.
12. Strategic alliances offering sources for referrals and joint marketing activities to extend our reach.
13. _____ (supplier name) is offering co-op advertising.
14. A competitor has overextended itself financially and is facing bankruptcy.
15. Similar companies in other markets have seen explosive growth.
16. Spinning off fee-based business concepts, such as dry-cleaning, tailoring, style consulting, software development, etc.
17. Celebrate partnerships with designers who have developed a newly 'green' source of raw materials, like sustainable natural fabric fiber.
18. _____

Threats

What trends or competitor actions could hurt us?
What threats do our weaknesses expose us to?
1. Another Subscription Clothing Rental Company could move into this area.
2. Further declines in the economic forecast.

3. Inflation affecting operations for gas, labor, and other operating costs.
4. Keeping trained efficient staff and key personnel from moving on or starting their own business ventures.
5. Imitation competition from similar indirect service providers, such as women's clothing boutiques.
6. Price differentiation is a significant competition factor.
7. The government could enact legislation that could affect operations.
8. Need to do a better job of assessing the strengths and weaknesses of all our competitors.
9. Sales of upscale designer clothing by mass discounters.
10. The traditionalism and conservatism surrounding the collecting of a designer wardrobe and pride of ownership.
11. _____

Recap:
We will use the following strengths to capitalize on recognized opportunities:
1. _____
2. _____

We will take the following actions to turn our weaknesses into strengths and prepare to defend against known threats.
1. _____
2. _____

6.4.0 Marketing Strategy

Our objective is to position _____ (company name) as the logical alternative to buying limited use designer clothing for work or play. The marketing strategy will be to create customer awareness, develop the customer base, and build customer loyalty and referrals.

The objective will be achieved through a multi-faceted marketing campaign, involving the use of online directories, Google Search and social media postings. Other marketing, such as press releases, sales brochures and fashion magazine ads, will serve to generate awareness. These ads will serve to generate visibility for the industry in general. While a national magazine has steep advertising rates, ___ (company name) will be entering into cooperative agreements with the other pioneers in the industry to help diffuse costs. This is attractive to the other market participants as it generates awareness for the industry as a whole.

The last facet of the communication campaign is the use of the marketing content on our website. The website will be useful for the dissemination of information because it allows people to collect information and educate themselves on their own time and schedule. The website will be a rich source of information regarding the designer selection and returns processes, rental prices and the subscription rental industry in general. These different communication methods will be useful in legitimizing the clothing rental concept and driving sales.

_____ (company name) will use the following mediums for the focus of our marketing campaign:

1. **Local Fashion Publications** - These include magazines that are used to promote fashion shows.
2. **Style Consultants** - By building relationships with local style and image consultants, we will have a direct referral source.
3. **Web Links** - Most designers offer a "store locator" on their web pages. Therefore, when available, we will be listed on the web sites of the designers whose lines we carry, with a link to our web site.
4. **Yellow Pages** - We will be listed under the "clothing rental" section of the yellow pages, so this will serve as a standard resource for members to find us.

Our Marketing strategy will focus on the following:

1. Developing a reputation for great selection, fast order processing, competitive member rental plan fees, mobile services, and exceptional customer service.
2. Developing strong relationships with our suppliers to help insure best wholesaler deals and fastest supplier services obtainable.
3. Keeping the staff focused, satisfied and motivated in their roles, to help keep our productivity and customer service at the highest obtainable levels.
4. Maintaining the visibility of our business through regular advertising to our target community.
5. Reaching out to potential alliance partners and community organizations, with commissioned independent sales reps.
6. Doing activities that can stimulate additional business: educational seminars designed to share fashion knowledge, publishing a newsletter, offering customer self-service through a website, free deliveries and return shipments, automatic and reminder ordering services and mobile shopping services.
7. Extending our market penetration beyond the physical boundaries of the physical location through home party plan sales, outside sales reps and an interactive e-commerce website.

_____ (company name) intends to actively seek out and attract new members, whose needs go beyond the need for convenience sales. Our online website will the primary focus of this incentive program. This service will be an interactive feature that will act as a database of our broad product selection and will primarily be focused on our high-end rental products. The goals for this service will be for it to serve as a compilation of our product selection, in which a user will be able to categorize our entire inventory in several different ways and then be able to view individual product descriptions and suggestions. The service is intended to make our members more comfortable with our rental lines. It will provide a way for our members to survey the attributes of our garments and accessories, so that they may be able to make an informed rental decision. This system seeks to create consumer demand through consumer education.

In phase one of our marketing plan, we will gain exposure to our target markets through the use of discounts and grand opening promotional tactics. We will be taking a very aggressive marketing stance in the first year of business in hopes of gaining customer loyalty. In our subsequent years, we will focus less resources on advertising as a whole. However, we do plan to budget for advertising promotions on a continual and season specific basis.

We will start our business with our known personal referral contacts and then continue our campaign to develop recognition among other groups, such as professional women. We will develop and maintain a database of our contacts in the field. We will work to maintain and exploit our existing relationships throughout the start-up process and then use our marketing tools to communicate with other potential referral sources, such as millennials. The marketing strategy will create awareness, interest and appeal from our target market. Its ultimate purpose is to encourage repeat rentals and get members to refer friends and professional contacts. To get referrals we will provide incentives and excellent service and build relationships with members by consistently caring about what the customer needs and wants.

Our marketing strategy will revolve around two different types of media; flyers and a website. These two tools will be used to make members aware of our broad range of rental plan offerings. One focus of our marketing strategy will be to drive members to our website for information about our clothing rental programs. A combination of local media and event marketing will be utilized. __ (company name) will create an identity-oriented marketing strategy with executions particularly in the local media and social media sites. Our marketing strategy will also utilize prime time radio spots, print ads, press releases, yellow page ads, and e-newsletter distribution. We will make effective use of direct response advertising and include coupons in all print ads to track return on investment.

We will use comment cards, newsletter sign-up forms and surveys to collect customer email addresses and feed our client relationship management (CRM) software system. This system will automatically send out, on a predetermined schedule, follow-up materials, such as article reprints, seminar invitations, email messages, surveys and e-newsletters. We will offset some of our advertising costs by asking our suppliers and other local merchants to place ads in our newsletter.

Marketing Budget

Our marketing budget will be a flexible $_____ per quarter. The marketing budget can be allocated in any way that best suits the time of year.

Marketing budget per quarter:

Newspaper Ads	$_____	Radio advertisement	$_____
Web Page	$_____	Customer raffle	$_____
Direct Mail	$_____	Sales Brochure	$_____
Fashion Shows	$_____	Seminars	$_____
Superpages	$_____	Google Adwords	$_____
Giveaways	$_____	Vehicle Signs	$_____
Business Cards	$_____	Flyers	$_____

Labels/Stickers	$ _____	Videos/DVDs	$ _____
Samples	$ _____	Newsletter	$ _____
Social Media Posts	$ _____	Email Campaigns	$ _____
Sales Reps Comm.	$ _____	Other	$ _____

Total: $ _____

Our objective in setting a marketing budget has been to keep it between ____ (5?) and ____ (7?) percent of our estimated annual gross sales.

Marketing Mix

New members will primarily come from word-of-mouth and our referral program. The overall market approach involves creating brand awareness through targeted advertising, public relations, co-marketing efforts with select alliance partners, direct mail, email campaigns (with constant contact.com), fashion shows, seminars and a website.

Host Focus Groups

We will host focus groups for professional women listed in local business magazines. This will help our company to learn about their needs, wants and priorities, and develop effective marketing ideas for reaching this target audience. Female business executives will welcome the opportunity to learn more about clothing rental industry trends and convey information about their fashion wish list.

Free Services

As a get acquainted, introductory offer, we will offer free style consulting services. This will help us to collect contact information and to build our database of qualified prospects.

Advertise Gift Registries

We will advertise our subscription clothing rental plan in gift registries to demonstrate our program benefits to gift recipients. These reciprocal marketing arrangements will reduce our advertising costs and provide an endorsement of our rental programs.

Hold Trunk Shows

We will arrange for the designers of selected fashion types to be present to speak directly to rental shoppers about their designs.

Video Marketing

We will link to our website a series of YouTube.com based video clips that talk about our range of clothing rental services and demonstrate our expertise with certain designers. We will create business marketing videos that are both entertaining and informational and improve our search engine rankings.

Note: Video business marketing is growing significantly in popularity because customers want to see the firm's facility or a product or service in action. Having a video incorporated into a web site or Facebook page can lead to increased views and sales. In fact, Google Business Views are very popular right now. Google Business View is a 360-

degree panoramic virtual tour added to a Google Business Page and Google Maps. It increases Search Engine Optimization (SEO) dramatically.
Resource: www.google.com/maps/about/partners/businessview/

The videos will include:
- **Client testimonials** - We will let our best members become our instant sales force, because people will believe what others say about us more readily than what we say about ourselves.
- **Product Demonstrations** - We will train and pre-sell our potential members on our most popular clothing rental services by talking about and showing them. Often, our potential members don't know the full range and depth of our products and services because we haven't taken the adequate time to show and tell them.
- **Include Business Website Address**
- **Owner Interview:** Discussion of company mission statement and unique value proposition.
- **Create Video Commercial**: To be distributed by CD as part of a direct mail package or played as an ad on a Local Style Cable TV Channel.
- **Frequently Asked Questions** - We will answer questions that we often get and anticipate objections we might get and give great reasons to convince potential members that we are the best Subscription Clothing Rental Company in the area.
- **Include a Call to Action** - We have the experience and the know-how to save working professionals a significant amount of ideal wardrobe money, so call us, right now, and let's get started.
- **Seminar** - Include a portion of a seminar on how money-saving clothing rental tips
- **Comment on industry trends and product news** - We will appear more in-tune and knowledgeable in our market if we can talk about what's happening in our industry and marketplace.

Resources: www.businessvideomarketing.tv
www.hotpluto.com
www.hubspot.com/video-marketing-kit
www.youtube.com/user/mybusinessstory

Video Advertising Bureau   www.thevab.com
Provides marketers with industry-defining data, actionable thought leadership and planning tools to navigate and optimize the ever-expanding world of premium multiscreen video content. In collaboration with their member partners, the VAB champions the undeniable power of premium video advertising.
Inc. Video   www.inc.com/christine-hunsicker/how-gwynnie-bee-is-redesigning-the-plus-size-industry.html
Examples:
www.youtube.com/watch?v=KhaZadQWVA
www.youtube.com/watch?v=tQvs-_XKBts
www.youtube.com/watch?v=eOjv_4hHKUY
How to Rent:
www.youtube.com/watch?v=OVG7L1G3jgk
www.youtube.com/watch?v=4FHufxIYApg

Top 11 places where we will share our videos online:

YouTube	www.youtube.com
Google Video	http://video.google.com/
Yahoo! Video	http://video.yahoo.com/
Revver	http://www.revver.com/
Blip.tv	http://blip.tv/
Vimeo	http://www.vimeo.com/
Metacafe	http://www.metacafe.com/
ClipShack	http://www.clipshack.com/
Veoh	http://www.veoh.com/
Jumpcut	http://download.cnet.com/JumpCut/3000-18515_4-10546353.html
DailyMotion	www.dailymotion.com

Business Cards

Our business card will include our company logo, complete contact information, name and title, association logos, slogan or markets serviced, and certifications. The center of our bi-fold card will contain a listing of the designers and rental services we offer. We will give out multiple business cards to friends, family members, and to each new member. We will also distribute business cards in the following ways:

1. Attached to invoices, surveys, flyers and door hangers.
2. Included in customer product packages.
3. We will leave a stack of business cards in a Lucite holder with the local Chamber of Commerce and any other businesses offering free counter placement.

We will use fold-over cards because they will enable us to list all our service benefits and complete contact instructions on the inside of the card. We will also give magnetic business cards to new members for posting on the refrigerator door.
Resource: www.vistaprint.com

Direct Mail Package

To build name recognition, demonstrate the expertise of our style consultants and to announce the opening of our Subscription Clothing Rental Company, we will create a mail package consisting of a tri-fold brochure containing a discount coupon to welcome our new subscribers. The mailing piece will also contain a composite photo of the likely garments contained in one of our shipping boxes. We will also present our competitive advantages, a simplistic overview of the subscription rental benefits to be realized and a basic flowchart of how the profiling, ordering, renting, shipping and returning processes work.

We also plan to include a magnetic business card for future easy reference. We plan to make a mailing to local subscribers of style and fashion-focused magazines, such as Glamour and InStyle Magazines. From those identified local members, we shall ask them to complete a survey and describe their perception of the ideal Subscription Clothing Rental Company, and any specific designers or services they would like to see added. Those members returning completed surveys would receive a premium (giveaway) gift.
Resources:

www.targetmarketingmag.com/post/5-ideas-for-subscription-box-direct-mail/
www.mytotalretail.com/article/le-tote-disrupts-fashion-direct-mail/
Example:
www.mytotalretail.com/resource/le-tote-uses-mail-to-reach-a-new-audience/

Trade Shows

We will exhibit at as many local trade shows per year as possible. These include Bridal Expos and Festivals, Fashion Shows, County Fairs, open exhibits in shopping malls, Business Expos, business spot-lights with our local Chamber of Commerce, and more. The objective is to get our company name and service out to as many people as possible. We will do our homework and ask other clothing rental businesses where they exhibit their products and services. When exhibiting at a trade show, we will put our best foot forward and represent ourselves as professionals. We will be open, enthusiastic, informative and courteous. We will exhibit our subscription services with sales brochures, logo-imprinted giveaways, sample products to review, a photo book for people to browse through and a computer to run our video presentation through. We will use a 'free drawing' for a gift basket prize and a sign-in sheet to collect names and email addresses. We will also develop a personal style questionnaire or survey that helps us to assemble an ideal customer profile and qualify the leads we receive. We will train our booth attendants to answer all type of fashion questions and to handle objections. We will also seek to present educational seminars at the show to gain increased publicity, and name and expertise recognition. Most importantly, we will develop and implement a follow-up program to stay-in-touch with prospects.

Resources:	www.tsnn.com	www.expocentral.com
	www.acshomeshow.com/	www.bridesclub.com/bridal-shows/
	www.eventinamerica.com	www.biztradeshows.com

Resource:
http://augustafreepress.com/trade-show-booth-ideas-rock-show/

New Homeowners / Movers

We will reach out to new movers in our immediate neighborhood. Marketing to new movers will help bring in more long-term members. And, because new movers are five times more likely to become loyal, this marketing program, will generate new, fresh members who are likely to turn in to the regular members. The value of a new loyal customer will be significant, as a new loyal customer who comes in ___ (#) times a month can be worth up to $_____ a year for standard services. Furthermore, many studies suggest that new movers typically stay in their new homes for an average of 5.6 years. We will also participate in local Welcome Wagon activities for new residents and assemble a mailing list to distribute sales literature from county courthouse records and Realtor supplied information. We will use a postcard mailing to promote a special get-acquainted clothing rental offer to new residents.

Resources:
Welcome Wagon	www.WelcomeWagon.com
Welcome Mat Services	www.WelcomeMatServices.com
Welcomemat Services uses specialized, patent-pending technology to store and log

customer demographics for use by the local companies it supports.

Bench Ads
These ads will provide us with an affordable way to improve our subscription clothing rental visibility.   Resource: www.BenchAds.net

Networking
Networking will be a key to success because referrals and alliances formed can help to improve our community image and keep our practice growing. We will strive to build long-term mutually beneficial relationships with our networking contacts and join the following types of organizations:
1. We will form a LeTip Chapter to exchange business leads.
2. We will join the local BNI.com referral exchange group.
3. We will join the Chamber of Commerce to further corporate relationships.
4. We will join the Rotary Club, Lions Club, Kiwanis Club, Church Groups, etc.
5. We will do volunteer work for American Heart Assoc. and Habitat for Humanity.
6. We will become an affiliated member of the local board of Realtors and the Women's Council of Realtors.
7. We will join local garden and women's clubs.
8. We will join women's business councils.

Resources:
National Women's Business Council   www.nwbc.org
Women's Business Enterprise National Council   www.wbenc.org
Resource:
Find Networking Events   http://findnetworkingevents.com/

We will use our metropolitan _____ (city) Chamber of Commerce to target prospective contacts. We will mail letters to each prospect describing our bridal products and services. We will follow-up with phone calls.
Resource: http://www.uschamber.com/chambers/directory/default

Newsletter
We will develop a one-page newsletter to be handed out to members to take home with them as they visit the store. The monthly newsletter will be used to build our brand and update members on special promotions. The newsletter will be produced in-house and for the cost of paper and computer time. We will include the following types of information:
1. Our involvement with charitable events.
2. New Service/Product Introductions
3. Featured employee/bride of the month.
4. New industry technologies and trends.
5. Customer endorsements/testimonials.
6. Classified ads from local sponsors and suppliers.
7. Announcements / Upcoming events and promotions.
8. Survey results.

Resources: Microsoft Publisher   www.aweber.com

Boomtrain   https://zetaglobal.com/zeta-hub-small-and-medium-businesses/
Helps companies to send individually relevant mobile apps, e-newsletters and email notifications at any scale.
Content Examples: www.frankandoak.com/handbook

Vehicle Signs
We will place magnetic and vinyl signs on our vehicles and include our company name, phone number, company slogan and website address, if possible. We will create a cost-effective moving billboard with high-quality, high-resolution vehicle wraps. We will wrap a portion of the vehicle or van to deliver excellent marketing exposure.
Resource: http://www.fastsigns.com/

Advertising Wearables
We will give all preferred club members an eye-catching T-shirt or sweatshirt with our company name and logo printed across the garment to wear about town. We will also give them away as a thank you for customer referral activities. We will ask all employees to wear our logo-imprinted shirts. We will also explore advertising and wearable technologies, which are clothing and accessories that incorporate computer and advanced electronics. They can come in a variety of forms, including smart watches, arm bands, glasses/heads-up displays, smart fabrics and jewelry.
Source: www.exactdrive.com/news/advertising-and-wearable-technology

Stage Events
We will stage events to become known in our community. This is essential to attracting referrals. We will schedule regular events, such as seminar talks about clothing design trends, business casualwear demonstrations, catered open house events and fundraisers. We will offer seminars through organizations to promote the health benefits of wardrobe management and the financial benefits of designer clothing rentals. We will use event registration forms, our website and an event sign-in sheet to collect the names and email addresses of all attendees. This database will be used to feed our automatic customer relationship follow-up program and e-newsletter service.

Sales Brochures
The sales brochure will enable us to make a solid first impression when pursing business. Our sales brochure will include the following contents and become a key part of our sales presentation folder and direct mail package:

- Contact Information
- Customer Testimonials
- Competitive Advantages
- Trial Coupon
- Key Designers Carried
- Business Description
- List of Subscription Benefits
- Owner Resume/Bio
- Style Consultant Resumes
- Rental Procedures and Policies

Sales Presentation Folder Contents
1. Resumes
2. Member Photos
3. Contract/Application
4. Frequently Asked Questions
5. Sales Brochure
6. Business Cards

7. Testimonials/References
8. Plan/Program Descriptions
9. Informative Articles
10. Referral Program
11. Company Overview
12. Operating Policies
13. Member Satisfaction Survey

Coupons

We will use coupons with limited time expirations to get prospects to try our subscription clothing rental service plans. We will also accept the coupons of our competitors to help establish new client relationships. We will run ads directing people to our Web site for a $___ coupon certificate. This will help to draw in new members and collect e-mail addresses for the distribution of a monthly newsletter. Research indicates that we can use our coupons to spark online searches of our website and drive sales. This will help to draw in new members and collect e-mail addresses for the distribution of a monthly newsletter. We will include a coupon with each garment rental or sale or send them by mail to our mailing list. We will also use them as thank you rewards when subscribers provide feedback.

We will use the following discounts to benefit our brand and also show customer appreciation:
- first time member's discount
- volume discount
- returning member discount
- teacher, senior, military or student discounts
- donation receipt discount

Resources:
http://www.businessknowhow.com/marketing/couponing.htm
https://www.constantcontact.com/features/coupons

We will use coupons selectively to accomplish the following:
1. To introduce a new product or service.
2. To attract loyal members away from the competition
3. To prevent customer defection to a new competitor.
4. To help celebrate a special event.
5. To thank members for a large order and ensure a repeat order within a certain limited time frame.

Examples:
https://dealhack.com/coupons/gwynnie-bee
https://coupons.businessinsider.com/
www.goodsearch.org/coupons/le-tote

Types of Coupons:
1. Courtesy Coupons — Rewards for repeat business
2. Cross-Marketing Coupons — Incentive to try other products/services.
3. Companion Coupon — Bring a friend incentive.

Resources: www.google.com/offers/business/how-it-works.html

Websites like Groupon.com, LivingSocial, Eversave, and BuyWithMe sell discount vouchers for services ranging from custom _____ to ____ consultations. Best known is Chicago-based Groupon. To consumers, discount vouchers promise substantial savings — often 50% or more. To merchants, discount vouchers offer possible opportunities for price discrimination, exposure to new members, online marketing, and "buzz." Vouchers are more likely to be profitable for merchants with low marginal costs, who can better accommodate a large discount and for patient merchants, who place higher value on consumers' possible future return visits over an extended period of time.
Example: www.groupon.com/deals/le-tote-nat-9

Cross-Promotions
We will develop and maintain partnerships with local businesses that cater to the needs of our members, such as beauty salons, nail salons, financial planners and executive recruiters, and conduct cross-promotional marketing campaigns. These cross-promotions will require the exchanging of customer mailing lists and endorsements.

Premium Giveaways
We will distribute logo-imprinted promotional products at events, also known as giveaway premiums, to foster top-of-mind awareness (www.promoideas.org). These items include business cards with magnetic backs, mugs with contact phone number, natural spot remover recipe booklets, season-based fashion tips, and calendars that feature important fashion show date reminders.

Local Newspaper Ads
We will use these ads to announce the opening of our subscription rental business and get our name established. We will adhere to the rule that frequency and consistency of message are essential. We will include a list of our top designer names and specialty service benefits. We will include a coupon to track the response in zoned editions of 'Shopper' Papers, Theater Bills, and Community Newsletters and Newspapers. We will use the ad to announce any weekly or monthly member specials.

Local Publications
We will place low-cost classified ads in neighborhood publications to advertise our included style consulting services. We will also submit public relations and informative articles to improve our visibility and establish our designer fashion rental expertise and trustworthiness. These publications include the following:
1. Neighborhood Newsletters
2. Church Bulletins
3. Local Restaurant Association Newsletter
4. Local Chamber of Commerce Newsletter
5. Realtor Magazines
6. Homeowner Association Newsletters
7. Fashion Magazines

Resource: Hometown News   www.hometownnews.com
           Pennysaver   www.pennysaverusa.com

Business Journals

We will consider placing display ads in business journals read by professionals and possibly rent a list of their local subscribers for a planned direct mailing. The mailing will describe our subscription clothing rental programs. We will use empirical data to prove how our targeted subscription programs can actually save company employees time and money.

Resource:
The Business Journals   www.bizjournals.com/
Examples:
www.bizjournals.com/newyork/news/2019/03/22/gwynnie-bee-unveils-tech-to-help-retailers-enter.html
www.bizjournals.com/newyork/news/2016/03/23/rent-the-runway-unlimited-subscription.html

Doorhangers

Our doorhangers will feature a calendar of 'Free Wardrobe Planning Seminars'. The doorhanger will include a list of all our subscription service categories, and info about our rental program options. We will also attach our business card to the doorhanger. Even if we have already used a direct mail campaign to reach consumers, the door hanger will be used as a reminder device to reinforce our upcoming fashion show event in the mind of the consumer. Our advertising message will be reinforced simply and effectively on our door hanger advertisements.

Resources:
https://www.psprint.com/resources/door-hanger-marketing-secrets/
https://www.adeasprinting.com/Door-Hangers/
www.prospectsplus.com/ProductCats.asp?cid=1117&itemname=One+Sided+Door+Hangers

Article Submissions

We will pitch articles to consumer fashion magazines, local newspapers, business magazines and internet articles directories to help establish our specialized fashion trend expertise and improve our visibility in the subscription clothing rental industry. Hyperlinks will be placed within written articles and can be clicked on to take the customer to another webpage within our website or to a totally different website. These clickable links or hyperlinks will be keywords or relevant words that have meaning to our Subscription Clothing Rental Company. We will create keyword-rich article titles that match the most commonly searched keywords for our topic. In fact, we will create a position whose primary function is to link our Subscription Clothing Rental Company with opportunities to be published in local publications.

Examples of General Publishing Opportunities:

1.	Document a new solution to old problem	2.	Publish a research study
3.	Mistake prevention advice	4.	Present a different viewpoint
5.	Introduce a local angle on a hot topic.	6.	Reveal a new trend.
7.	Share specialty niche expertise.	8.	Share money-saving secrets.

Examples of Specific Article Titles:
1. "Everything You Ever Wanted to Know About Renting a Dress for Work"
2. "How to Evaluate and Compare Subscription Clothing Rental Companies"
3. "The Reputations of the Top Business Casual Dress Designers"
4. "Special Occasion Dress Rental Tips"
5. "How You Can Afford a Top Designer Dress"
6. "New Designer Clothing Rental Trends"
7. "The Top 10 Reasons to Rent Your Next Evening-Out Dress".
8. "Better Wardrobe Management Types Via Subscription Rentals"

Possible Magazines and Blogs to submit ads and articles include:

1.	Modern Bride Magazine	2.	Today's Bride Magazine
3.	New York Magazine - Weeding Edition	4.	Cosmopolitan
5.	Vogue	6.	Us Magazine
7.	Glamour	8.	Town & Country - Weddings
9.	The Oprah Magazine	10.	Lucky Magazine
11.	Marie Claire	12.	In-Style Magazine
13.	Teen Vogue	14.	Fast Company
15.	Los Angeles Magazine	16.	Parent Magazine
17.	Bridal Show Magazine	18.	Womansday.com
19.	The Bride	20.	Martha Stewart's Weddings
21.	Style Me Pretty	22.	Elle
23.	Harper's BAZAAR	24.	Allure
25.	Redbook		

Ezines:
http://eco-beautifulweddings.com/ezine/
http://ny.racked.com
www.businessinsider.com
www.refinery29.com/get-smart-budget-wise-wedding-rentals
www.stylemepretty.com/2012/05/15/little-borrowed-dress-2/
www.allyoucanread.com/top-10-fashion-magazines/

Specialized Websites:

1.	TheKnot.com	2.	Style.com
3.	CosmoGirl.com	4.	Elle.com
5.	Webcastr.com		

General Business Websites:

1.	USAToday.com	2.	FoxBusiness.com
3.	NYTimes.com	4.	WSJ.com
5.	Inc.com	6.	Forbes.com

Resources: Writer's Market   www.writersmarket.com
                Directory of Trade Magazines   www.techexpo.com/tech_mag.html

Internet article directories include:

http://ezinearticles.com/	http://www.mommyshelpercommunity.com
http://www.wahm-articles.com	http://www.ladypens.com/
http://www.articlecity.com	http://www.amazines.com
http://www.articledashboard.com	http://www.submityourarticle.com/articles
http://www.webarticles.com	http://www.articlecube.com
http://www.article-buzz.com	http://www.free-articles-zone.com
www.articletogo.com	http://www.content-articles.com
http://article-niche.com	http://superpublisher.com
www.internethomebusinessarticles.com	http://www.site-reference.com
http://www.articlenexus.com	www.articlebin.com
http://www.articlefinders.com	www.articlesfactory.com
http://www.articlewarehouse.com	www.buzzle.com
http://www.easyarticles.com	www.isnare.com
http://ideamarketers.com/	//groups.yahoo.com/group/article_announce
http://clearviewpublications.com/	www.ebusiness-articles.com
http://www.goarticles.com/	www.authorconnection.com/
http://www.webmasterslibrary.com/	www.businesstoolchest.com
http://www.connectionteam.com	www.digital-women.com/submitarticle.htm
http://www.MarketingArticleLibrary.com	www.searchwarp.com
http://www.dime-co.com	www.articleshaven.com
http://www.allwomencentral.com	www.marketing-seek.com
http://www.reprintarticles.com	www.articles411.com
http://www.articlestreet.com	www.articleshelf.com
http://www.articlepeak.com	www.articlesbase.com
http://www.simplysearch4it.com	www.articlealley.com

Online Classified Ad Placement Opportunities

The following free classified ad sites, will enable our Subscription Clothing Rental Company to thoroughly describe the benefits of our using our services:

1. **Craigslist.org**
2. Ebay Classifieds
3. Classifieds.myspace.com
4. KIJIJI.com
5. //Lycos.oodle.com
6. Webclassifieds.us
7. USFreeAds.com
8. www.oodle.com
9. Backpage.com
10. stumblehere.com
11. Classifiedads.com
12. gumtree.com
13. Inetgiant.com
14. www.sell.com
15. Freeadvertisingforum.com
16. Classifiedsforfree.com
17. www.olx.com
18. www.isell.com
19. Base.google.com
20. www.epage.com
21. Chooseyouritem.com
22. www.adpost.com
23. Adjingo.com
24. Kugli.com

Sample Classified Ad:
Are You Looking for a Better Job? Do You Need to Dress Better for a Coming Special Interview or the First Week at a New Place of Employment....at a Reasonable Price?

We have been serving the _____ area since _____ (year) with money-saving business casualwear rentals. We also have the largest selection of Rental Designer Outfits in the _____ area. Give us a call at _____ to arrange a private style consultation or visit us at _____ (Website) for our fashion expo schedule or to get acquainted with our simple rental process and operating policies.

Two-Step Direct Response Classified Advertising
We will use 'two-step direct response advertising' to motivate readers to take a step or action that signals that we have their permission to begin marketing to them in step two. Our objective is to build a trusting relationship with our prospects by offering a free unbiased, educational report in exchange for permission to continue the marketing process. This method of advertising has the following benefits:

1. Shorter sales cycle.
2. Eliminates need for cold calling.
3. Establishes expert reputation.
4. Better qualifies prospects
5. Process is very trackable.
6. Able to run smaller ads.

Sample Two Step Lead Generating Classified Ad:
FREE Report Reveals "How to Save Money with Rented Designer Clothing"
Or….. "How to Choose a Subscription Clothing Rental Company".
Call 24 hour recorded message and leave your name and address.
Your report will be sent out immediately.

Yellow Page Ads
Research indicates that the use of the traditional Yellow Page Book is declining, but that new residents or people who don't have many personal acquaintances will look to the Yellow Pages to establish a list of potential businesses to call upon. Even a small 2" x 2" boxed ad can create awareness and attract the desired target client, above and beyond the ability of a simple listing.
Resource: www.superpages.com   www.yellowpages.com
Examples: www.yellowpages.com/hialeah-fl/wedding-dress-rental
Ad Information:
- Book Title: _____
- Yearly Fee: $_____
- Renewal date: _____
- Coverage Area: _____
- Ad Size: _____ page
- Contact: _____

Cable Television Advertising
Cable television will offer us more ability to target certain affluent market niches or demographics with specialty programming. We will use our marketing research survey to determine which cable TV channels our members are watching. It is expected that many watch the Home & Garden TV channel, and that people with surplus money watch the Style Channel and the Food Network. Our plan is to choose the audience we want, and to hit them often enough to entice them to take action. We will also take advantage of the fact that we will be able to pick the specific areas we want our commercial to air. Ad pricing will be dependent upon the number of households the network reaches, the ratings the particular show has earned, contract length and the supply and demand for a particular network.
Resource:

Spot Runner　　　　　　　　www.spotrunner.com
Television Advertising　　　http://televisionadvertising.com/faq.htm

Comcast Spotlight　　　　www.comcastspotlight.com/
An advertising sales company providing video solutions to local, regional and national businesses through television and digital advertising. Comcast Spotlight provides local market coverage across multiple platforms (cable TV, satellite, telco, online, VOD) and can target customers geographically, demographically and by message to more efficiently and effectively reach specific audience segments.

Radio Advertising

We will use non-event- based radio advertising. This style of campaign is best suited for non-promotional sales driven retail businesses, such as our Subscription Clothing Rental Company. We will utilize a much smaller schedule of ads on a consistent long-range basis (48 to 52 weeks a year) with the We will use non-event- based radio advertising. This style of campaign is best suited for non-sales driven retail businesses, such as our company. We will utilize a much smaller schedule of ads on a consistent long-range basis (48 to 52 weeks a year) with the objective of continuously maintaining top-of-mind-awareness. This will mean maintaining a sufficient level of awareness to be either the number one or number two choice when a triggering-event, such as a new job, moves the consumer into the market for services and forces "a consumer choice" about which company in the consumer's perception might help them the most. This consistent approach will utilize only one ad each week day (260 days per year) and allow our company to cost-effectively keep our message in front of consumers once every week day. The ad copy for this non-event campaign, called a positioning message, will not be time-sensitive. It will define and differentiate our business' "unique market position" and will be repeated for a year.

Note: On the average, listeners spend over 3.5 hours per day with radio.

　　Resources:　　Radio Advertising Bureau　　　www.RAB.com
　　　　　　　　　Radio Locator　　　　　　　　　www.radio-locator.com
　　　　　　　　　Radio Directory　　　　　　　　www.radiodirectory.com

Ad Information:
　　Length of ad "spot": ___ seconds　　Development costs: $____ (onetime fee)
　　Length of campaign: __ (#) mos.　　Runs per month: Three times per day
　　Cost per month.: $_____　　　　　Total campaign cost: $_____.

Resources:
www.lfmaudio.com/best-practises-for-creating-radio-ads-your-listeners-will-respond-to/
https://fitsmallbusiness.com/radio-advertising-ideas/

Script Resources:
https://voicebunny.com/blog/5-tips-make-radio-ads-grab-attention-sell/
www.voices.com/documents/secure/voices.com-commercial-scripts-for-radio-and-television-ads.pdf
http://smallbusiness.chron.com/say-30second-radio-advertising-spot-10065.html
https://voicebunny.com/blog/5-tips-make-radio-ads-grab-attention-sell/

Blog Talk Radio

National Public Radio (www.NPR.org) plays host to a radio program called _____. The program features _____ (type of experts) who talk and blog about dress rental tips. This will help to establish our _____ (fashion?) expertise and build the trust factor with potential members. Even if we can't get our own nationally syndicated talk show, we will try to make guest appearances and try our hand with podcasting by using apps like Spreaker or joining podcasting communities like BlogTalkRadio.

Resources:
Spreaker   http://www.spreaker.com/
Blog Talk Radio   http://www.blogtalkradio.com/
With BlogTalkRadio, people can either host their own live talk radio show with any phone and a computer or listen to thousands of new shows created daily.
Example: www.blogtalkradio.com/rice10tailor
Resource: https://blogtalkradio.knoji.com/alternatives/

Press Release Overview:
We will use market research surveys to determine the media outlets that our demographic members read and then target them with press releases. We will draft a cover letter for our media kit that explains that we would like to have the newspaper print a story about the start-up of our new Subscription Clothing Rental Company or a milestone that we have accomplished. And, because news releases may be delivered by feeds or on news services and various websites, we will create links from our news releases to content on our website. These links which will point to more fashion trend information or a special offer and will drive our prospects into the sales process. They will also increase search engine ranking on our site. We will follow-up each faxed package to the media outlet with a phone call to the lifestyle or fashion section editor.

Media Kit
We will compile a media kit with the following items:
1. A pitch letter introducing our company and relevant impact newsworthiness for their readership.
2. A press release with helpful newsworthy story facts.
3. Biographical fact sheet or sketches of key personnel.
4. Listing of new designer and/or service features and benefits to members.
5. Photos and digital logo graphics
6. Copies of media coverage already received.
7. Frequently Asked Questions (FAQ)
8. Customer testimonials
9. Sales brochure
10. Media contact information
11. URL links to these online documents instead of email attachments.
12. Our blog URL address.

Resources:
http://www.ehow.com/how_2043935_write-press-release.html
https://blog.hubspot.com/marketing/press-release-template-ht

Press Releases

We will use well-written press releases to not only catch a reader's attention, but also to clearly and concisely communicate our business' mission, goals and capabilities.

The following represents a partial list of some of the reasons we will issue a free press release on a regular basis:

1. Announce Grand Opening Event and the availability of subscription rental services.
2. Planned Open House or Fashion Show Event
3. Addition of new designer releases or service introduction.
4. Support for a Non-profit Cause or other local event, such as a Blood Drive.
5. Presentation of a free seminar or workshop on clothing renting tips.
6. Report Survey Results
7. Publication of an article or book on subscription clothing rental benefits.
8. Receiving an Association Award.
9. Additional training/certification/licensing received.
10. Signing of a new celebrity designer, endorser or influencer.

Example:

Olivia Culpo and online fashion service Le Tote today announced the launch of *Olivia Culpo x Le Tote,* a summer capsule collection available exclusively at www.letote.com/olivia. A brand ambassador and style influencer to millions, this collection marks a milestone for Culpo as the debut of her first-ever collection.

Source:
www.businesswire.com/news/home/20170606005223/en/Olivia-Culpo-Le-Tote-Launch-Exclusive-Design

Examples:
https://closet.gwynniebee.com/pages/press
https://www.armoire.style/press/
www.marketwired.com/press-release/le-tote-experience-one-kind-shopping-platform-continues-evolve-as-company-with-new-personalization-1924646.htm

We will use the following techniques to get our press releases into print:

1. Find the right contact editor at a publication, that is, the editor who specializes in lifestyle issues.
2. Understand the target publication's format, flavor and style and learn to think like its readers to better tailor our pitch.
3. Ask up front if the journalist is on deadline.
4. Request a copy of the editorial calendar--a listing of targeted articles or subjects broken down by month or issue date, to determine the issue best suited for the content of our news release or article.
5. Make certain the press release appeals to a large audience by reading a couple of back issues of the publication we are targeting to familiarize ourselves with its various sections and departments.
6. Customize the PR story to meet the magazine's particular style.
7. Avoid creating releases that look like advertising or self-promotion.
8. Make certain the release contains all the pertinent and accurate information the journalist will need to write the article and accurately answer the questions "who,

what, when, why and where".
9. Include a contact name and telephone number for the reporter to call for more information.

Distribution: www.1888PressRelease.com   www.ecomwire.com
               www.prweb.com   www.WiredPRnews.com
               www.PR.com   www.eReleases.com
               www.24-7PressRelease.com   www.NewsWireToday.com
               www.PRnewswire.com   www.onlinePRnews.com
               www.digitaljournal.com   www.PRLog.org
               www.businesswire.com   www.marketwire.com
               www.primezone.com   www.primewswire.com
               www.xpresspress.com/   www.ereleases.com/index.html
               www.webwire.com   www.Mediapost.com

Journalist Lists: www.mastheads.org   www.easymedialist.com
                    www.helpareporter.com

Media Directories
    Bacon's –   www.bacons.com/   AScribe –   www.ascribe.org/
    Newspapers – www.newspapers.com/   Gebbie Press – www.gebbieinc.com/

Support Services
    PR Web -   http://www.prweb.com
    Yahoo News –   http://news.yahoo.com/
    Google News –   http://news.google.com/

Media Resource Expert

We will send email and mail to local media outlets, like our local TV news stations, Local Newspapers, and News Radio Stations, to advise them that we are a readily available resource for subscription related new stories. We will include our areas of specialty, and how we can contribute to media stories about _____ and home tasting and cocktail parties in general. We will also indicate our willingness to share our knowledge on how the public can prevent from being scammed by unethical _____. We will always be on the look-out for opportunities to interview with local and national reporters. We will sign up for the following services that notify companies of reporters looking for interviews:

Reporter Connection   http://reporterconnection.com/
ProfNet Connection   http://www.profnetconnect.com/
Muck Rack   https://muckrack.com/benefits
News Wise   www.newswise.com/
Pitch Rate   http://pitchrate.com/
Experts   www.experts.com
News Basis   http://newsbasis.com/

Help A Reporter Out   www.helpareporter.com/
HARO is an online platform that provides journalists with a robust database of sources for upcoming stories. It also provides business owners and marketers with opportunities

to serve as sources and secure valuable media coverage.
Resources:
http://www.thebuzzfactoree.com/journalists-seeking-sources/
http://ijnet.org/en/blog/5-ways-find-sources-online

Direct Mail Campaign

A direct mail package consisting of a tri-fold brochure, letter of introduction, and reply card will be sent to a list of new businesses in _____ County. This list can be obtained from International Business Lists, Inc. (Chicago, IL) and is compiled from Secretary of State incorporation registrations, business license applications, announcements from newspaper clippings, and tax records. The letter will introduce _____ (company name) and describe our competitive advantages. The package will also include a promotional offer—the opportunity to sample our subscription clothing rental services. Approximately ten days after the mailing, a telephone follow-up will be conducted to make sure the brochure was received, whether the client has any questions, or would like to schedule a sample shipment of rentable designer clothing.

Resources:
www.23kazoos.com/17-essential-elements-successful-direct-mail-marketing-campaign/
www.dmnews.com/channel-marketing/article/13038513/tailor-marketing-strategies-to-customer-preferences
www.directmailquotes.com/rfq/quote1.cfm?affiliate=14
http://www.listgiant.com/

Postcards

1. We will use a monthly, personalized, newsletter styled postcard, that includes healthy meal suggestions, to stay-in-touch with prospects and members.
2. Postcards will offer cheaper mailing rates, staying power and attention-grabbing graphics, but require repetition, like most other advertising methods.
3. We will develop an in-house list of potential members for routine communications from open house events, seminar registrations, direct response ads, etc.
4. We will use postcards to encourage users to visit our website and take advantage of a special rental or purchase offer.
5. We will grab attention and communicate a single-focus message in just a few words.
6. The visual elements of our postcard (color, picture, symbol) will be strong to help get attention and be directly supportive of the message.
7. We will facilitate a call to immediate action by prominently displaying our phone number and website address.
8. We will include a clear deadline, expiration date, limited quantity, or consequence of inaction that is connected to the offer to communicate immediacy and increase response.

Resources:
www.Postcardmania.com   www.printsmadeeasy.com
www.businesscardsusa.net   www.printplace.com

Flyers

We will clearly show off the designers we offer by creating a collage-like flyer design with the different labels of the designer clothing we want to feature.

1. We will seek permission to post flyers on the bulletin boards in local businesses, community centers, party supply stores, beauty salons, and local colleges.
2. We will also insert flyers into our direct mailings.
3. We will use our flyers as part of a handout package at open house events.
4. The flyers will feature a discount coupon and our fashion-focused seminar schedule.
5. The flyers will contain a listing of our bridal rental service categories.

Resources: www.tweak.com

Referral Program

We understand the importance of setting up a formal referral network through contacts with the following characteristics:

1. We will give a premium reward based simply on people giving referral names on the registration form or customer satisfaction survey.
2. Send an endorsed testimonial letter from a loyal patient to the referred prospect.
3. Include a separate referral form as a direct response device.
4. Provide a space on the response form for leaving positive comments that can be used to build a testimonial letter, that will be sent to each referral.
5. We will clearly state our incentive rewards, and terms and conditions.
6. We will distribute a newsletter to stay in touch with our members and include articles about our referral program success stories.
7. We will encourage our staff at weekly meetings to seek referrals from their personal contacts.

We will offer an additional donation of $ _____ to any organization whose member use a referral coupon to become a client. The coupon will be paid for and printed in the organization's newsletter.

Sample Referral Program

We want to show our appreciation to established members and business network partners for their kind referrals to our business. _____ (company name) wants to reward our valued and loyal members who support our _____ Programs by implementing a new referral program. Ask any of our team members for referral cards to share with your family and friends to begin saving towards your next _____ (product/service) purchase. We will credit your account $___ (?) for each new customer you refer to us as well as give them 10% off their first visit. When they come for their first visit, they should present the card upon arrival. We will automatically set you up a referral account.

The Referral Details are as Follows:

1. You will receive a $___ (?) credit for every customer that you refer for _____ (products/services). Credit will be applied to your referral account on their initial visit.

2. We will keep track of your accumulated reward dollars and at any time we can let you know the amount you have available for use in your reward account.
3. Each time you visit ____ (company name), you can use your referral dollars to pay up to 50% of your total charge that day
4. Referral dollars are not applicable towards the purchase of ____ products.
5. All referral rewards are for _ services and cannot be used towards _ services.

Example:
Ready to earn $25 in LL Rental Bucks?
Just tell a friend about Lending Luxury and when they make their first purchase using your referral link, we will credit your account with $25 towards your next rental!
Source: https://lendingluxury.com/customer/account/login/

Example:
Earn referral credits on your account and share discounts with your friends. For each referral you sign up, you'll receive $25 back to use towards your Armoire subscription. The more friends who sign up, the more money back you get. Referred friends get perks too: they'll receive $50 off their first month's subscription.
Source: www.armoire.style/refer/
Ambassador Program: www.armoire.style/ambassadors
https://www.thebalance.com/how-to-get-testimonials-and-referrals-1794616

Resources:
http://brightsmack.com/marketing-strategies/37-referral-ideas-to-grow-your-business/
http://www.nisacards.com/Business-Referral-Marketing-Cards.aspx
https://www.referralsaasquatch.com/resources/
https://www.referralcandy.com/blog/47-referral-programs/
www.consultingsuccess.com/10-referral-strategies-to-grow-your-consulting-business

Resources:
Referral Program Software Packages
   www.invitebox.com
   www.referralsaasquatch.com/
   www.referralcandy.com/
   www.getambassador.com/

Statistics that support referral programs include:
92% of consumers trust peer recommendations, 40% trust advertising in search results, 36% trust online video ads, 36% trust sponsored ads on social networking sites and 33% trust online banner ads. The average value of a referred customer is at least 16% higher than that of a non-referred customer with similar demographics and time of acquisition.
Examples:
www.extole.com/blog/an-epic-list-of-75-besties-referral-programs-for-2019/

Refer-A-Friend
We will setup an aggressive invite-a-friend referral program. We will encourage new members or newsletter subscribers, during their initial registration process, to upload and

send an invitation to multiple contacts in their email address books. We will encourage them by providing an added incentive, such as a free _____.
Example: www.extole.com/blog/an-epic-list-of-50-referral-program-examples/

Customer Reward/Loyalty Program
As a means of building business by word-of-mouth, members will be encouraged and rewarded as repeat members. This will be accomplished by offering a discounted _____ to those members who sign-up for our frequent buyer card and purchase $___ of products and services within a ___ (#) month period.

Frequent Rental/Buyer Program Types:
1.   Punch Cards   Receive something for free after __? purchases.
2.   Dollar-for-point Systems Accrue points toward a free product.
3.   Percentage of Purchase   Accrue points toward future purchases.

Resources:
http://www.refinery29.com/best-store-loyalty-programs
https://thrivehive.com/customer-retention-and-loyalty-programs/
http://blog.fivestars.com/5-companies-loyalty-programs/
www.americanexpress.com/us/small-business/openforum/articles/10-cool-mobile-apps-that-increase-customer-loyalty/
https://squareup.com/loyalty
www.consumerreports.org/cro/news/2013/10/retailer-loyalty-rewards-programs/index.htm

Online Directory Listings
The following directory listings use proprietary technology to match members with industry professionals in their geographical area. The local search capabilities for specific niche markets offer an invaluable tool for the customer. These directories help member businesses connect with purchase-ready buyers, convert leads to sales, and maximize the value of customer relationships. Their online and offline communities provide a quick and easy low or no-cost solution for members to find a transcription specialist quickly. We intend to sign-up with all no cost directories and evaluate the ones that charge a fee.
1.   www.findsubscriptionboxes.com/box/le-tote-select/
2.   www.mysubscriptionaddiction.com/best-subscription-boxes/best-womens-clothing-boxes
3.   www.subscriptionboxmom.com/2014/10/le-tote-first-month-free-clothing-rental-subscription.html
4.   https://boxes.hellosubscription.com/womens-clothing-subscription-boxes/
5.   www.bestweddingsites.com
6.   //wedding.theknot.com
7.   www.weddingvendorsdirectory.com
8.   www.theweddingdirectory.us
9.   http://greenweddingshoes.com/vendor-categories/rentals/
10. http://cybercommmarketing.com/categories/wedding_services/wedding_dress_rentals/wedding_dress_rentals1.htm

Other General Directories Include:

Listings.local.yahoo.com	Switchboard Super Pages
YellowPages.com	MerchantCircle.com
Bing.com/businessportal	Local.com
Yelp.com	BrownBook.com
InfoUSA.com	iBegin.com
Localeze.com	Bestoftheweb.com
YellowBot.com	HotFrog.com
InsiderPages.com	MatchPoint.com
CitySearch.com	YellowUSA.com
Profiles.google.com/me	Manta.com
Jigsaw.com	LinkedIn.com
Whitepages.com	PowerProfiles.com
Judysbook.com	Company.com
Google.com	Yahoo.com

Get Listed — http://getlisted.org/enhanced-business-listings.aspx
Universal Business Listing — https://www.ubl.org/index.aspx
www.UniversalBusinessListing.org

Universal Business Listing (UBL) is a local search industry service dedicated to acting as a central collection and distribution point for business information online. UBL provides business owners and their marketing representatives with a one-stop location for broad distribution of complete, accurate, and detailed listing information.

E-mail Marketing

We will use the following email marketing tips to build our mailing list database, improve communications, boost customer loyalty and attract new and repeat business.

1. Define our objectives as the most effective email strategies are those that offer value to our subscribers: either in the form of educational content or promotions. To drive sales, a promotional campaign is the best format. To create brand recognition and reinforce our expertise in our industry we will use educational newsletters.
2. A quality, permission-based email list will be a vital component of our email marketing campaign. We will ask members and prospects for permission to add them to our list at every touch-point or use a sign-in sheet.
3. We will listen to our members by using easy-to-use online surveys to ask specific questions about members' preferences, interests and satisfaction.
4. We will send only relevant and targeted communications.
5. We will reinforce our brand to ensure recognition of our brand by using a recognizable name in the "from" line of our emails and including our company name, logo and a consistent design and color scheme in every email.

Every ___ (five?) to ____ (six?) weeks, we will send graphically-rich, permission-based, personalized, email marketing messages to our list of members who registered on our website or responded to an ad or attended a fashion expo event. The emails will alert members in a ___ mile radius to limited-time promotions as well as fashion show events sponsored by our Subscription Clothing Rental Company. This service will be provided by either ExactTarget.com or ConstantContact.com. The email will announce a special event and contain a short sales letter. The message will invite recipients to click on a link to our website to checkout more information about the event, then print out the page and bring it with them to the event. The software offered by these two companies will automatically personalize each email with the customer's name. The software also provides detailed click-through behavior reports that will enable us to evaluate the success of each message. The software will also allow us to dramatically scale back our direct mail efforts and associated costs. Our company will send a promotional e-mail about a promotion that the customer indicated was important to them in their registration application. Each identified market segment will get notified of new products, services, specials and offers based on past buying patterns and what they've clicked on in our previous e-newsletters or indicated on their surveys. The objective is to tap the right customer's need at the right time, with a targeted subject line and targeted content.

Example:
A/B testing gave Gwynnie Bee valuable insights, but they needed a faster approach. They realized that to nurture longer-term relationships with prospects, Gwynnie Bee needed editorial content, like styling tips and fashion lookbooks, which made potential members more likely to join the service. And so Gwynnie Bee moved to Mailchimp's automation workflows to deploy emails based on behavioral characteristics. The team continuously tests, and segments users based on how far along they are in their timeline, since signing up, such as a campaign that went out to members who had recently nixed their membership. Using data to show all the styles and features they'd missed since opting out, Gwynnie Bee saw an uptick in users coming back.

Gwynnie Bee has also incorporated a strategy that brands typically use on Twitter. "Flock to unlock" is a way to entice users to retweet something a certain number of times to "unlock" new content. To translate that into email, Gwynnie Bee challenged a certain number of users to join, and if they did, they'd unlock a special prize on top of it. It was one of their most successful campaigns to date.

The company also created 'GB Flash' which is an e-newsletter that doubles as a digital stylist, giving tips and tricks, like how to layer for the winter, or what to wear for your next office party. They feature their favorite plus-size bloggers, staffers, and members that have inspired them, and they do photo shoots multiple times a week.
Source:
https://mailchimp.com/resources/stitching-together-data-with-gwynnie-bee/

Resources:
http://www.verticalresponse.com/blog/10-retail-marketing-ideas-to-boost-sales/
www.constantcontact.com/pricing/email-marketing.jsp

Google Reviews
We will use our email marketing campaign to ask people for reviews. We will ask people what they thought of our subscription business and encourage them to write a Google Review if they were impressed. We will incorporate a call to action (CTA) on our email auto signature with a link to our Google My Review page.
Source: https://superb.digital/how-to-ask-your-clients-for-google-reviews/

Resources:
https://support.google.com/business/answer/3474122?hl=en
https://support.google.com/maps/answer/6230175?co=GENIE.Platform%3DDesktop&hl=en
www.patientgain.com/how-to-get-positive-google-reviews

Example:
We will tell our customers to:
1. Go to https://www.google.com/maps
2. Type in your business name, select the listing
3. There's a "card" (sidebar) on the left-hand side. At the bottom, they can click 'Be the First to Write a Review' or 'Write a Review' if you already have one review.
Source: www.reviewjump.com/blog/how-do-i-get-google-reviews/

Voice Broadcasting
A web-based voice broadcast system will provide a powerful platform to generate thousands of calls to members and members or create customizable messages to be delivered to specific individuals.
Resources:
www.voiceshot.com/public/outboundcalls.asp
www.callfire.com/common-uses/voicemail-broadcasting

Facebook.com
We will use Facebook to move our businesses forward and stay connected to our members in this fast-paced world. Content will be the key to staying in touch with our members and keeping them informed. The content will be a rich mix of fashion trend information, before and after photos, interactive questions, current fashion expo events, industry facts, education, promotions and specials, humor and fun.

We will use the following step system to get prospective members from Facebook.com:
1. We will open a free Facebook account at Facebook.com.
2. We will begin by adding Facebook friends. The fastest way to do this is to allow Facebook to import our email addresses and send an invite out to all our members.
3. We will post a video to get our members involved with our Facebook page. We will post a video called "How to Select the Perfect Business Outfit." The video will be first uploaded to YouTube.com and then simply be linked to our Facebook page. Video will be a great way to get people active and involved with our Facebook page.

4. We will send an email to our members base that encourages them to check out the new video and to post their feedback about it on our Facebook page. Then we will provide a link, driving members to our Facebook page.
5. We will respond quickly to feedback, engage in the dialogue and add links to our response that direct the author to a structured mini-survey.
6. We will optimize our Facebook profile with our business keyword to make it an invaluable marketing tool and become the "go-to" expert in our fashion industry
7. On a monthly basis, we will send out a message to all Facebook fans with a special offer, as Fan pages are the best way to interact with members and potential members on Facebook,
8. We will use Facebook as a tool for sharing success stories and relate the ways in which we have helped our members.
9. We will use Facebook Connect to integrate our Facebook efforts with our regular website to share our Facebook Page activity. This will also give us statistics about our website visitors and add social interaction to our site.

Resources:
www.facebook.com/advertising/
https://www.facebook.com/pages/create.php
http://www.wordstream.com/blog/ws/2015/01/28/facebook-ad-targeting
www.socialmediaexaminer.com/how-to-set-up-a-facebook-page-for-business/
www.socialmediaexaminer.com/how-to-build-a-better-target-audience-for-your-facebook-ads/
http://smallbizsurvival.com/2009/11/6-big-facebook-tips-for-small-business.html
www.forbes.com/sites/jaysondemers/2015/06/16/50-free-ways-to-increase-your-facebook-page-likes/#31f62040566e

Examples:
www.facebook.com/GwynnieBee
www.facebook.com/letote
www.facebook.com/fashionpass

Facebook Profiles represent individual users and are held under a person's name. Each profile should only be controlled by that person. Each user has a wall, information tab, likes, interests, photos, videos and each individual can create events.

Facebook Groups are pretty similar to Fan Pages but are usually created for a group of people with a similar interest and they are wanting to keep their discussions private. The members are not usually looking to find out more about a business - they want to discuss a certain topic, such as fashion trends.

Facebook Fan Pages are the most viral of your three options. When someone becomes a fan of your page or comments on one of your posts, photos or videos, that is spread to all of their personal friends. This can be a great way to get your information out to lots of people...and quickly! In addition, one of the most valuable features of a business page is that you can send "updates" about new products and content to fans and your home building brand becomes more visible.

Facebook Live lets people, public figures and Pages share live video with their followers and friends on Facebook.
Source: https://live.fb.com/about/
Resources:
https://www.facebook.com/business/a/Facebook-video-ads
http://smartphones.wonderhowto.com/news/facebook-is-going-all-live-video-streaming-your-phone-0170132/

Facebook Business Page
Resources:
https://www.facebook.com/business/learn/set-up-facebook-page
https://fitsmallbusiness.com/how-to-create-a-facebook-business-page/
https://blog.hootsuite.com/steps-to-create-a-facebook-business-page/
https://www.pcworld.com/article/240258/how_to_make_a_facebook_page_for_your_small_business.html
https://blog.hubspot.com/blog/tabid/6307/bid/5492/how-to-create-a-facebook-business-page-in-5-simple-steps-with-video.aspx

Small Business Promotions
This group allows members to post about their products and services and is a public group designated as a Buy and Sell Facebook group.
Source: https://www.facebook.com/groups/smallbusinesspronotions/
Resource:
https://www.facebook.com/business/a/local-business-promotion-ads
https://www.facebook.com/business/learn/facebook-create-ad-local-awareness
www.socialmediaexaminer.com/how-to-use-facebook-local-awareness-ads-to-target-customers/

Facebook Ad Builder
https://waymark.com/signup/db869ac4-7202-4e3b-93c3-80acc5988df9/?partner=fitsmallbusiness

Facebook Lead Ads   www.facebook.com/business/a/lead-ads
A type of sponsored ad that appears in your audience's timeline just like other Facebook ads. However, the goal with lead ads is literally to capture the lead's info without them leaving Facebook. These ads don't link to a website landing page, creating an additional step.

Facebook Local Reach Ads
www.facebook.com/business/learn/facebook-create-ad-reach-ads
www.facebook.com/business/help/906073466193087?ref=fbb_reach

We will use Facebook in the following ways to market our Subscription Clothing Rental Company:

1. Promote our blog posts on our Facebook page
2. Post a video of our service people in action.
3. Make time-sensitive offers during slow periods
4. Create a special landing page for coupons or promotional giveaways
5. Create a Welcome tab to display a video message from our owner. Resource: Pagemodo.
6. Support a local charity by posting a link to their website.
7. Thank our members while promoting their businesses at the same time.
8. Describe milestone accomplishments and thank members for their role.
9. Give thanks to corporate accounts.
10. Ask members to contribute stories about _____ occurrences.
11. Use the built-in Facebook polling application to solicit feedback.
12. Use the Facebook reviews page to feature positive comments from members, and to respond to negative reviews.
13. Introduce members to our staff with resume and video profiles.
14. Create a photo gallery of unusual _____ (requests/jobs?) to showcase our expertise.

We will also explore location-based platforms like the following:
- FourSquare
- Facebook Places
- GoWalla
- Google Latitude

As a Subscription Clothing Rental Company serving a local community, we will appreciate the potential for hyper-local platforms like these. Location-based applications are increasingly attracting young, urban influencers with disposable income, which is precisely the audience we are trying to attract. People connect to geo-location apps primarily to "get informed" about local happenings.
Example: www.facebook.com/pages/HIT-Wedding-Gown-Rental/122935697758574

Foursquare.com
A web and mobile application that allows registered users to post their location at a venue ("check-in") and connect with friends. Check-in requires active user selection and points are awarded at check-in. Users can choose to have their check-ins posted on their accounts on Twitter, Facebook, or both.
Resource: https://foursquare.com/business/

Instagram
Instagram.com is an online photo-sharing, video-sharing and social networking service that enables its users to take pictures and videos, apply digital filters to them, and share them on a variety of social networking services, such as Facebook, Twitter, Tumblr and Flickr. A distinctive feature is that it confines photos to a square shape, similar to Kodak Instamatic and Polaroid images, in contrast to the 16:9 aspect ratio now typically used by mobile device cameras. Users are also able to record and share short videos lasting for up to 15 seconds.
Resources:
http://www.wordstream.com/blog/ws/2015/01/06/instagram-marketing

We will use Instagram in the following ways to help amplify the story of our brand, get people to engage with our content when not at our store, and get people to visit our store or website:

1. Let our members and fans know about clothing availability for specific occasions.
2. Tie into trends, events or holidays to drive awareness.
3. Let people know we are open, and our dress selection is spectacular.
4. Run a monthly contest and pick the winning hash-tagged photograph to activate our customer base and increase our exposure.
5. Encourage the posting and collection of happy customer photos with testimonials.
6. Encourage subscribers to use the hashtag #OOTD, or 'outfit of the day' to photo-document their prized rentals.

Examples:
www.instagram.com/gwynniebee/
www.instagram.com/letote/
www.instagram.com/fashionpass/

SnapChat.com

This is a photo messaging app for iPhone and Android mobile devices. Users can take a picture or video and add text, drawings, and a variety of filters. They set a designated time limit, 1-10 seconds, and send to selected contacts from their list. Users can also set a "story" – a Snap that pins to their profile and is viewable for 24 hours after posting. Snapchat photos display for a maximum of 10 seconds (for 24 hours, in the case of a snap story) before becoming permanently inaccessible. The user may choose to save their snaps, but this will only save it to their local device. If the receiver uses the screenshot function on their phone, or chooses to replay a snap, the sender is notified. The point of Snapchat is to be fun and quirky, enticing and engaging your contacts with visual snippets of whatever you are doing. Teen and millennial users enjoy using Snapchat where they would traditionally send a text message.

Resources:
www.forbes.com/sites/forbesagencycouncil/2017/06/22/should-your-business-use-snapchat-stories-or-instagram-stories/#6a03082ce26c
http://adage.com/article/cmo-strategy/booze-brands-rush-snapchat-navigating-age-risks/304880/
www.adweek.com/digital/michaelaaron-flicker-xenopsi-guest-post-snapchat-alcohol/

Snapchat is not useful as a lead generating tool, but it is exceptionally useful for client engagement and retention. When we meet with a client and exchange mobile contact information, we will ask if they use Snapchat and if we can add them to keep them updated on class schedules. The beauty of the Snap is that is draws the client into the environment and makes them want to see or learn more. We will use this limitation to our advantage and make our client feel compelled to request and attend more demonstrations and fashion expo appearances. Snapchat is also a phenomenal tool to engage with existing clients. It will make buyers feel connected to the sales agent and the garment searching process, which is conducive to converting sales and retaining these clients in the future. While the primary user demographic is in the millennial age range, the app is popular with many adults as well. Incorporating Snapchat into our client communication strategy will aid our ability to close enrolments swiftly and form long term client relationships.

Resources:

www.godaddy.com/garage/snapchat-tips-for-your-business-and-how-to-get-started/

https://blog.hootsuite.com/smart-ways-to-use-snapchat-for-business/

https://blogs.constantcontact.com/ideas-for-snapchat/

http://smallbiztrends.com/2014/10/how-businesses-can-use-snapchat.html

http://nymag.com/selectall/2016/04/the-snapchat-101-the-best-coolest-smartest-weirdest-accounts.html

Examples:

https://www.snapchat.com/add/gwynniebee

LinkedIn.com

LinkedIn ranks high in search engines and will provide a great platform for sending event updates to business associates. To optimize our LinkedIn profile, we will select one core keyword. We will use it frequently, without sacrificing consumer experience, to get our profile to skyrocket in the search engines. LinkedIn provides options that will allow our detailed profile to be indexed by search engines, like Google. We will make use of these options, so our business will achieve greater visibility on the Web. We will use widgets to integrate other tools, such as importing your blog entries or Twitter stream into your profile, and go market research and gain knowledge with Polls. We will answer questions to show our expertise and ask questions to get a feel for what members and prospects want or think. We will publish our LinkedIn URL on all our marketing collateral, including business cards, email signature, newsletters, and web site. We will grow our network by joining industry and alumni groups related to our business. We will update our status examples of recent work and link our status updates with our other social media accounts. We will start and manage a group or fan page for our product, brand or business. We will share useful articles that will be of interest to members, and request LinkedIn recommendations from members willing to provide testimonials. We will post our presentations on our profile using a presentation application. We will ask our first-level contacts for introductions to their contacts and interact with LinkedIn on a regular basis to reach those who may not see us on other social media sites. We will link to articles posted elsewhere, with a summary of why it's valuable to add to our credibility and list our newsletter subscription information and archives. We will post discounts and package deals. We will buy a LinkedIn direct ad that our target market will see. We will find vendors and contractors through connections.

Examples:

https://www.linkedin.com/company/gwynnie-bee/

http://www.linkedin.com/company/so-llc

Podcasting

Our podcasts will provide both information and advertising. Our podcasts will allow us to pull in a lot of members. Our monthly podcasts will be heard by ___ (#) eventual subscribers. Podcasts can now be downloaded for mobile devices, such as an iPod. Podcasts will give our company a new way to provide information and an additional way to advertise. Podcasting will give our business another connection point with members. We will use this medium to communicate on important issues, what is going on with a planned fashion event, and other things of interest to our fashion-conscious members. The programs will last about 10 minutes and can be downloaded for free on iTunes. The purpose is not to be a mass medium. It is directed at a niche market with an above-average educational background and very special interests. It will provide a very direct and a reasonably inexpensive way of reaching our targeted audience with relevant information about our bridal rental services.

Examples:
https://blog.monicaandandy.com/podcast/mentor-files/christine-hunsicker/

Resources:
www.apple.com/itunes/download/
www.cbc.ca/podcasting/gettingstarted.html
www.bizjournals.com/southflorida/blog/2014/11/south-florida-entrepreneurs-how-podcasting-helped.html
www.smarttimeonline.com/category/podcast/

Blogging

We will use our blog to keep members and prospects informed about products, events and services that relate to our Subscription Clothing Rental Company, new releases, contests, and specials. Our blog will show readers that we are a good source of expert fashion information that they can count on. With our blog, we can quickly update our members anytime our company releases a new designer line, the holding of a contest or are placing for-sale items on special pricing. We will use our blog to share customer testimonials and meaningful clothing usage stories. We will use the blog to supply advice on creative cocktail party suggestions. Our visitors will be able to subscribe to our RSS feeds and be instantly updated without any spam filters interfering. We will also use the blog to solicit outfit usage recommendations and future designer collection addition suggestions. Additionally, blogs are free and allow for constant ease of updating.

Our blog will give our company the following benefits:
1. A cost-effective marketing tool.
2. An expanded network.
3. A promotional platform for new fitting services.
4. An introduction to people with similar interests.
5. Builds credibility and expertise recognition.

We will use our blog for the following purposes:
1. To share customer testimonials, experiences and meaningful success stories.
2. Update our members anytime our company releases a new service.
3. Supply advice on new rental options.
4. Discuss research findings.
5. To publish helpful content.
6, To welcome feedback in multiple formats.
7. Link together other social networking sites, including Twitter.
8. To improve Google rankings.

9.   Make use of automatic RSS feeds.

Resources: www.blogger.com   www.blogspot.com   www.wordpress.com

Influential Bloggers: https://ravishly.com/plus-size-rent-the-runway

Possible Blog Topics:

Your Guide to Summer Fashion

Example: https://blog.letote.com/2019/07/09/your-guide-to-summer-fashion/

Five Ways to Wear a Jumpsuit

Example: https://blog.letote.com/2019/05/14/five-ways-to-wear-a-jumpsuit/
                www.armoire.style/curatedcolumn/
                www.pinterest.com/LETOTE/
                https://blog.thefashionpass.com/
                www.foundrentals.com/blog/tag/los-angeles-wedding/

Example: Gwynnie Bee's blog, "The Hive," builds a community that its subscribers want to be part of. It offers sizing tips, style ideas, and lots of subscriber-shared photos featuring Gwynnie Bee fashions.   Source: http://blog.gwynniebee.com/

Examples:

Fashion blogger Kelly Augustine shares how she turned her love of fashion into a full-time job with Gwinnie Bee, a clothing subscription rental service for sizes 10 – 32. While growing her fashion blog, Kelly Augustine began sharing fashion pieces from GB, a clothing subscription clothing rental service for sizes 10-32. She fell in love with the brand and got the courage to ask for a full-time job with the company. Now she manages influencer relations while sharing her style insight. See her fashion and career tips for success. She serves as a liaison between influencers and the marketing and merchandising departments at GB. She engages with influencers on various levels, from creating editorial content and hosting events to reviewing all the garments on the site.
Source: www.essence.com/lifestyle/money-career/essence-network-fashion-blogger-turned-style-influencer-major-brand-shares-her-career/

Influencer Blogger Example:
If you'd like to try Gwynnie Bee they're still offering your first month for free. Just click here (that's my referral link and I'll get an extra item free if you use that link!) or go to GwynnieBee.com. Again, this is not a sponsored post, nor did I get anything for writing it, I was just having fun with the clothes and thought I would share.
Source: www.katesullivanblog.com/2014/05/big-gwynnie-bee-post/

Influencer Blogger Example:
I wear A LOT of Gwynnie Bee (I've been a member for over 5 years now), and thought it'd be cool to create a Gwynnie Bee Review Fashion File of all my looks. Gwynnie Bee is a monthly subscription service for clothes sizes 0-32 (woo!) Wear, return, repeat. More info below. I have tried so many styles I wouldn't have before, and it's really helped me push my style limits without going broke.
Source: https://authenticallyemmie.com/?s=gwynnie+bee

Resources:
http://www.bloggersideas.com/tips-for-small-business-blogging-success/
http://www.blogwritersbootcamp.com/

Independent Blogger Advertising and Reviews

Bloggers are online influencers and will help to spread great words about our subscription clothing rental company. Their blog posts rule the search engines, social media, and even the mobile world. We will connect with and make friends with influential bloggers in the celebrity, entertainment, fashion and lifestyle niches by exchanging thoughtful ideas and fashion sensibilities. Bloggers usually own a digital camera for taking beautiful photos about their experiences with the designer clothing they review. Some of the topics covered by alternative bloggers are garment reviews, designer interviews, alternative fashion trends, a community for the holistic and 'giveback' obsessed, and sample giveaways.

Guest Blogging

We will guest blog on other blogs largely related, or semi-related to our websites niche. Opening other peoples' eyes to our name and our website will always be good promotion. Additionally, networking with other bloggers will be great for business as well.

Twitter

We will use 'Twitter.com' as a way to produce new business from existing members and generate prospective members online. Twitter is a free social networking and micro-blogging service that allows its users to send and read other users' updates (otherwise known as tweets), which are text-based posts of up to 140 characters in length. Updates are displayed on the user's profile page and delivered to other users who have signed up to receive them. The sender can restrict delivery to those in his or her circle of friends, with delivery to everyone being the default. Users can receive updates via the Twitter website, SMS text messaging, RSS feeds, or email. We will use our Twitter account to respond directly to questions, distribute news, solve problems, post updates, and offer special discounts on rental services. We will also add our website, company logo, personal photo and/or blog on our profile page.
Examples:
https://twitter.com/gwynniebee
https://twitter.com/letote
https://twitter.com/BrideDresses
http://twitter.com/#!/BloggerBrides/wedding-dress

Bag and Box Advertising

We will purchase printed bags and storage boxes for member shipments. The bags will be sized to standard garment dimensions and contain our advertising message, logo and contact information.

Google Maps

We will first make certain that our business is listed in Google Maps. We will do a search

for our business in Google Maps. If we don't see our business listed, then we will add our business to Google Maps. Even if our business is listed in Google Maps, we will create a Local Business Center account and take control of our listing, by adding more relevant information. Consumers generally go to Google Maps for two reasons: Driving Directions and to Find a Business.
Resource: http://maps.google.com/

Bing Maps   www.bingplaces.com/
This will make it easy for members to find our business.

Yelp.com
We will use Yelp.com to help people find our local business. Visitors to Yelp write local reviews, over 85% of them rating a business 3 stars or higher In addition to reviews, visitors can use Yelp to find events, special offers, lists and to talk with other Yelpers. As business owners, we will setup a free account to post offers, photos and message our members. We will also buy ads on Yelp, which will be clearly labeled "Sponsored Results". We will also use the Weekly Yelp, which is available in 42 city editions to bring news about the latest business openings and other happenings.
Example: https://www.yelp.com/biz/le-tote-san-francisco-4

Other Review Sites:
www.highya.com/gwynnie-bee-reviews
www.sitejabber.com

Proactive Management of Online Reviews
Resources:
http://www.fiveyellow.com/
www.reputationdefender.com/blog/online-reviews/how-remove-negative-reviews-internet

Pay-Per-Click Advertising
Google AdWords, Yahoo! Search Marketing, and Microsoft adCenter are the three largest network operators, and all three operate under a bid-based model. Cost per click (CPC) varies depending on the search engine and the level of competition for a particular keyword. Google AdWords are small text ads that appear next to the search results on Google. In addition, these ads appear on many partner web sites, including NYTimes.com (The New York Times), Business.com, Weather.com, About.com, and many more. Google's text advertisements are short, consisting of one title line and two content text lines. Image ads can be one of several different Interactive Advertising Bureau (IAB) standard sizes. Through Google AdWords, we plan to buy placements (ads) for specific search terms through this "Pay-Per-Click" advertising program. This PPC advertising campaign will allow our ad to appear when someone searches for a keyword related to our business, organization, or subject matter. More importantly, we will only pay when a potential customer clicks on our ad to visit our website. For instance, since we operate a Subscription Clothing Rental Company in ___ (city), _____ (state), we will target people using search terms such as "Subscription Clothing Rental Company, rent dresses, business casual attire rentals, dress rentals, designer fashion

rentals, premium fashion rentals, jewelry rentals, fashion accessories in ____ (city), ____ (state)". With an effective PPC campaign our ads will only be displayed when a user searches for one of these keywords.

Resources: http://adwords.google.com/support/aw/?hl=en
www.wordtracker.com
http://www.google.com/support/analytics/
http://www.wordstream.com/local-online-marketing
https://www.wordstream.com/keywords
https://adwords.google.com/KeywordPlanner

Yahoo Local Listings

We will create our own local listing on Yahoo. To create our free listing, we will use our web browser and navigate to http://local.yahoo.com. We will first register for free with Yahoo and create a member ID and password to list our business. Once we have accessed http://local.yahoo.com, we will scroll down to the bottom and click on "Add/Edit a Business" to get onto the Yahoo Search Marketing Local Listings page. In the lower right of the screen we will see "Local Basic Listings FREE". We will click on the Get Started button and log in again with our new Yahoo ID and password. The form for our local business listing will now be displayed. When filling it out, we will be sure to include our full web address (http://www.companyname.com). We will include a description of our Subscription Clothing Rental Company products and services in the description section.

Affiliate Marketing

Affiliate marketing is a form of online advertising that is based upon revenue sharing between websites. The affiliate websites display an online ad of another website and are compensated when the Internet traffic is driven to the other website upon clicking of the ad. The payment could be based on pay-per-click or for the time the ad is displayed, depending upon the mutual understanding between the companies. We will create an affiliate marketing program to broaden our reach. We will first devise a commission structure, so affiliates have a reason to promote our business. We will give them ___ (10)% of whatever sales they generate. We will go after event planner bloggers or webmasters who get a lot of web traffic for our keywords. These companies would then promote our products/services, and they would earn commissions for the sales they generated. We will work with the following services to handle the technical aspects of our program.

ConnectCommerce	www.connectcommerce.com/
Commission Junction	www.cj.com
ShareASale	www.shareasale.com/
Share Results	
LinkShare	www.linkshare.com
Clickbank	www.clickbank.com
Affiliate Scout	http://affiliatescout.com/
Affiliate Seeking	www.affiliateseeking.com/
Clix Galore	www.clixgalore.com/
Pepperjam	www.pepperjam.com

They created a transparent affiliate marketing platform that enables easy relationship creation and connection building.

Post Affiliate Pro   www.postaffiliatepro.com/
Affiliate software is software that lets users track clicks and signups and assign them to the right affiliates with the option of reports and payouts.

Contract Example:
http://www.lendingluxury.com/affiliate/affiliates/
www.google.com/affiliatenetwork/ntn.html?advid=223777

Sample Programs:
Sign up with Pepperjam and apply to be a Gwynnie Bee Affiliate.
Display our ads, banners, and links. Review our service and collections and advertise our promotions. Get Paid.
Source: https://closet.gwynniebee.com/pages/become-an-affiliate

Frank and Oak is part of the Rakuten Linkshare affiliate network, which is home to thousands of trusted affiliates and merchants. You can make money by offering your readers exclusive promotions, sales, and a curated shop. It's free to register and payments are sent out monthly. To learn more about our brand, our demographics or how we work with affiliates download our media kit.
Source: https://www.frankandoak.com/affiliate
https://media.frankandoak.com/media/assets/v3/affiliate/Affiliate-MediaKit.pdf

Corporate Incentive / Employee Rewards Program
Our Employee Rewards Program will motivate and reward the key resources of local corporations – the people who make their business a success. We will use independent sales reps to market these programs to local corporations. It will be a versatile program, allowing the corporate client to customize it to best suit the following goals:
1. Welcome New Hires
2. Introduce an Employee Discount Program for our clothing rental services.
3. Reward increases in sales or productivity with an Employee Incentive Program
4. Thank Retirees for their service to the company

Cause Marketing
Cause marketing or cause-related marketing refers to a type of marketing involving the cooperative efforts of a "for profit" business and a non-profit organization for mutual benefit. The possible benefits of cause marketing for business include positive public relations, improved customer relations, and additional marketing opportunities.
Our business objective will be to generate highly cost-effective public relations and media coverage for the launch of a marketing campaign focused on _____ (type of cause), with the help of the _____ (non-profit organization name) organization.
Resources: www.causemarketingforum.com/
              www.cancer.org/AboutUs/HowWeHelpYou/acs-cause-marketing

Speaking Engagements

We will consider a "problem/solution" format where we describe a challenge and tell how our expertise achieved an exceptional solution. We will use speaking engagements as an opportunity to expose our styling, fashion and design expertise to prospective members. By speaking at conferences and forums put together by professional and industry trade groups, we will increase our firm's visibility, and consequently, its prospects for attracting new business. Public speaking will give us a special status and make it easier for our speakers to meet prospects. We will identify speaking opportunities that will let us reach our targeted audience. We will designate a person who is responsible for developing relationships with event and industry associations, submitting proposals and, most importantly, staying in touch with contacts. We will tailor our proposals to the event organizers' preferences.

Speaking Proposal Package:
1. Speech Topic/Agenda/Synopsis
2. Target Audience: Community and Civic Groups
3. Speaker Biography
4. List of previous speaking engagements
5. Previous engagement evaluations

Possible Targets:
1. AARP Groups
2. Chamber of Commerce
3. YMCAs
4. Executive Meetup Groups
5. Women's Business Councils
6. Event Planners

Possible Speech Topics:
1. The Financial Benefits of Renting Your Wardrobe
2. How to Evaluate the Quality of a Subscription Clothing Rental Company

Speaking Engagement Package
1. Video or DVD of prior presentation.
2. Session Description
3. Learning Objectives
4. Takeaway Message
5. Speaking experience
6. Letters of recommendation
7. General Biography
8. Introduction Biography

Resource: www.toastmasters.com

Meet-up Group

We will form a meet-up group to encourage people to participate in our wine tasting programs.

Resource: www.meetup.com/create/
www.bluesteps.com/blog/meetup-executive-job-search.aspx

Examples: https://www.meetup.com/topics/executives/
www.meetup.com/en-AU/topics/fashion/all/

Marketing Associations/Groups

We will set up a marketing association comprised of complementary businesses. We will market our Subscription Clothing Rental Company as a member of a group of complementary companies. Our marketing group will include a job recruiter, image consultant, an event planner, and an office supply store. Any business that provides event services will be a likely candidate for being a member of our marketing group. The group will joint advertise, distribute joint promotional materials, exchange mailing lists, and develop a group website. The obvious benefit is that we will increase our marketing effectiveness by extending our reach.

BBB Accreditation

We will apply for BBB Accreditation to improve our perceived trustworthiness. BBB determines that a company meets BBB accreditation standards, which include a commitment to make a good faith effort to resolve any consumer complaints. BBB Accredited Businesses pay a fee for accreditation review/monitoring and for support of BBB services to the public. We will place the BBB Accreditation Logo in all our ads. Example: www.bbb.org/us/ny/new-york/profile/clothing/rent-the-runway-inc-0121-119824/complaints

Sponsor Events

The sponsoring of events, such as fashion shows and job fairs will allow our company to engage in what is known as experiential marketing, which is the idea that the best way to deepen the emotional bond between a company and its members is by creating a memorable and interactive experience. We will ask for the opportunity to prominently display our company signage and the set-up of a booth from which to handout sample products and sales literature. We will also seek to capitalize on networking, speech giving and workshop presenting opportunities. We will also sponsor a local team, such as dance competitions, the local soccer club or a bowling group. We will then place our company name on the uniforms or shirts in exchange for providing the equipment and/or uniforms.

Mobile iPhone Apps

We will use new distribution tools like the iPhone App Store to give us unprecedented direct access to consumers, without the need to necessarily buy actual mobile *ads* to reach people. Thanks to Apple's iPhone and the App Store, we will be able to make cool mobile apps that may generate as much goodwill and purchase intent as a banner ad. We will research Mobile Application Development, which is the process by which application software is developed for small low-power handheld devices, such as personal digital assistants, enterprise digital assistants or mobile phones. These applications are either pre-installed on phones during manufacture, or downloaded by members from various mobile software distribution platforms. iPhone apps make good marketing tools. The bottom line is iPhones and smartphones sales are continually growing, and people are going to their phones for information. Apps will definitely be a lead generation tool because it gives potential members easy access to our contact and business information and the ability to call for more information while they are still "hot". Our apps will contain: directory of staffers, publications on relevant issues, office location, videos, etc.

Resources: http://www.apple.com/iphone/apps-for-iphone/

Software Development:
  http://iphoneapplicationlist.com/apps/business/
  http://www.mutualmobile.com/
  http://www.avenuesocial.com/mob-app.php#
  http://www.biznessapps.com/

Resource: www.appolicious.com/pages/services

Examples:
https://itunes.apple.com/us/app/gwynnie-bee-an-endless-closet/id981897219?mt=8
https://play.google.com/store/apps/details?id=com.gwynniebee.gbcloset&hl=en_US
https://itunes.apple.com/us/app/rent-the-runway/id672853806

Gift Certificates/ Cards

We will offer for sale Gift Certificates via our website. This will provide an excellent way to be introduced to new members and improve our cash flow position. An e-commerce platform for small businesses.

Resources:
  Boom Time   https://ps1419.boomtime.com/lgift
  Gift Cards   www.giftcards.com
  Gift Card Café   www.TheGiftCardCafe.com

Examples:
https://closet.gwynniebee.com/pages/give-a-gift
https://blog.letote.com/2019/09/13/10-insider-tips-to-get-the-most-out-of-le-tote/
www.renttherunway.com/giftcards   www.frankandoak.com/giftcard
https://lendingluxury.com/gift-cards.html   www.armoire.style/gifts/

e-Gift Card Example:
Style Plan e-gift cards are sent by email and applicable on any Style Plan purchase. You must be signed in as a Frank and Oak client to apply them to your account. After being redeemed, the amount of the gift card is automatically credited to your Style Plan invoice, or to any Frank And Oak purchase. If you return products purchased with a gift card, your corresponding store credits will be re-credited to your account. Style Plan e-Gift cards are non-refundable.
Source: https://www.frankandoak.com/faq/styleplan

Publish e-Book

Ebooks are electronic books which can be downloaded from any website or FTP site on the Internet. Ebooks are made using special software and can include a wide variety of media such as HTML, graphics, Flash animation and video. We will publish an e-book to establish our subscription clothing rental expertise and reach people who are searching for ebooks on how to make better use our products and/or services. Included in our ebook will be links back to our website, product or affiliate program. Because users will have permanent access to it, they will use our ebook again and again, constantly seeing a link or banner which directs them to our site. The real power behind ebook marketing will be the viral aspect of it and the free traffic it helps to build for our website. ebook directories include:
www.e-booksdirectory.com/
www.ebookfreeway.com/p-ebook-directory-list.html

www.quantumseolabs.com/blog/seolinkbuilding/top-5-free-ebook-directories-subscribers/
Resource: www.free-ebooks.net/

e-books are available from the following sites:
    Amazon.com   Createspace.com
    Lulu.com   Kobobooks.com
    BarnesandNoble.com   Scribd.com
    AuthorHouse.com   e-junkie.com

Resource: www.smartpassiveincome.com/ebooks-the-smart-way/

Testimonial Marketing

We will either always ask for testimonials immediately after a completed rental service or contact our clients once a quarter for them. We will also have something prepared that we would like the client to say that is specific to the subscription service we offer, or anything relevant to advertising claims that we have put together. For the convenience of the client we will assemble a testimonial letter that they can either modify or just sign off on. Additionally, testimonials can also be in the form of audio or video and put on our website or mailed to potential clients in the form of a DVD or Audio CD. A picture with a testimonial is also excellent. We will put testimonials directly on a magazine ad, slick sheet, brochure, or website, or assemble a complete page of testimonials for our sales presentation folder.

Examples:
http://www.goldwilldigger.com/clothing-rental-review/
https://www.highya.com/gwynnie-bee-reviews
https://retrohousewifegoesgreen.com/le-tote-review

We will collect customer testimonials in the following ways:
1. Our website – A page dedicated to testimonials (written and/or video).
2. Social media accounts – Facebook fan pages offer a review tab, which makes it easy to receive and display customer testimonials.
3. Google+ also offers a similar feature with Google+ Local.
4. Local search directories – Ask customers to post more reviews on Yelp and Yahoo Local.
5. Customer Satisfaction Survey Forms

We will pose the following questions to our customers to help them frame their testimonials:
1. What was the obstacle that would have prevented you from buying this service?
2. What was your main concern about buying this subscription service?
3. What did you find as a result of buying this clothing rental service?
4. What specific feature did you like most about this clothing rental program?
5. What would be three other key benefits about this service?
6. Would you recommend this service? If not, why?
7. Are there any comments you'd like to add?

Resource:

https://smallbiztrends.com/2016/06/use-customer-testimonials.html

Business Logo

Our logo will graphically represent who we are and what we do, and it will serve to help brand our image. It will also convey a sense of uniqueness and professionalism. The logo will represent our company image and the message we are trying to convey. Our business logo will reflect the philosophy and objective of the Subscription Clothing Rental Company.

Example: https://99designs.com/logo-design/fashion
Resources: www.freelogoservices.com/   www.hatchwise.com
             www.logosnap.com   www.99designs.com
             www.fiverr.com   www.freelancer.com
             www.upwork.com

Logo Design Guide:
www.bestfreewebresources.com/logo-design-professional-guide
www.creativebloq.com/graphic-design/pro-guide-logo-design-21221

Fundraisers

Community outreach programs involving charitable fundraising and showing a strong interest in the local school system will serve to elevate our status in the community as a "good corporate citizen" while simultaneously increasing store traffic. We will execute a successful fundraising program for our Subscription Clothing Rental Company and build goodwill in the community, by adhering to the following guidelines:

1. Keep It Local
2. Plan It
3. Contact Local Media
4. Contact Area Businesses
5. Get Recipient Support
6. Give Out Bounce Backs
7. Be Ready with plenty of product and labor on hand for the event.

Resource: www.thefundraisingauthority.com/fundraising-basics/fundraising-event/

Billboards

We will use billboard advertising to create brand awareness and strong name recognition. We will design Billboards that are eye-catching and informative and use easy to read fonts like Verdana. We will include our business name, location, a graphic, standout border and no more than eight words. In designing the billboard, we will consider the fact that the eye typically moves from the upper left corner to the lower right corner of a billboard. We will use colors that can be viewed by color blind people, such as yellow, black and blue, and pictures to contrast with the sky and other surroundings. We will keep the layout uncluttered and the message simple and include a direct call to action.

Example: Rent Your Clothing and Save the Planet…
Resources:
Outdoor Advertising Association of America   www.oaaa.org

EMC Outdoor, Inc.   www.emcoutdoor.com

Theater Advertising
Theater advertising is the method of promoting our clothing rental business through in-theatre promotions. The objective of theater advertising is to expose the movie patron to our advertising message in various ways throughout the theater. Benefits include; an engaged audience that can't change the channel, an audience that is in a quiet environment, an audience that is in a good mood and receptive, advertising that is targeted to our local geographic area, full color video advertising on a 40 foot screen, and a moving and interactive ad with music and voiceover.

Resources: Velocity Cinema Advertising   www.movieadvertising.com/index.html
             NCM   www.nationalcinemedia.com/intheatreadvertising/
             ScreenVision   www.screenvision.com
             AMC Theaters   www.amctheatres.com
             Regal Entertainment Group   www.regmovies.com

Business Card Exchanges
We will join our Chamber of Commerce or local retail merchants' association and volunteer to host a mixer or business card exchange. We will take the opportunity to invite social and business groups to our offices to enjoy wine tastings, and market to local businesses. We will also build our email database by collecting the business cards of all attendees.

Pinterest.com
The goal of this website is to connect everyone in the world through the 'things' they find interesting. They think that a favorite style book or fashion designer can reveal a common link between two people. With millions of new pins added every week, Pinterest is connecting people all over the world based on shared tastes and interests. What's special about Pinterest is that the boards are all visual, which is a very important marketing plus. When users enter a URL, they select a picture from the site to pin to their board. People spend hours pinning their own content, and then finding content on other people's boards to "re-pin" to their own boards. We will use Pinterest for remote personal shopping appointments. When we have a customer with specific needs, we will create a board just for them with clothing items we rent and sell that would meet their needs, along with links to other tips and content. We will invite our customer to check out the board on Pinterest and let them know we created it just for them.

Examples:
www.pinterest.com/gwynniebee/
www.pinterest.com/amber1279/gwynnie-bee-love/
www.pinterest.com/gwynniebee/style-inspiration/
www.pinterest.com/LETOTE/
www.pinterest.com/LETOTE/outfits-from-le-tote-ladies/
www.pinterest.com/rentthedress/wedding-dresses/
www.pinterest.com/thefashionpass/

Survey Marketing

We will conduct a door-to-door survey in our target area to illicit opinions to our proposed business. This will provide valuable feedback, lead to prospective members and serve to introduce our Subscription Clothing Rental Company before we begin actual operations.

'Green' Marketing

We will target environmentally friendly members to introduce new members to our business and help spread the word about going "green". We will use the following 'green' marketing strategies to form an emotional bond with our members:

1. We will use clearly labeled 'Recycled Paper' and Sustainable Packaging, such as receipts and storage containers.
2. We will use "green", non-toxic cleaning supplies.
3. We will install 'green' lighting and heating systems to be more eco-friendly.
4. We will use web-based Electronic Mail and Social Media instead of using paper advertisements.
5. We will find local suppliers to minimize the carbon footprint that it takes for deliveries.
6. We will use products that are made with organic ingredients and supplies.
7. We will document our 'Green' Programs in our sales brochure and website.
8. We will be a Certified Energy Star Partner.
9. We will install new LED warehouse lighting, exit signs, and emergency signs.
10. We will install motion detectors in low-traffic areas both inside and outside of warehouses.
11. We will implement new electricity regulators on HVAC units and compressors to lower energy consumption.
12. We will mount highly supervised and highly respected recycling campaigns.
13. We will start a program for waste product to be converted into sustainable energy sources.
14. We will start new company-wide document shredding programs.
15. We will use of water-based paints during the finishing process to reduce V.O.C.'s to virtually zero.
16. We will install very energy-efficient dry-cleaning and laundering equipment.
17. We will only use hybrid or electric vehicles for transport purposes.

Sticker Marketing

Low-cost sticker, label and decal marketing will provide a cost-effective way to convey information, build identity and promote our company in unique and influential ways. Stickers can be affixed to almost any surface, so they can go and stay affixed where other marketing materials can't; opening a world of avenues through which we can reach our target audience. Our stickers will be simple in design, and convey an impression quickly and clearly, with valuable information or coupon, printed optionally as part of its backcopy. Our stickers will handed-out at fashion shows and special events, mailed as a postcard, packaged with product and/or included as part of a mailing package. We will insert the stickers inside our product or hand them out along with other marketing tools such as flyers or brochures. Utilizing a strong design, in a versatile size, and with an eye-catching shape, that is, relevant to our business, will add to the perceived value of our promotional stickers.

USPS Every Door Direct Mail Program
Every Door Direct Mail from the U.S. Postal Service® is designed to reach every home, every address, every time at a very affordable delivery rate. Every business and resident living in the _____ zip code will receive an oversized post card and coupon announcing the _____ (company name) grand opening 7-days before the grand opening:
Resource: https://eddm.usps.com/eddm/customer/routeSearch.action

Price – USPS Marketing Mail™ Flats up to 3.3 oz
EDDM Retail® USPS Marketing Flats $0.177 per piece
EDDM BMEU USPS Marketing Mail at $0.156 per piece
Resource:
https://www.usps.com/business/every-door-direct-mail.htm
https://eddm.usps.com/eddm/customer/routeSearch.action

ZoomInfo.com
Their vision is to be the sole provider of constantly verified information about companies and their employees, making our data indispensable — available anytime, anywhere and anyplace the customer needs it.
Example: https://www.zoominfo.com/c/flyrobe/370368079

Google+
We will pay specific attention to Google+, which is already playing a more important role in Google's organic ranking algorithm. We will create a business page on Google+ to achieve improved local search visibility. Google+ will also be the best way to get access to Google Authorship, which will play a huge role in SEO. Aside from having all the necessary information like hours and contact information, quality photos and visuals will be essential on our Google+ local page. To go above the basics, we will have a local Google photographer visit and create a virtual tour.
Resources: https://plus.google.com/pages/create
                            https://plus.google.com/+GoogleBusiness/posts
Examples: https://plus.google.com/+fashionpass

Google My Business Profile   www.google.com/business/befound.html
We will have a complete and active Google My Business profile to give our subscription clothing rental company a tremendous advantage over the competition, and help potential customers easily find our company and provide relevant information about our business. This is a free listing that connects to Google Maps. It's the primary way that Google knows where our service area is located, so we can come up for local searches. We will optimize our descriptions with keywords and try to get customer reviews to increase our ranking.

Google My Business will let us:
- Manage business listing info for search, maps and Google+

- Upload photos and/or a virtual tour of our business
- Share content and interacting with followers on Google+
- See reviews from across the web and responding to Google+ reviews
- Integrate with AdWords Express to create and track campaigns
- Access Insights reports, the <u>new social analytics tool for Google+</u>
- See information about our integrated YouTube and Analytics accounts
- Resource:
- https://www.wordstream.com/blog/ws/2014/06/12/google-my-business

Reddit.com
An online community where users vote on stories. The hottest stories rise to the top, while the cooler stories sink. Comments can be posted on every story, including stories about startup clothing rental companies.
Example:
www.reddit.com/r/FrugalFemaleFashion/comments/98mb9x/have_you_guys_tried_clothing_subscription_boxes/

6.4.1 Strategic Alliances

We will form strategic alliances to accomplish the following objectives:
1. To share marketing expenses.
2. To realize bulk buying power on wholesale purchases.
3. To engage in barter arrangements.
4. To collaborate with industry experts.
5. To set-up mutual referral relationships.

_____ (company name) will seek out opportunities to establish viable strategic alliances, such as co-marketing with companies that cater to the needs of professional women and millennials. We will develop referral relationships with businesses that have an affluent clientele. Talent agents, business executives, jewelers, realtors, lawyers and insurance agents are all in this category. We will network with a reputable person in each type of business and send referrals to them, or co-sponsor special events and other promotions to generate publicity and build awareness.

We will develop strategic alliances with the following service providers by conducting introductory 'cold calls' to their offices and making them aware of our clothing rental capabilities by distributing our brochures and business cards:

1.	Party Supply Stores	2.	Senior Daycare Centers
3.	Dance Schools	4.	Gourmet Food Stores
5.	Day Spas	6.	Boutiques
7.	Health Clubs	8.	Beauty Salons
9.	Nail Salons	10.	Bridal Centers
11.	Caterers	12.	Event Planners
13.	Corporate Offices	14.	Style Consultants

15.	Studio Photographers		16.	Restaurants
17.	Catering Halls		18.	Caterers
19.	Printing Companies		20.	Music DJs
21.	Tailor Shops		22.	Dry Cleaners
23.	Travel Agents		24.	Jewelry Stores
25.	Image Consultants		26.	Realtors
27.	Gift Stores		28.	Furniture Store

We will assemble and present a sales presentation package that includes sales brochures, business cards, and a DVD presentation of party planning tips, and client testimonials. We will include coupons that offer a discount or other type of introductory deal. We will ask to set-up a take-one display for our sales brochures at the business registration counter. We will also use their services in exchange for their referrals and marketing support.

We will promptly give the referring business any one or combination of the following agreed upon reward options:
1. Referral fees
2. Free services
3. Mutual referral exchanges

We will monitor referral sources to evaluate the mutual benefits of the alliance and make certain to clearly define and document our referral incentives prior to initiating our referral exchange program.

6.4.2 Monitoring Marketing Results

To monitor how well _____ (company name) is doing, we will measure how well the advertising campaign is working by taking customer surveys. What we would like to know is how they heard of us and how they like and dislike about our subscription clothing rental services. In order to get responses to the surveys, we will give discounts as thank you rewards.

Response Tracking Methods
Coupons: ad-specific coupons that easily enable tracking
Landing Pages: unique web landing pages for each advertisement
800 Numbers: unique 1-800-# per advertisement
Email Service Provider: Instantly track email views, opens, and clicks
Address inclusion of dept # or suite #.

Our financial statements will offer excellent data to track all phases of sales. These are available for review on a daily basis. _____ (company name) will benchmark our objectives for sales promotion and advertising in order to evaluate our return on invested marketing dollars and determine where to concentrate our limited advertising dollars to realize the best return. We will also strive to stay within our marketing budget.

Key Marketing Metrics
We will use the following two marketing metrics to evaluate the cost-effectiveness of our marketing campaign:
1. The cost to acquire a new customer: The average dollar amount invested to get one new client. Example: If we invest $3,000 on marketing in a single month and end the month with 10 new members, our cost of acquisition is $300 per new customer.
2. The lifetime value of the average active customer. The average dollar value of an average customer over the life of their business with you. To calculate this metric for a given period of time, we will take the total amount of revenue our business generated during the time period and divide it by the total number of members we had from the beginning of the time period.
3. We will track the following set of statistics on a weekly basis to keep informed of the progress of our business:
   - A. Number of total referrals.
   - B. Percentage increase of total referrals (over baseline).
   - C. Number of new referral sources.
   - D. Number of new members/month.

Key Marketing Metrics Table
We've listed some key metrics in the following table. We will need to keep a close eye on these, to see if we meet our own forecasted expectations. If our numbers are off in too many categories, we may, after proper analysis, have to make substantial changes to our marketing efforts.

Key Marketing Metrics	2019	2020	2021
Revenue			
Leads			
Leads Converted			
Avg. Transaction per Customer			
Avg. Dollars per Customer			
Number of Referrals			
Number of PR Appearances			
Number of Testimonials			
Number of New Club Members			
Number of Returns			
Number of BBB Complaints			
Number of Completed Surveys			
Number of Blog readers			
Number of Twitter followers			
Number of Facebook Fans			

Metric Definitions
1. Leads: Individuals who are likely to consider making a purchase.
2. Leads Converted: Percent of individuals who actually make a purchase.
3. Average Transactions Per Customer: Number of purchases per customer per

month. Expected to rise significantly as members return for more and more designer clothing items per month
4. Average $ Per Customer: Average dollar amount of each transaction. Expected to rise along with average transactions.
5. Referrals: Includes customer and business referrals.
6. PR Appearances: Online or print mentions of the business that are not paid advertising. Expected to be high upon opening, then drop off and rise again until achieving a steady level.
7. Testimonials: Will be sought from the best and most loyal members. Our objective is ___ (#) per month) and they will be added to the website. Some will be sought as video testimonials for posting to YouTube.
8. New Loyalty Club Members: This number will rise significantly as more members see the value in repeated visits and the benefits of club membership.
9. Number of BBB Complaints: Our goal is zero.
10. Number of Completed Surveys: We will provide incentives for members to complete customer satisfaction surveys.

6.4.3 Word-of-Mouth Marketing

We plan to make use of the following techniques to promote word-of-mouth advertising:
1. Repetitive Image Advertising
2. Provide exceptional customer service.
3. Make effective use of loss leaders.
2. Schedule activities, such as demonstrations or fashion shows.
3. Make trial easy with a coupon or introductory discount.
4. Initiate web and magazine article submissions.
5. Utilize a sampling program.
6. Add a forward email feature to our website.
7. Share relevant and believable testimonial letters.
8. Publish owner profiles and staff bios.
9. Make product/service upgrade announcements.
10. Hold contests or sweepstakes.
12. Organize involvement with community events.
13. Pay suggestion box rewards
14. Distribute a monthly e-newsletter
15. Share easy-to-understand fashion trend information (via an article or seminar).
16. Make personalized marketing communications.
17. Structure our referral program with real incentives.
18. Sharing of Community Commonalities
19. Invitations to join our community of shared interests.
20. Publish Uncensored Customer Reviews
21. Enable Information Exchange Forums
22. Provide meaningful comparisons with competitors.
23. Clearly state our member benefits.

24. Make and honor ironclad guarantees
25. Provide superior post-sale support, including access to style consultants.
26. Provide support in the pre-sale decision making process.
27. Host Free Informational Seminars or Workshops.
28. Get involved with local business organizations that support female executives.
29. Issue Press Release coverage of charitable involvements.
30. Hold traveling company demonstrations/exhibitions/competitions.

6.4.4   Customer Satisfaction Survey

We will design a customer satisfaction survey to measure the "satisfaction quotient" of our Subscription Clothing Rental Company members. By providing a detailed snapshot of our current customer base, we will be able to generate more repeat and referral business and enhance the profitability of our Subscription Clothing Rental Company.

Our Customer Satisfaction Survey will include the following basics:
1. How do our members rate our business?
2. How do our members rate our competition?
3. How well do our members rate the value of our products or services?
4. What new customer needs and trends are emerging?
5. How loyal are our members?
6. What can be done to improve customer loyalty and repeat business?
7. How strongly do our members recommend our business?
8. What is the best way to market our business?
9. What new value-added services would best differentiate our business from that of our competitors?
10. How can we encourage more referral business?
11. How can our pricing strategy be improved?
12. Why did our best customers first come to our business and why they continue to come back?
13. Where do they live and what is their basic life situation?

Our customer satisfaction survey will help to answer these questions and more. From the need for continual new products and services to improved customer service, our satisfaction surveys will allow our business to quickly identify problematic and underperforming areas, while enhancing our overall customer satisfaction.

We will advise customers that:
By submitting this survey form, I understand my testimonial may be used in connection with publicizing and promoting _____ (company name). I authorize ____ (company name) to use my name and the testimonial as defined on this form. I hereby irrevocably authorize ____ (company name) to copy, exhibit, publish or distribute the testimonial for purposes of publicizing _____'s (company name) programs or for any other lawful purpose. These statements may be used in printed publications, multimedia presentations, on websites or in any other distribution media. I agree that I will make no monetary or other claim against ____ (company name) for the use of the statement. In addition, I waive any right to inspect or approve the finished product, including written copy,

wherein my likeness or my testimonial appears.

Examples:
https://subscriptionly.net/gwynnie-bee-reviews/
Resources:
https://survicate.com/customer-satisfaction/survey/most-popular-questions/
https://www.survata.com/
https://www.google.com/insights/consumersurveys/use_cases
https://www.surveymonkey.com/mp/customer-satisfaction-survey-questions/
http://www.smetoolkit.org/smetoolkit/en/content/en/6708/Customer-Satisfaction-Survey-Template-
http://smallbusiness.chron.com/common-questions-customer-service-survey-1121.html
http://smallbiztrends.com/2014/11/tailoring-survey-questions-for-your-industry.html
http://www.amplituderesearch.com/customer-satisfaction-surveys.shtml

6.4.5 Marketing Training Program

Our Marketing Training Program will include both an initial orientation and training, as well as ongoing continuing education classes. Initial orientation will be run by the owner until an HR manager is hired. For one week, half of each day will be spent in training, and the other half shadowing the store's operation manager. Training will include:

Learning the entire selection of wedding dress rental products and services.
Understanding our Mission Statement, Value Proposition, Position Statement and Unique Selling Proposition.
Appreciating our competitive advantages.
Understanding our core message and branding approach.
Learning our store's policies; returns processing, complaint handling, etc.
Learning our customer services standards of practice.
Learning our customer and business referral programs.
Learning our Membership Club procedures, rules and benefits.
Becoming familiar with our company website, and online ordering options.
Service procedures specific to the employee's role.

Ongoing workshops will be based on customer feedback and problem areas identified by mystery buyers, which will better train employees to educate members. These ongoing workshops will be held _____ (once?) a month for _____ (three?) hours.

6.4.4.1 Exit Survey

We will develop an Exit Survey that will be given to members who cancel their memberships. It will include the following types of questions to provide our studio with constructive feedback that we can act upon:

1. How long have you been a member?

2. Reason for cancelling? (moving, changing service providers, can't afford it, not enough time, family circumstances, Other: _____).
3. How would you rate the style consultant? (include categories for knowledge, friendliness, approachability, availability, etc., and rate 1 to 5)
4. How would you rate the shipments received? (cleanliness, range of styles, fit accuracy, comfort, fashion trendiness, style match, fabric suitability, designer preference, etc., and rate 1 to 8)
5. Any other comments or feedback?

6.5 Sales Strategy

The development of our sales strategy will start by developing a better understanding of our customer needs. To accomplish this task, we will pursue the following research methods:

1. Join the associations that our targeted members belong to.
2. Contact the membership director and establish a relationship to understand their member's needs, challenges and concerns.
3. Identify non-competitive suppliers who sell to our customer to learn their challenges and look for partnering solutions.
4. Work directly with our customer and ask them what their needs are and if our business may offer a possible solution.

We will utilize the following sales strategies:
1. Members need to be acknowledged and attended to right away to capture and maintain interest.
2. Our expertise will help members stay focused. The process of choosing everyday business casual attire can be overwhelming, because it is such a significant purchase, and because there are so many variables. Therefore, it will be critical to educate and navigate the customer through the profile building process efficiently.
3. In addition to renting and selling goods, we will be delivering a shopping experience. If we provide a positive experience, word of mouth will grow exponentially.
4. Sales goals will be set for our employees, and achievement of those goals will be rewarded monetarily.
5. We will constantly educate our members as to how they can realize the most benefits from their subscription clothing rental membership.
Resource:
https://blog.letote.com/2019/09/13/10-insider-tips-to-get-the-most-out-of-le-tote/

The Management of our business will focus on daily sales revenue goals and explaining any variances. Best value products will be identified to assist members with smart rental and purchase selections. Deliveries will be geared to the customer's convenience. The situation will be monitored to ensure that the company invests adequately in its own delivery operations.

Sales feedback will be elicited to stimulate ideas, approaches, relate success stories, instruct in new techniques, share news, and implement improvements. Major referral accounts will be solicited through networking, neighborhood solicitations via sales agents, and opportunistic fashion show encounters at any time by management.

Our focus will be on making the rental services we offer of the highest possible quality. Only when those services are well-established, will we consider expanding our range of products and services offered. We will become a one-stop shop for subscription clothing rental services, and specialized program offerings. We will also be very active in the community, building a solid reputation with professionals and community leaders.

Our members will be primarily obtained through word-of-mouth referrals, but we will also advertise introductory offers to introduce people to our preferred club membership programs. The combination of the perception of higher-quality designer fashions, exceptional purchase guidance, innovative returns processing and the recognition of superior value should turn referral leads into satisfied members.

The company's sales strategy will be based on the following elements:
- Advertising in the Yellow Pages - two inch by three-inch ads describing our services will be placed in the local Yellow Pages.
- Placing classified advertisements in the regional editions of fashion magazines.
- Word of mouth referrals - generating sales leads in the local community through customer referrals.

Our basic sales strategy is to:
- Develop a website for lead generation by _____ (date).
- Provide exceptional customer service and style consulting services.
- Accept payment by all major credit cards, cash, PayPal and check.
- Survey our members regarding products and services they would like to see added.
- Sponsor charitable and other community events.
- Provide tours of the facility so members can learn how to be discriminating members and build a trust bond with our operations.
- Motivate employees with a pay-for-performance component to their straight salary compensation package, based on profits and customer satisfaction rates.
- Build long-term customer relationships by putting the interests of members first.
- Establish mutually beneficial relationship with local businesses serving the ____ (image/styling?) needs of local residents.

6.5.1 Customer Retention Strategy

We will use the following techniques to reduce controllable subscriber churn, improve customer retention and long-term member value (LTV), foster referrals and improve the long-term profitability of our subscription clothing rental business:
1. Keep the Subscription Clothing Rental Company well-supported with state-of-

the-art software to facilitate the efficient, on-time processing of complete orders.
2. Use only well-trained sales associates and styling consultants.
3. Actively solicit customer feedback and promptly act upon their inputs.
4. Tell members how much you appreciate their business.
5. Call regular members by their first names.
6. Send thank you notes.
7. Offer free new product trial samples.
8. Change displays and sales presentations on a regular basis.
9. Practice good phone etiquette
10. Respond to complaints or issues promptly.
11. Reward referrals.
12. Publish a weekly/monthly opt-in direct response newsletter with customized content, dependent on the recipient's stated information preferences to stay top-of-mind.
13. Develop and publish a list of frequently asked questions.
14. Issue Preferred Customer Membership Cards at three different benefit levels.
15. Hold informational seminars and workshops.
16. Provide an emergency hotline number.
17. Publish code of ethics and service guarantees.
18. Help members to make accurate competitor comparisons.
19. Build a stay-in-touch (drip marketing) communications calendar.
20. Keep marketing communications focused on our competitive advantages.
21. Offer repeat user discounts and incentives.
22. Be supportive and encouraging, and not judgmental.
23. Measure customer retention and look at recurring revenue and customer surveys.
24. Build a community of shared interests by offering a website forum or discussion group for professionals and members to facilitate knowledge sharing.
25. Offer club membership benefits above and beyond those of our competitors.
26. Issue reminder emails and holiday gift cards.
27. Provide a free (freemium) or discounted basic service with incentives to upgrade to a service with more curated choices and/or personalized recommendations.
28. Develop a ____ (one/two/three?) year contractual agreement that rewards customers for their long-term commitment.
Examples: Faster services, rebate program, higher purchase discounts, new designer notifications, more personalized services, price increase protections, exclusive designer access, concierge services, giveaways (T-shirts), milestone achievement notifications, exclusive offers, etc.
29. Offer a range of price points for differentiated subscription program benefits, with the option to either downgrade or upgrade.
30. Learn how to pre-qualify the most likely loyal subscribers to best monetize the relationship over time.
31. Develop a new member onboarding process that gets them started realizing the core value benefits right away.
32. Offer instant savings and rewards based on past purchases.
33. Consistently exceed customer expectations.
34. Develop exclusive relationships with emerging designers.

35. Invest in the original design, marketing and branding of own, exclusive private labels.
36. Do not use price increases or marketing expenditure cutbacks to mitigate revenue losses due to churn.
37. Continually strive to find the right mix between the offering of popular designer fashions and original creations.
38. Continually leverage member profiles, member purchasing patterns (transaction data) and member satisfaction (interview) surveys to provide a more personalized experience and understand why churn happens in the first place.
39. Develop a recommendation software engine that suggests complete outfit packages, including accessories and jewelry for specific types of occasions.
40. Empower front-line, customer facing staff to do what is right by the customer first.
41. Develop ways to predict when customers may need some help or want to upgrade their membership.
42. Create a memorable experience that members cannot get anywhere else.
43. Encourage members to post positive testimonials via videos, podcasts, forums, discussion pages and blogs on their social media sites and company websites.
44. Start with a minor membership fee so subscribers will value their membership and use the service more frequently to lower the average fee cost per transaction.
45. Develop a way to spot the early warning signs of pending churn and take the appropriate corrective actions.
46. Find a way to become a repository of stored value, that will drive a bigger need to stay connected to the company, such as a rebate or loyalty program or an information source for tax filings or gift giving.
47. Find ways to make the usage of the service a hassle-free habit or a part of an information gathering or money-saving routine.
48. Achieve long-term retention by continually improving the value-added proposition or the perceived value of rewards.
49. Develop a cancellation survey to understand and track when and how they were originally acquired and why they cancelled, such as limited access to a preferred fashion designer or the inability to schedule a shipment for a special event.
50. Develop solutions for cancellation reasons, generate a series of 'missing-you' email communications and issue incentives to come back.
51. Develop a system to designate some members as high-status or frequent users, or community influencers, because this will confer a special social recognition.
52. Give members the option to pick and choose specialized plan features, rather than forcing all subscribers to pay for 'feature bloat'.
53. Develop a structured, ongoing onboarding process that moves subscribers along a well-defined, features learning curve.

6.5.2 Sales Forecast

Our sales projections are based on the following:
1. Actual sales volumes of local competitors
2. Interviews with Subscription Clothing Rental Company owners and managers
3. Observations of sales and traffic at competitor establishments.

4. Government and fashion industry trade statistics
5. Local population demographics and projections.

___ percent will be a sensible estimate for the first year of operations. There are currently about ___ (#) Subscription Clothing Rental Companies in _____ County that carry some or all the items offered at ___ (company name). Assuming that the customer base was divided evenly among these businesses, each would have about a _____ percent market share. However, because this will be the first year of operations for _____ (company name), that "even share" of the market is not expected right away. It is expected that by year two, the market share will increase to ___ percent, and by year three, the market share will exceed _____ (#) percent. This will happen as _____ (company name) becomes known as the place to rent or buy designer fashions and/or other accessories.

Costs of sales assumes that for clothing, the wholesale cost will average about 45% of the retail price, and for accessories, the wholesale cost will average about 30% of the retail price. For the clothing items, there is a two-month lag in cost of sales because the inventory takes two to three months to arrive from the day it is ordered, and the store does not pay for custom-ordered items until they are shipped.

Our sales forecast is an estimated projection of expected sales over the next three years, based on our chosen marketing strategy, local economic conditions and assumed competitive environment. Sales are expected to be below average during the first year, until a regular customer base has been established. It has been estimated that it takes the average Subscription Clothing Rental Company a minimum of two years to establish a significant customer base. After the customer base is built, sales will grow at an accelerated rate from word-of-mouth referrals and continued networking efforts. We expect sales to steadily increase as our marketing campaign, employee training programs and contact management system are executed. By using advertising, especially discounted introductory coupons, as a catalyst for this prolonged process, ____(company name) plans to attract more members sooner. Throughout the first year, it is forecasted that sales will incrementally grow until profitability is reached toward the end of year ___(one?). Year two reflects a conservative growth rate of ____ (20?) percent. Year three reflects a growth rate of _____ (25?) percent. We expect to be open for business on ____ (date). With our unique designer fashion collections, along with our thorough and aggressive marketing strategies, we believe that sales forecasts are actually on the conservative side.

Table: Sales Forecast

Sales	Annual Sales 2019	2020	2021
Membership Fees			
Clothing Rentals			
Clothing Sales			
Maternity Rentals			
Children's Rentals			
Formalwear Rentals			

Jewelry Rentals
Jewelry Sales
Other Accessories
Gift Merchandise
Tailoring Services
Laundering Services
Consulting Services
Misc.
Total Unit Sales

Direct Cost of Sales:
Membership Fees
Clothing Rentals
Clothing Sales
Maternity Rentals
Children's Rentals
Formalwear Rentals
Jewelry Rentals
Jewelry Sales
Other Accessories
Gift Merchandise
Tailoring Services
Laundering Services
Consulting Services
Misc.
Subtotal Direct Cost of Sales

6.5.3 Sales Programs

Our sales staff will have a level of fashion style knowledge that will position _____ (company name) to address customer needs better than our competition. The company will support the sales staff with education tuition assistance, and we will recruit our sales staff from students of fashion institutes. A proprietary website address has been registered, and a website will be built to enhance customer service, and direct sales. Peripheral sales and marketing collaterals will be used to expand product lines and customer awareness of our business, including playing cards, and calendars.
A sophisticated proprietary software app will be developed to enhance the customer renting experience with product knowledge matched to our members' tastes and stated fashion preferences.

6.6 Merchandising Strategy

Merchandising is that part of our marketing strategy that is involved with promoting the sales of our merchandise, as by consideration of the most effective means of selecting, pricing, displaying, and advertising items for sale in our business. Through proper product placement, space allocation, and in-store outlet promotions, sales space will be geared towards high profit margin products.

To be successful, our retail area must be impressive and compelling. It must have sufficient space, excellent inventory and beautiful display furnishings.

The décor of the merchandising area is extremely important to sales. Display units are primary, but lighting, furniture, wall surfaces, window treatments, carpeting, accessories and countertops will all play important supporting roles. We will monitor our sales figures and data to confirm that products in demand are well-stocked and slow-moving fashions are phased-out. We will improve telephone skills of employees to boost phone orders. We will attach our own additional business labels to all products to promote our line of services and location.

6.7 Pricing Strategy

When setting prices, we will consider the following factors:
1. Direct Costs: labor, time and supplies
2. Indirect Costs: rent, utilities, taxes and expenses.
3. Demand: economic conditions, demographics, consumer behavior, etc.
4. Marketing Promotions
5. Level of Competition
6. Positioning Image
7. Goals: profit objectives, return on investment, growth objectives.

Pricing will also be heavily influenced by the demand for the individual garment, for example, the higher the demand the higher the rent will be. Product pricing will also be based on competitive parity guidelines. Prices will be consistent with those of other subscription clothing rental businesses in ____ region, with the exception of very high-volume operations who have more powerful pricing leverage. Pricing will be monitored continuously against other competitive sources who we can readily research. Our plan is to discount thematically, that is, tied to an event theme.

Examples:
We will offer monthly membership plans starting at $69/month for Classic and $79/month for Maternity.

Shipping will always be free, both ways. We will provide a USPS prepaid shipping label and return bag with every shipment to send back pieces. To avoid being charged for an item, we will offer optional insurance for $5/month to cover all repairable damages, like stains or missing buttons.

Sample Rental Pricing Schedule Range

We will offer several subscription plans to fit any budget. We will have plans from 1 item at a time to 10 items out at a time. All plans will include unlimited exchanges, shipping both ways, and cleaning, and will be cancellable at any time by the subscriber.

Number of Items in Shipment	Monthly Subscription Price
1	$49
2	$69
3	$95
4	$120
5	$139
6	$159
7	$179
8	$185
9	$190
10	$199

Source: https://closet.gwynniebee.com/pages/pricing-update

We are not interested in being the low-price leader, as our pricing strategy plays a major role in whether we will be able to create and maintain members for a profit. Our revenue structure must support our cost structure, so the salaries we pay to our staff are balanced by the revenue we collect.

The number of competitors in the area largely determines what type of pricing we will have. We don't want to be known as the highest price place in town, but it is equally important not to be the cheapest. We will continuously try to expand our selection. If a customer asks for a garment type of fashion designer that we don't have, we will write it down, monitor other requests for similar items and then attempt to get it for them.

Price List Comparison

Competitor	Service/Product	Our Price	Competitor Price	B/(W) Competitor

We will adopt the following pricing guidelines:
1. We must ensure that our price plus service equation is perceived to be an exceptional value proposition.
2. We must refrain from competing on price, but always be price competitive.
3. We must develop value-added services, and bundle those with our products to create offerings that cannot be easily price compared.
4. We must focus attention on our competitive advantages.
5. Development of a pricing strategy based on our market positioning strategy, which is ____ (mass market value leadership/exceptional premium niche value?)
6. Our pricing policy objective, which is to _____ (increase profit margins/ achieve revenue maximization to increase market share/lower unit

7. We will use marketplace intelligence and gain insights from competitor pricing.
8. We will solicit pricing feedback from members using surveys and interviews.
9. We will utilize limited time pricing incentives to penetrate niche markets
10. We will conduct experiments at prices above and below the current price to determine the price elasticity of demand. (Inelastic demand or demand that does not decrease with a price increase, indicates that price increases may be feasible.)
11. We will keep our offerings and prices simple to understand and competitive, based on market intelligence.
12. We will consider a price for volume strategy on certain items and study the effects of price on volume and of volume on costs, as when in a recession, trying to recover these costs through a price increase can be fatal.

Determining the costs of servicing business is the most important part of covering our expenses and earning profits. We will factor in the following pricing formula:
Product Cost + Materials + Overhead + Labor + Profit + Tax = Price

We will develop a pricing strategy that will reinforce the perception of value to the member and manage profitability, especially in the face of rising inflation. To ensure our success, we will use periodic competitor and customer research interviews and surveys to continuously evaluate our pricing strategy. We intend to review our revenue trendlines and profit margins every six months.

6.8 Differentiation Strategies

We will use differentiation strategies to develop and market unique subscription plans for different customer segments. To differentiate ourselves from the competition, we will focus on the assets, creative ideas and competencies that we have that none of our competitors has. The goal of our differentiation strategies will be to be able to charge a premium price for our products and services and/or to promote loyalty and assist in retaining our members.

1. Due to the increase in female employment, many service-oriented businesses are leaning toward differentiating themselves on the basis of convenience. Therefore, we plan to provide more services via an interactive website.
2. We will utilize software systems that will enable us to personalize each customer's buying experience, including easy access to customer transaction history, stated preference profile and detailed information about all the products of interest to that client.
3. We will enable the automatic online re-ordering of our products and services.
4. We will be able to feature more high-end designer clothing because afford can afford a $100 rental fee more often than they can afford to purchase a $1,000 outfit.
5. We will promote the fact that we can ship the rented dress directly to the preferred temporary location of the member, saving them transportation costs and hassles.

6. We will allow members to make the final edit decision on the contents of the shipment they receive, and they will have the option to rent, buy or immediately return those items.
7. We will efficiently enable intimate one-on-one communication between our customers and our certified stylists and customer service representatives.
8. We will partner with Zendesk.com to have access to a more robust platform that streamlines customer service operations and creates a personalized and consistent experience across different service touch points.
9. We will use the customer feedback aggregated from Zendesk to improve the e-Commerce experience, as well as marketing and merchandising tactics.
10. We will continuously work to combine the best features of cashflow friendly subscription e-commerce, technology-based "personalized shopping," and stylist-assisted collaborative consumption.

Other differentiation strategies include the following:
1. Exclusive private label and designer branded products and services.
2. We will offer mobile at-home and office services.
3. We will build an extensive profile on members to capture information about their lifestyle, style preferences and key occasion reminder dates.
4. We will develop a referral program that turns our members into referral agents.
5. We will use regular member satisfaction surveys to collect feedback, improvement ideas, referrals and testimonials.
6. We will promote our "green" practices, such as establishing a garment recycling program, refurbishing garments for resale, purchasing recycled-content office goods, installing highly efficient laundering equipment, using non-toxic detergents and responsibly handling hazardous wastes.
7. We will customize our offerings according to the language, cultural influences, customs, interests and preferences of local markets to create loyalty and increase sales.
8. We will develop the expertise to satisfy the needs of targeted market segments, such as pregnant women, with customized and exceptional rental support services.

6.9 Milestones (select)

The Milestones Chart is a timeline that will guide our company in developing and growing our subscription clothing rental business. It will list chronologically the various critical actions and events that must occur to bring our business to life. We will make certain to assign real, attainable dates to each planned action or event.

_____ (company name) has identified several specific milestones which will function as goals for the company. The milestones will provide a target for achievement as well as a mechanism for tracking progress. The dates were chosen based on realistic delivery times and necessary construction times. All critical path milestones will be completed within their allotted time frames to ensure the success of contingent milestones. The following table will provide a timeframe for each milestone.

Table: Milestones

Milestones	Start Date	End Date	Budget	Responsibility
Business Plan Completion				
Secure Permits/Licenses				
Locate & Secure Space				
Conduct Lease Negotiations				
Obtain Insurance Coverage				
Secure Additional Financing				
Get Start-up Inventory Quotes				
Obtain BBB Certification				
Purchase Office Equipment				
Renovate Space				
Define Marketing Programs				
Install Racking Equipment				
Install Subscription Software				
Other Technology Systems				
Set-up Accounting System				
Develop Office Policies				
Develop Procedures Manual				
Arrange Support Service Providers				
Finalize Media Plan				
Create Facebook Business Page				
Open Twitter Account				
Conduct Blogger Outreach				
Develop Personnel Plan				
Develop Staff Training Programs				
Hire/Train Staff				
Implement Marketing Plan				
Get Website Live				
Develop SEO Campaign				
Form Strategic Alliances				
Open Accounts with Designers				
Attend Fashion Shows				
Purchase Start-up Inventory/Supplies				
Press Release Announcements				
Advertise Grand Opening				
Kickoff Advertising Program				
Participate in trade shows				
Join Community Orgs./Network				
Conduct Satisfaction Surveys				
Evaluate/Revise Plan				
Monitor Social Media Networks				
Respond Positively to Reviews				
Measure Return on Marketing $$$				
Devise Growth Strategy				
Revenues Exceed $_____				

| Reach Profitability | _____ |
| Totals: | _____ |

7.0 Website Plan Summary

_____ (company name) is currently developing a website at the URL address www. (company name).com. We will primarily use the website to promote an understanding of the bridal rental services we offer by posting helpful articles, circulate information about coming events and to enable online rental order placement. Visitors will be able to receive information about the designers we carry as well as basic company information, such as shipment location. The site will also be a resource for all members. Through a secure, password-protected log in, they will be able to provide the necessary information to register and place their clothing rental order. They will also be able to supply detailed feedback on the contents of the shipment received. Supplying the visitors to our websites with this information will make a huge difference in turning our website visitors into new members.

We will also provide multiple incentives to sign-up for various benefits, such as our newsletters and promotional sale notices. This will help us to build an email database, which will supply our automated customer follow-up system. We will create a personalized drip marketing campaign to stay in touch with our customers and prospects.

We will develop our website to be a resource for web visitors who are seeking knowledge and information about brand comparisons, with a goal to service the knowledge needs of our customers and generate leads. Our home page will be designed to be a "welcome mat" that clearly presents our service offerings and provides links through which visitors can gain easy access to the information they seek. We will use our website to match the problems our customers face with the solutions we offer.

We will use the free tool, Google Analytics (http://www.google.com/analytics), to generate a history and measure our return on investment. Google Analytics is a free tool that can offer insight by allowing the user to monitor traffic to a single website. We will just add the Google Analytics code to our website and Google will give our firm a dashboard providing the number of unique visitors, repeat traffic, page views, etc. This will help to stop wasting our company's money on inefficient marketing. Using an analytic program will show exactly which leads are paying off, and which ones to do without. We will find out what's bringing our site the most traffic and how to improve upon that.

To improve the readability of our website, we will organize our website content in the following ways.
1. Headlines
2. Bullet points
3. Callout text
4. Top of page summaries

To improve search engine optimization, we will maximize the utilization of the following;

1.	Links	2.	Headers
3.	Bold text	4.	Bullets
5.	Keywords	6.	Meta tags

This website will serve the following purposes:

About Us	How We Work/Our Philosophy
Contact Us	Customer service contact info
How Our Subscription Rentals Work	
Membership Plan Options	Pricing
Operating Policies	Returns/Turnaround/Cleaning/Other
Help Center	
Size Advisor Tool	
Fit Guide	
Styling Tips and Tricks	
Clothing Categories	
Specialty Services	
Accessories Catalog	Online Ordering/Shopping Cart
Featured Designers	Bios
Now Trending	
Top Rated Style Inspirations	
Style Gallery	
Create Virtual Closet	
Garment Care Instructions	
Give a Gift	
Gift Certificate	Order Form
Coupons	
New Arrivals	New Releases/Pre-Sales
Special Offers	
Meet Our Style Consultants	
Trunk Show Schedule	
Frequently Asked Questions	FAQs
VIP Club Membership	Mailing List Sign-up
Newsletter Sign-up	Join Mailing List
Newsletter Archives	Fashion Articles
Upcoming Events/Promotions	Fashion/Trunk Shows
Member Testimonials	Letters w/photos
Referral Program	Details
Customer Satisfaction Survey	Feedback
Hours of Operation	
Press Releases	Community Involvement
Strategic Alliance Partners	Links to Local Vendors
Resources	Professional Associations
Our Blog	Accept comments
Refer-a-Friend	Viral marketing

Video/Photo Gallery   Fashion Show/Testimonials
Guarantees
Code of Ethics
Terms of Service   Ex: ww.renttherunway.com/pages/termsofservice
Career Opportunities
My Account
Classified Ads

Classified Ads
By joining and incorporating a classified ad affiliate program into our website, we will create the ultimate win-win-win. We will provide our members with a free benefit, increase our rankings with the search engines by incorporating keyword hyperlinks into our site, attract additional markets to expose to our fashions, create an additional income source as they upgrade their ads, and provide our members with a reason to return to our web site again and again.

Resources:
App Themes	www.appthemes.com/themes/classipress/
e-Classifieds	http://www.e-classifieds.net/
Noah's Classifieds	http://www.noahsclassifieds.org/
Joom Prod	http://www.joomprod.com/
Flynax	http://www.flynax.com/
Market Grabber	http://www.marketgrabber.com/

7.1 Website Marketing Strategy

Our online marketing strategy will employ the following distinct mechanisms:

1. Search Engine Submission
   This will be most useful to people who are unfamiliar with _____ (company name) but are looking for a local Subscription Clothing Rental Company. There will also be searches from members who may know about us, but who are seeking additional information.

   SEO is a very important digital marketing strategy because search engines are the primary method of finding information for most internet users. SEO is simply the practice of improving and promoting a website in order to increase the number of visitors a site receives from search engines. Basic SEO techniques will range from the naming of webpages to the way that other websites link to our website. We will also need to get our business listed on as many relevant online directories as possible, such as Google, Yelp, Kudzu and Yahoo Local, write a blog that solicit comments and be active on social media sites.
   We will also try to incorporate local terms potential clients would use, such as "_____ (city) subscription rental clothing" or "_____ (city) rent/buy fashion designer clothing." This will make it more likely that local customers will find us close to the top of their search.
   Resource;

https://www.semrush.com/
www.officerreports.com/blog/wp-content/uploads/2014/11/SEOmoz-The-Beginners-Guide-To-SEO-2012.pdf

2. Website Address (URL) on Marketing Materials
   Our URL will be printed on all marketing communications, business cards, letterheads, faxes, and invoices and product labels. This will encourage a visit to our website for additional information.

3. Online Directories Listings
   We will list our website on relevant, free and paid online directories and manufacturer website product locators.
   The good online directories possess the following features:
   Free or paid listings that do not expire and do not require monthly renewal.
   Ample space to get your advertising message across.
   Navigation buttons that are easy for visitors to use.
   Optimization for top placement in the search engines based on keywords that people typically use to find Online Subscription Clothing Rental Companies.
   Direct links to your website, if available.
   An ongoing directory promotion campaign to maintain high traffic volumes to the directory site.

4. Strategic Business Partners
   We will use a Business Partners page to cross-link to prominent _____ (city) area wedding services web sites as well as the city Web sites and local recreational sites. We will also cross-link with brand name suppliers and designers.

5. YouTube Posting
   We will produce a video of testimonials from several of our satisfied members and educate viewers as to the range of our services and products. Our research indicates that the YouTube video will also serve to significantly improve our ranking with the Google Search Engine.

6. Exchange of links with strategic marketing partners.
   We will cross-link to non-profit businesses that accept our gift certificate donations as in-house run contest prize awards.

7. E-Newsletter
   Use the newsletter sign-up as a reason to collect email addresses and limited profiles and use embedded links in the newsletter to return readers to website.

8. Create an account for your photos on flickr.com
   Use the name of your site on flickr so you have the same keywords and your branded.

9. Geo Target Pay Per Click (PPC) Campaign
   Available through Google Adwords program. Example keywords include Subscription Clothing Rental Company, Fashion designer clothing rentals, Business casual attire rentals and _____ (city).

10. Post messages on Internet user groups and forums.
    Get involved with fashion related discussion groups and forums and develop a descriptive signature paragraph.
    Example: www.weforum.org/agenda/2019/08/clothing-rental-could-be-the-key-to-a-stylishly-sustainable-fashion-industry
11. Write up your own LinkedIn.com and Facebook.com profiles.
    Highlight your background and professional interests.
12. Facebook.com Brand-Building Applications:
    As a Facebook member, we will create a specific Facebook page for our business through its "Facebook Pages" application. This page will be used to promote who we are and what we do. We will use this page to post alerts when we have new articles to distribute, news to announce, etc. Facebook members can then become fans of our page and receive these updates on their newsfeed as we post them. We will create our business page by going to the "Advertising" link on the bottom of our personal Facebook page. We will choose the "Pages" tab at the top of that page, and then choose "Create a Page." We will upload our logo, enter our company profile details, and establish our settings. Once completed, we will click the "publish your site" button to go live. We will also promote our Page everywhere we can. We will add a Facebook link to our website, our email signatures, and email newsletters. We will also add Facebook to the marketing mix by deploying pay-per-click ads through their advertising application. With Facebook advertising, we will target by specifying sex, age, relationship, location, education, as well as specific keywords.
13. Blog to share our success stories and solicit feedback comments.
    Blogging will be a great way for us to share information, expertise, and news, and start a conversation with our members, the media, suppliers, and any other target audiences. Blogging will be a great online marketing strategy because it keeps our content fresh, engages our audience to leave comments on specific posts, improves search engine rankings and attracts links. In the blog we will share fun wedding party tips. We will also provide a link to our Facebook.com page.
    Resource: www.blogger.com

7.2 Development Requirements

A full development plan will be generated as documented in the milestones. Costs that _____ (company name) will expect to incur with development of its new website include:

Development Costs
    User interface design $_____.
    Site development and testing $_____
    Site Implementation $._____

Ongoing Costs
    Website name registration $_____ per year.
    Site Hosting $_____ or less per month.
    Site design changes, updates and maintenance are considered part of Marketing.

Initially, the _____ (company name) website will be developed with few technical resources. A simple hosting provider will host the site and provide the technical back end. We will work with a contracted web page designer to develop a simple, yet classy, site. The most technically complex portion of the site will be the ordering portion. For this, a secure site must be created so that credit card information can be transmitted safely. In addition, it will need to be designed in such a way that employees will be able to set up the necessary profiles for members to log in.

The site will be developed by _____ (company name), a local start-up company. The user interface designer will use our existing graphic art to come up with the website logo and graphics. We have already secured hosting with a local provider, _____ (business name). Additionally, they will prepare a monthly statistical usage report to analyze and improve web usage and return on investment. The plan is for the website to be live by ___(date). Basic website maintenance, including update and data entry will be handled by our staff. Site content, such as images and text will be maintained by _____ (owner name). In the future, we may need to contract with a technical resource to build the trackable article download and newsletter capabilities.
Resource:
www.fatbit.com/fab/launch-designer-dress-rental-portal-with-top-website-features/

Ecommerce Platform Builder:
www.shopify.com
www.godaddy.com/garage/offer-a-clothing-rental-service-heres-what-you-need-to-know/

7.3 Sample Frequently Asked Questions

We will use the following guidelines when developing the frequently asked questions for the ecommerce section of the website:
1. Use a Table of Contents: Offer subject headers at the top of the FAQ page with a hyperlink to that related section further down on the page for quick access.
2. Group Questions in a Logical Way and group separate specific questions related to a subject together.
3. Be Precise with the Question: Don't use open-ended questions.
4. Avoid Too Many Questions: Publish only the popular questions and answers.
5. Answer the Question with a direct answer.
6. Link to Resources When Available: via hyperlinks so the customer can continue with self-service support.
7. Use Bullet Points to list step-by-step instructions.
8. Focus on Customer Support and Not Marketing.
9. Use Real and Relevant Frequently Asked Questions from actual members.
10. Update Your FAQ Page as members continue to communicate questions.

The following frequently asked questions will enable us to convey a lot of important information to our members in a condensed format. We will post these questions and answers on our website and create a hardcopy version to be included on our sales presentation folder.

What are some advantages to renting a dress instead of buying?
Here are just a few of the many reasons to rent instead of buying:
- You can choose from thousands of designer dresses for a quarter of the retail price.
- You can wear the same fashion names featured in current fashion magazines or worn by your favorite celebrity.
- You can shop for the season's hottest new dresses from the comfort of your home without travel to big cities or trendy boutiques.
- You can save money by resisting the urge to accumulate a closet full of dresses that cost a fortune – but are quickly outdated.
- You never have to be concerned about laundering clothing or shipping charges.
- You can also purchase rental garments at a significant discount.

Source: https://lendingluxury.com/faq

How does the free or discounted trial work?
The __ (#) day free trial is a great way for new users of our rental service to see if a subscription is right for them, with absolutely no risk! Try our service out free for ____ (30?) days. Wear, return, and repeat as often as you'd like, on us, for the 2 items at a time plan. Shipping both ways and cleaning is included in this trial. The ___ (30?) day free trial is applicable on the 2 items plan for new members. Your credit card is necessary upon signup however you will not be charged until the __ (30?) day free trial ends. You can cancel your membership anytime during your free trial.

How does your subscription clothing rental service work?
Our service works in the following way:
1. Browse our collection of thousands of items from top designers.
2. Add all the styles you like to your ____ (company name) virtual closet. You're in control, and there's no limit to how many items you can add.
3. We will ship your first box within 2-3 days of filling your closet application to the minimum level. You'll receive a shipping notification and tracking information.
4. Wear the items and enjoy fashion without commitment.
5. Using the pre-paid shipping bags included with your shipment, send back what you like, when you like. You can return any number of pieces at a time. Or, if you receive something from us that you can't part with, you have the option of purchasing it directly from your virtual closet.
6. Repeat the process as we handle the cleaning while you enjoy unlimited style.

How much does it cost?
_____ (company name) offers several subscription plans to fit any budget. We have plans from 1 item at a time (costing $49) to 10 items out at a time (costing $199). All plans include unlimited exchanges, free shipping both ways, and free cleaning.
Example:

https://support.gwynniebee.com/hc/en-us/articles/207752033-How-much-does-it-cost-

What kind of clothing and accessories can I rent?
We offer women's clothing and accessories (jewelry, handbags, shoes, gloves and scarves) for rent. We have thousands of on-trend and classic styles, including those for the workday, the weekend and special events. There are also maternity styles if you are expecting. We carry hundreds of brands, including Karen Kane, Vince Camuto, Calvin Klein, Ann Taylor and French Connection, and our sizes range from 0-32 (XS-XXL).

How long do I get to keep these items?
You can keep the items for as long as you're a member in good standing. Keep them for a week or an entire season — it's up to you! You can swap your items for new ones as often as you want, so you're able to get multiple orders each month. You must return all your items at the same time unless you want to purchase one or more of your items. If you cancel your membership, you must either return or purchase the items in your possession.

How do I exchange pieces?
Place the items you wish to exchange in the provided 'Return Bag' and drop your package off at any USPS blue collection boxes, give it to your USPS carrier, or take it to a USPS-approved service provider. Sending items back triggers the preparation of your next shipment.

How do I know my dress is clean?
We'll only ship dresses that receive a 100% fresh seal of approval. Our dry cleaner is an expert in eco-friendly, luxury dry cleaning. They utilize an environmentally safe process that certifies that every garment is thoroughly cleaned and cared for, maintaining the impeccable quality of the garment while being kind to the environment. Our packaging method is also specially designed to fully protect the dresses during shipment.

How frequently are your dresses cleaned?
Dresses are cleaned after each rental. They are carefully inspected, cleaned, sanitized & packaged beautifully so all you have to do is get dressed.

Is the clothing new or used?
Because we are a fashion rental service, the pieces you rent are also gently used by other ____ (company name) members. We inspect each item when it is sent back to make sure it's still like new, and we use the most state-of-the-art dry-cleaning equipment to restore the sanitary freshness of the garment.

Will the dresses need to be pressed upon arrival?
We do our best to ensure everything arrives wrinkle free! Each dress is steamed and pressed before packaging where it is then sealed in plastic on a hanger and wrapped in a garment bag. Certain fabrics are more prone to wrinkle, so if you receive a dress with slight creases please try steaming the garment on low heat.

What if I accidentally stain or damage the dress?
We understand that some wear and tear may be inevitable and beyond your control. Our dry cleaner can take care of most minor damage, and the $5 insurance charge included on each dress you rent will cover these types of situations. Although very rare, significant destruction or theft is obviously not permitted. Unfortunately, if the dress cannot be repaired and we are unable to rent it to future members, your credit card will be charged immediately for the retail price of the dress.

Do I get to pick the pieces that I receive?

Yes. After we have recommended your style selections, you get to look through everything available in your size at that time and pick items you want to rent. Our technology makes suggestions based on what you tell us in your style profile, how you've rated previously rented items and what is trending—but you will ultimately choose what you get.

How do I know the clothes will fit my body?
Based on the information you provide on your 'Style Profile', our stylist will select a closet of items for you that will work for your body/preferences. As you rent more items and give feedback, the automated component of the curation process will select like brands, sizes and silhouettes that will work best for you. All selections will then be reviewed and tweaked by a stylist and sent to you to choose your favorites.

How much does shipping cost?
Shipping is always free.

Do you deliver outside the continental United States?
At this time, we only ship and deliver orders within the continental United States. Similarly, orders must be returned to us from within the continental U.S.

Do you offer overnight shipping?
Yes. We offer overnight 10:30am and 8pm delivery options for an added fee.

What if I want my package delivered to a hotel or location other than my home?
No problem—just provide the exact address to which you want the dress shipped. If you're shipping to a hotel, please put the hotel name in the company field and address it to the person whose name is on your reservation. It must be a secure location, not a PO Box, and please make sure the hotel concierge is expecting your delivery.

Is a signature required for delivery?
Our UPS packages do not require a signature, but ___ (city) members are required to sign for our courier deliveries. Concierge, mail rooms and front desks are able to sign on behalf of the customer.

How do I return my order?
We'll take care of everything you need to make returning your rental entirely hassle-free. Simply follow the 3 easy steps on the Return Instruction Card:
1. Check the tag included on the dress to verify your selected return date.
2. Place the dress(es) in the enclosed bubble-padded return envelope. There's no need to iron or clean the dress—we'll take care of any reasonable wear and tear. To return accessories without damage, please package the items back exactly the way they were sent to you. No need to return the garment bag, hangers or any special samples we send your way.
4. Drop your return envelope in any United States Postal Service blue mailbox just like a letter. Make sure to drop off your package no later than noon on your return date. If your return date falls on a Sunday or holiday, it must be postmarked first thing the following day. It is important that we receive the dress back on time so we can ensure availability to other members.

What if I misplace/lose my return shipping envelope?
We give each customer a pre-paid return envelope lined with protective bubble wrap, ready to just pop into the mailbox. If you misplace the envelope and return shipping

label, it is your responsibility to send the order back to us by the due date at your own expense.

Do I need to wash the clothes?
No. Just send everything back and we'll wash the clothes and sterilize the accessories before putting them back into rotation. Plus, we have developed a very 'green' and efficient apparel cleaning process that uses biodegradable detergents.

What if I want to keep or purchase a dress?
We only offer our dresses and accessories for rent at this time—otherwise we wouldn't be able to offer other members the experience of trying out new styles. We will host Semi-Annual Clearance Sales where you can purchase select designer styles. We will send email announcements for such sales.

Can I rent accessories alone or do I have to rent them with a dress?
You can absolutely rent accessories to update a dress that you already own and love. You don't have to rent a dress to rent accessories.

How do I add accessories to an order that I already placed?
Call us at _____ or Email us at _____ with the accessories you'd like to add to your existing order. Please contact us at least one week prior to your reservation start date so we have time to adjust the order before it ships.

How do I know my accessories are clean and sanitized?
All of the jewelry is hand cleaned at our warehouse by our jewelry specialists. Additionally, members receive alcohol wipes with all earrings and new earring backs with pierced earrings.

Can I rent some items longer and return everything else?
You must return all items you don't want to purchase together in the enclosed return bag; you will be charged for any missing pieces. Remember, you can always rent favorite pieces again.

What if I fall in love and want to buy an accessory that I rented?
If you are interested in purchasing an accessory, contact our Stylists and we will do our best to help you locate where to purchase it.

What are the beauty products?
Because no party dress is complete without the trendiest lip shade, we're excited to offer a unique selection of _____ (brand name) beauty products to the site for purchase.

How many items do you have in stock?
We have approximately _____ (12500?) rental garments on some days in stock and hundreds more available for special order. The number of available outfits may frequently vary based on previous rental reservations, alterations, cleaning, warehoused merchandise, etc. We offer a vast array of colors, styles and types of clothing all for rent.

Can members skip a month and if so, for how long?
Yes, Members can pause their membership for up to _____ (three?) months at a time by either reaching out to our Membership Experience team by email, telephone _____, or Live Chat. Select members, have exclusive access to activating the Pause feature online on their Account Settings. You must pause your membership on or before the ___ (14?) th day of each month in order to not be charged for that month.

What if I want to take a break or cancel my membership?
There is no commitment with a _____ (company name) membership, so you can pause or cancel at any time.

What Payment Options are available when renting my Wedding Gown?
The following payment options are available: Cash, Master Card, Visa, Discover Card, Checks as well as your Visa Debit Card is acceptable.
Do you offer express delivery?
Yes. Except bare-in-mind that these are available in limited style and colors.
How will I be notified when my clothes arrive?
We will notify you via email or Text message.
Do you do alterations?
Yes, professional alternations are available on-site at reasonable rates
Examples:
https://www.armoire.style/faq

7.4 Website Performance Summary

We will use web analysis tools to monitor web traffic, such as identifying the number of site visits. We will analyze customer transactions and take actions to minimize problems, such as incomplete sales and abandoned shopping carts. We will use the following table to track the performance of our website:

Category	2019 Fcst	2019 Act	2020 Fcst	2020 Act	2021 Fcst	2021 Act
No. of Members						
New Newsletter Subscribers						
Unique Visitors						
Avg. Time on Site						
Pages per Visit						
Percent New Visits						
Bounce Rate						
No. of Products						
Product Categories						
Number of Incomplete Sales						
Conversion Rate						
Affiliate Sales						
Customer Satisfaction Score						

7.5 Website Retargeting/Remarketing

Research indicates that for most websites, only 2% of web traffic converts readers on the first visit. Retargeting will keep track of people who have visited our website and displays our ads to them as they browse online. This will bring back 98% of users who don't convert right away by keeping our brand at the top of their mind. Setting up a remarketing tracking code on our website will allow us to target past visitors who did not convert or take the desired action on our site. After people have been to our website and are familiar with our brand, we will market more aggressively to this 'warm traffic.'
Resource: www.marketing360.com/remarketing-software-retargeting-ads/

8.0 Operations Plan

Operations include the business aspects of running our business, such as conducting quality assessment and improvement activities, auditing functions, cost-management analysis, and customer service. Our operations plan will present an overview of the flow of the daily activities of the rental business and the strategies that support them. It will focus on the following critical operating factors that will make the business a success:

1. We will enjoy the following advantages in the sourcing of our inventory: _____

2. We will utilize the following technological innovations in the customer relationship management (CRM) process: _____

3. We will make use of the following advantages in our distribution process: _____

4. We will develop the following in-house training program to improve worker productivity: _____

5. We will utilize the following system to better control inventory carrying costs. _____

6. We will implement the following quality control plan: _____

Quality Control Plan

Our Quality Control Plan will include a review process that checks all factors involved in our operations. The main objectives of our quality control plan will be to uncover defects and bottlenecks, and reporting to management level to make the decisions on the improvement of the whole production process. Our review process will include the following activities:

- Quality control checklist
- Structured walkthroughs
- Testing process
- Finished rental service review
- Statistical sampling

Operations Planning

We will use Microsoft Visio to develop visual maps, which will piece together the different activities in our organization and show how they contribute to the overall "value stream" of our business. We will rightfully treat operations as the lifeblood of our business. We will develop a combined sales and operations planning process where sales and operations managers will sit down every month to review sales, at the same time creating a forward-looking 12-month rolling plan to help guide the product development and manufacturing processes, which can become disconnected from sales. We will approach our operations planning using a three-step process that analyzes the company's current state, future state and the initiatives it will tackle next. For each initiative, such as launching a new product or service, the company will examine the related financials, talent and operational needs, as well as target customer profiles. Our management team will map out the cost of development and then calculate forecasted return on investment and revenue predictions.

Our Subscription Clothing Rental Process:
1. Fill out a quick profiling, styling and sizing quiz.
2. Choose the desired subscription plan, which describes the number of items shipped in each box.
3. Choose the payment plan option.
4. Fill up the assigned 'Virtual Closet Wishlist' online with desired favorite items.
5. Review the items in the pending shipment within 48 hours of it being ready and swap out anything not wanted before it ships.
6. Confirm shipment contents.
7. Wait for it to come in the mail.
8. Check shipper progress online.
9. Receive garment box in the mail
10. Open box and wear garments as long as desired.
11. Remember that no washing is required.
12. If something is 'liked' and do not want to return it, just return everything else, and be charged a discounted rate for the items kept (prices listed online).
13. Keep them all and the next months' subscription fee is waived.
14. Log in and tell them you want to keep the whole box and they will ship the next box out.
15. When done wearing all the garments and want a new batch of clothes sent, mail them back in the enclosed pre-paid envelope.
16. As soon as the return shipment barcode has been scanned at the mail drop-off location, the company is notified to ship out the next box.
17. Take online survey so company can make the necessary changes to profile and preferences.
18. Wait for email informing that the next box has been stylized
19. Swap out items as desired, confirm, and wait for the next box shipment.
20. Repeat this process until submitting a 'pause' by the month or a permanent 'cancel membership' request.
21. Take survey to supply feedback on reason(s) for cancellation.

Supply Chain Relationships

We will seek to establish good working relationships with our vendors and encourage suppliers to provide more special deals to help improve sales of products. We will also encourage our suppliers to provide merchandising/marketing ideas, lower wholesale prices and other types of promotional support.

The business will be run as a team, with each employee playing an integral part in the success or failure of the business. Employees will be given whatever tools and training is deemed necessary to carry out their assignments. An emphasis on process improvement will be instilled in each of the "teammates" by offering bonuses or special privileges. Teammates will be rewarded both monetarily and non-monetarily for jobs well done. Effective communication will be stressed in the business. This will cut down on misunderstandings and miscommunications among members, employees, and managers. Weekly meetings will be held to discuss the weekly agenda, and to give a report of last week's happenings. Teammates will be given the opportunity to add input at these meetings in the form of suggestions, comments, and complaints. Teammates will have defined tasks but are to be open to doing whatever requests outside of their set guidelines need to be done to bring success to the business. Finally, we plan to offer perks to employees to keep them satisfied and willing to give the business 100 percent.

We will consolidate the number of suppliers we deal with to reduce the volume of paperwork and realize volume discounts. We will conduct a quality improvement plan, which consists of an ongoing process of improvement activities and includes periodic samplings of activities not initiated solely in response to an identified problem. Our plan will be evaluated annually and revised as necessary. Our client satisfaction survey goal is a ___ (98.0)% satisfaction rating. We also plan to develop a list of specific interview questions and a worksheet to evaluate, compare and pre-screen potential suppliers. We will also check vendor references and their rating with the Hoovers.com.

We plan to write and maintain an Operations Manual and a Personnel Policies Handbook. The Operating Manual will be a comprehensive document outlining virtually every aspect of the business. The operating manual will include management and accounting procedures, hiring and personnel policies, and daily operations procedures, such as opening and closing the store, and how to _____. The manual will cover the following topics:

- Community Relations
- Media Relations
- Vendor Relations
- Competition Relations
- Environmental Concerns
- Intra Company Procedures
- Banking and Credit Cards
- Computer Procedures
- Quality Controls
- Open/Close Procedures
- Software Documentation
- Customer Relations
- Employee Relations
- Government Relations
- Equipment Maintenance Checklist
- Inventory Controls
- Accounting and Billing
- Financing
- Scheduling Procedures
- Safety Procedures
- Security Procedures
- Subscription Policies

We will also develop a personnel manual. Its purpose is to set fair and equal guidelines in print for all to abide. It's the playbook detailing specific policies, as well as enforcement, thereby preventing any misinterpretation, miscommunication or ill feelings. This manual will reflect only the concerns that affect our personnel. A companion policy and procedure manual will cover everything else. We plan to create the following business manuals:

	Manual Type	**Key Elements**
1.	Operations Manual	Process flowcharts
2.	Employee Manual	Benefits/Appraisals/Practices
3.	Managers Manual	Job Descriptions
4.	Customer Service Policies	Inquiry Handling Procedures

We plan to develop and install a computerized customer tracking system that will enable us to target members who are likely to have an interest in a particular type of store promotional event.

Resource:
Quickbooks Accounting System   www.quickbooks.com   www.intuit.com

9.0   Management Summary

The Management Plan will reveal who will be responsible for the various management functions to keep the business running efficiently. It will further demonstrate how that individual has the experience and/or training to accomplish each function. It will address who will do the planning function, the organizing function, the directing function, and the controlling function.

At the present time ___ (owner name) will run all operations for ____ (company name). _____ (His/Her) background in _____ (business management?) indicates an understanding of the importance of financial control systems. There is not expected to be any shortage of qualified staff from local labor pools in the market area.

_____ (owner name) will be the owner and operations manager of _____ (company name). His/her general duties will include the following:
1. Oversee the daily operations
2. Ordering inventory and supplies.
3. Develop and implementing the marketing strategy
4. Purchasing equipment.
5. Arranging for the routine maintenance and upkeep of the facility.
6. Hiring, training and supervision of new assistants.
7. Scheduling and planning of seminars and other special events.
8. Creating and pricing products and services.
9. Managing the accounting/financial aspect of the business.
10. Contract negotiation/vendor relations.

9.1 Owner Personal History

The owner has been working in the _____ industry for over ___(#) years, gaining personal knowledge and experience in all phases of the industry. ____(owner name) is the founder and operations manager of _____ (company name). The owner holds a degree from the University of _____ at _____ (city). _____ (owner name) also earned a Higher Certificate with Distinction from the ____ and a ____ degree from the _____ (organization name). He/she began his/her career as a _____ .

Over the last _ (#) years, ___ (owner name) became quite proficient in a wide range of management activities and responsibilities, becoming an operations manager for ___ (former employer name) from __ to _ (dates). There he/she was able to achieve _____. For ____ years he/she has managed a business similar to _____ (company name). _____ (His/her) duties included _____. Specifically, the owner brings _____ (#) years of experience as a ____ , as well as certification as a _____ from the _____ (National _____ Association). He/she is an experienced entrepreneur with ____ years of small business accounting, finance, marketing and management experience. Education includes college course work in business administration, banking and finance, investments, and commercial credit management. The owner will draw an annual salary of $___ from the business although most of this goes to repay loans to finance business start-up costs. These loans will be paid-in-full by _____ (month) of _____ (year).

9.2 Management Team Gaps

Despite the owner's and manager's experience in the _____ (?) industry, the company will also retain the consulting services of _____ (consultant company name). This company has over _____ (#) years of experience in the _____ industry and has successfully opened dozens of Subscription Clothing Rental Companies across the country. The Consultants will be primarily used for certification approval, market research, customer satisfaction surveys and to provide additional input in the evaluation of new business opportunities. The company also expects to retain the services of a local CPA to help the owner manage cash flow. Additionally, the business will make use of the following advisory board to provide support for strategic planning and human resource related issues.

The Board of Advisors will provide continuous mentoring support on business matters. Expertise gaps in legal, tax, marketing and personnel will be covered by the Board of Advisors. The owner will actively seek free business advice from SCORE, a national non-profit organization with a local office. This is a group of retired executives and business owners who donate their time to serve as business counselors to new business owners.

Advisory Resources Available to the Business Include:

	Name	Address	Phone
CPA/Accountant			
Attorney			
Insurance Broker			
Banker			
Additional Assistance			
Wholesale Suppliers			
Trade Association			
Realtor			
SCORE.org			
Business Consultant			
Advisors			
Other			

9.2.1 Management Matrix

Note: See appendix for attached management resumes.

Name	Title	Credentials	Functions	Responsibilities

9.2.2 Outsourcing Matrix

Company Name	Functions	Responsibilities	Cost

9.3.0 Employee Requirements

1. **Recruitment**
Experience suggests that personal referrals from contractors and manufacturer reps are an excellent source for experienced associates We will also place newspaper ads and use our Yellow Page Ad to indicate what types of staff we use and what types of members we serve. We will also make effective use of our newsletter to post positions available and contact local trade schools for possible job candidates. We will give a referral bonus to existing employees.

2. **Training and Supervision**
Training is largely accomplished through hands-on experience and by manufacturer product reps with supplemental instruction. Additional knowledge is gained through our policy and Operations Manuals and attending manufacturer and trade association seminars. We will foster professional development and independence in all phases of our business. Supervision is task-oriented and the quantity is dependent on the complexity of the job assignment. Employees are called team members because they are part of Team _____ (company name). To help them succeed and confidently handle customer questions, employees will receive assistance with our internal certification program. They will also participate in our written training modules and receive regular samples to evaluate.

3. **Salaries and Benefits**
Staff will be basically paid a salary plus commission basis on product sales. Good training and incentives, such as cash bonuses handed out monthly to everyone for reaching goals, will serve to retain good employees. An employee discount of __ percent on personal sales is offered. As business warrants, we hope to put together a benefit package that includes insurance, and paid vacations. The personnel plan also assumes a 5% annual increase in salaries. We will also set up a retirement plan for our employees. We will either roll out a SEP-IRA, SIMPLE-IRA, or a traditional 401(k).
Resource:
https://gusto.com/framework/hr/how-do-i-set-up-a-401k-for-my-company/

4. **Incentive Plan**
All employees will qualify for a quarterly bonus (equal to as much as ____ (10) % of their salary) based on several performance measures, including input from clients. In fact, ___ (40) % of the potential bonus is tied to customer feedback. Four times a year, as well as at the conclusion of major projects, management will call ___ (25) or so active clients. clients will be asked if they're satisfied with their assigned team's ability to communicate, solve problems, and respond to their needs, and, if so, would they be willing to serve as a reference? After talking to clients, the manager rates employees on a scale of one to five for each area of customer service. Dissatisfied clients are weighed more heavily.

5. **Feedback Mechanism**
   We will provide incentives for employees to provide improvement suggestions and enhance our quality, innovativeness and productivity.

9.4.0 Job Descriptions

Job Description— Operations Manager

This position plans, organizes, and directs the operations of a Subscription Clothing Rental Company. Incumbents monitor sales and inventory trends to forecast sales and maintain adequate stock levels. They order supplies, monitor and evaluate cost effectiveness and efficiency of store operations, prepare and balance daily reports and maintain and balance inventory records on a computerized point-of-sale system. Incumbents provide customer service and specialized information regarding products and policies, and procedures governing subscription issues. Incumbents utilize effective public relations to provide services to members, respond to inquiries, handle complaints or resolve problems. This position is responsible for the efficient operations of the business. Incumbents determine staffing needs, prepare work schedules, establish and implement work procedures and priorities, and recommend changes to policies. They supervise staff including hiring and training employees, assigning work, preparing and conducting performance evaluations, and handling employee problem solving issues. The operations manager must possess proven management skills, and the ability to drive operational efficiencies. Must have a passion for people development and delivering excellent customer service. Must be capable of delivering performance through their teams and drive customer service through high retail standards, availability and presentation.

Key Accountabilities:
  Exceptional customer focus.
  Excellent Interpersonal skills.
  Monitor production flows.
  Effective planning and organizational skills.
  Influencing and negotiation skills.
  Budget management
  Supportive and persuasive management style.
  Tactical and strategic planning and implementation skills are a must.
  Clear vision and a determination to succeed.

Job Description -- Chief Customer Officer

Primarily responsible for finding ways to improve the customer experience.
- Managing the conversion optimization strategy from data-driven ideation, execution of the testing and feature roadmap, reporting and analysis.
- Owning and communicating the testing roadmap that identifies testing opportunities and all pertinent information regarding those tests including hypotheses, success metrics, testing requirements, timelines, features/user stories, testing platform, etc.
- Collaborate with internal resources to execute UX design tests (legal, compliance, technology, and test and learn teams)

- Actively optimize the user journey, reporting and taking action on key metrics and KPIs, through continuous website testing and user experience improvements
- Work with end-to-end PMOs to manage all Customer Experience-led build timelines.

Job Description – Chief Revenue Officer

Responsible for finding ways to improve the revenue generating processes. Participates actively in strategic and business unit planning to develop reasonable and thorough revenue projections for annual budgets and multi-year projections.

Duties and Responsibilities:
1. Create a standardized outreach for current and future clients and coordinate its implementation across sales channels, client management, and marketing and communications.
2. Develop growth strategies.
3. Create accountability within the company by developing appropriate metrics and coordinating compensation and promotions with these metrics.
4. Prospect and close relationships with key target clients.
5. Monitor the revenue pipeline and leads, adjusting as necessary to create sustainable growth.
6. Establish both short-term results and long-term strategy, including revenue forecasting.
7. Monitor the strategies and processes across the revenue cycle from customer acquisition to engagement to success.
8. Fill management gaps by building and training individuals and teams in Sales and Account Management.
9. Develop and implement robust sales management processes – pipeline, account planning, and proposals.
10. Oversee all Channel/Partner Development -- adding new sales channels and 3rd party resellers and partners.
11. Drive a "lean startup" style environment of constant experimentation and learning.
12. Leverage customer research to provide strategic leadership for brand architecture and positioning.

Job Description – Customer Analytics Manager

Duties and Responsibilities:
Driving the consolidation, standardization and consistency of reporting and analytics.
Providing business intelligence reporting for various teams across the organization.
Daily, weekly, monthly review and updates to key performance metrics.
Simplifying complex data into easy to comprehend analysis.
Identifying and communicating anomalies in performance and proposed solutions.
Creating complex excel models, macros and reporting tools to enable timely and accurate sales alignment, reporting and analysis.
Developing reporting tools, including dashboards and visualizations, to explain business insights.

Reporting Order/Revenue Intake, Market Data, Funnel Analysis, Forecast Updates, etc.
Switching between macro and micro analysis to highlight patterns.
Challenging existing processes to further enhance and automate reporting efforts through process improvement initiatives.
Building on current reporting to provide further intelligence.
Partnering with leadership to establish performance measures and frequency of reporting.
Providing leading indicators for potential performance gaps.
Adjusting and customizing presentations for intended audience.
Creating a systematic and repeatable approach to report creation and data audits.
Ongoing data validation and quality control checks.
Managing project timelines and expectations.

Job Description – Platform Infrastructure Manager

- Manage and set priorities for the design, maintenance, development, and evaluation of all infrastructure systems, including LANs, WANs, Internet, intranet, security, wireless implementations, etc.
- Design and enforce request handling and escalation policies and procedures.
- Establish and enforce Service Desk service levels agreements in consultation with end users to establish problem resolution expectations and timeframes.
- Monitor and test fixes to ensure problems have been adequately resolved.
- Access software updates, drivers, knowledge bases, and frequently asked questions resources on the Internet to aid in problem resolution.
- Assess need for any system reconfigurations based on request trends and make recommendations.
- Practice IT asset management, including maintenance of component inventory and related documentation.
- Direct and administrate a contingent of internal and external network analysts and technicians, and where necessary, conduct performance reviews and corrective action.
- Manage the processing of incoming calls to the Service Desk via both telephone and e-mail to ensure courteous, timely, and effective resolution of end user issues.
- Design and enforce request handling and escalation policies and procedures.
- Establish and enforce Service Desk service levels agreements in consultation with end users to establish problem resolution expectations and timeframes.
- Coordinate and manage all incidents and requests at the end user workstation level, including installing and upgrading software, installing hardware, implementing file backups, and configuring systems and applications.
- Analyze performance of the Service Desk activities and documented resolutions, identify problem areas, and devise and deliver solutions to enhance quality

Job Description -- Fashion Buyers

They visit clothing, shoe and accessory manufacturers and attend trade shows in order to determine what fashion items the company will carry each season. Because of the need to stay current with trends and offer competitive pricing, the work is generally quick-paced and aggressive. Many fashion buyers travel internationally on a regular basis to foreign manufacturing sites and glamorous fashion shows. A typical fashion buyer works with clothing suppliers to make and select the proper clothing pieces for the target market. They are responsible for deciding between the current fashion trends, as well as the classic traditional pieces which sell quite well. Fashion buyers maintain good relations with suppliers, while being able to negotiate prices with them. A fashion buyer is also the one who makes sure that suppliers deliver the new stocks on time. Fashion buyers also monitor the best-selling pieces and make sure that they are always available for consumers. The median salary is 55K.

Job Description – Software Engineer

The ideal candidate is a hands-on platform builder with significant experience in developing scalable data platforms. They have experience in business intelligence, analytics, data science and data products. They have strong, firsthand technical expertise in a variety of configuration management and big data technologies and the proven ability to fashion robust scalable solutions that can manage large data sets. They must be at ease working in an agile environment with little supervision. They are driven by a passion for continuous improvement and test-driven development.

Responsibilities for Software Engineer
- Analyze, design and develop tests and test-automation suites.
- Design and develop a processing platform using various configuration management technologies.
- Test software development methodology in an agile environment.
- Provide ongoing maintenance, support and enhancements in existing systems and platforms.
- Collaborate cross-functionally with data scientists, business users, project managers and other engineers to achieve elegant solutions.
- Provide recommendations for continuous improvement.
- Work alongside other engineers on the team to elevate technology and consistently apply best practices.

Job Description – Marketing Manager

Primary Duties and Responsibilities:
1. Lead generation for new customer sales.
2. Portfolio management for all the company offers.
3. Customer analytics that inform offer development and offer success.
4. Creates a pipeline of well-educated prospects for the self-service website and land sales channels to work against.
5. Responsible for educating existing subscribers on the newly acquired products and service-driven capabilities they should consider getting involved with.
6. Focused on acquiring new customers and selling new offer types.

Job Description – Customer Success Manager

Responsible for customer adoption, cost-effective renewals and account expansion.
- Drive adoption of our offerings by the customer.
- Provides customization assistance.
- Manage the on-boarding experience for customers.
- Become the internal voice of the customer.

- Take ownership for each customer's success and ROI with our services.
- Proactively consult to fully understand their needs and actively solve pain points.
- Build strong trust-based relationships with users and customer sponsors.
- Respond quickly to customer-submitted questions and requests.
- Maintain portfolio and monitoring analytics, reports and KPIs.
- Create internal and customer-facing reports.
- Solicit references, referrals and testimonials from customers.
- Collaborate internally with product, marketing and sales teams to communicate customer needs to design ideal offering/features.
- Manage the customer renewal process and identify up sell opportunities.

Job Description – Service Account Specialists
Responsible for servicing customer inquiries and achieving subscription renewals from existing customers.

Job Description -- Seamstresses
Used to repair garments between rentals.
Completes proper packaging of all special orders.
Conducts proper and safe use of all equipment.
Ability to safely operate all sewing equipment.
Ability to reach, stoop, bend, and lift as needed to stock or pull product for processing.
Other duties and responsibilities may be added to meet business demands.

Job Description – Style or Fashion Consultants
Personal stylists work with individuals, groups, classes or companies to educate members about general fashion apparel and accessories. Consultants make an evaluation of their client's physical attributes, lifestyle, and fashion style in order to make recommendations on which fashion choices will help the client achieve and maintain their desired image. Personal stylists may often shop for their members and pick out items that suit their image.
Duties and Responsibilities:
Advise customers and clients in making fashion decisions.
Make recommendations on individual pieces, entire outfits, color palettes, styles and fabrics.
Listen to the customer's needs and understand each individual client to personalize and tailor suggestions to the client's aesthetic preferences and personal style, body type, price range and the occasion for which the customer is dressing.
Work for a company as a customer service and sales representative to help sell additional merchandise, increasing overall customer satisfaction and company profit.
Remains up-to-date with marketplace trends and current fashions while maintaining a timeless knowledge of fashion principles.
Analyze seasonal trends and implement them into their client's new recommendations.

9.4.1   Job Description Format
Our job descriptions will adhere to the following format guidelines:
1.   Job Title   2.   Reports to:

3. Pay Rate
4. Job Responsibilities
5. Travel Requirements
5. Supervisory Responsibilities
6. Qualifications
7. Work Experience
8. Required Skills
10. Salary Range
11. Benefits
12. Opportunities

9.5 Personnel Plan
1. We will develop a system for recruiting, screening and interviewing employees.
2. Background checks will be performed as well as reference checks and drug tests.
3. We will develop an assistant training course.
4. We will keep track of staff scheduling.
5. We will develop client satisfaction surveys to provide feedback and ideas.
6. We will develop and perform semi-annual employee evaluations.
7. We will "coach" all our employees to improve their abilities and range of skills.
8. We will employ temporary employees via a local staffing agency to assist with one-time special projects.
9. Each employee will be provided an Employee Handbook, which will include detailed job descriptions and list of business policies, and be asked to sign these documents as a form of employment contract.
10. Incentives will be offered for reaching quarterly financial and enrollment goals, completing the probationary period and passing county inspections.
11. Customer service awards will be presented to those employees who best exemplify our stated mission and exceed customer expectations.

Our Employee Handbook will include the following sections:
1. Overview
2. Introduction to the Company
3. Organizational Structure
4. Employment and Hiring Policies
5. Performance Evaluation and Promotion Policies
6. Compensation Policies
7. Time Off Policies
8. Training Programs and Reimbursement Policies
9. General Rules and Policies
10. Termination Policies.

9.6 Staffing Plan
The following table summarizes our personnel expenditures for the first three years, with compensation costs increasing from $____ in the first year to about $_____ in the third year, based on ____ (5?) % payroll increases each year. The payroll includes tuition reimbursement, pay increases, vacation pay, bonuses and state required certifications.

_____ (company name) will have a sales force that includes the owner and ____ (#) _____ (part-time/full-time) employees. The store will have ____ (#) sales associates in the store on weekdays, and ____ (#) associates in the store on weekends. Sales associates will be paid an hourly wage. In years two and three, the sales associates' hours will increase to accommodate the planned increase in sales; thus, the wages in years two and three increase significantly. The owner, ___, will not be paid a salary, but will take distributions from the company profits while maintaining a positive cash balance. The financials in this plan do not yet include the owner's draw.

Table: Personnel Plan

	Number of Employees	Hourly Rate	2019	2020	2021
Owner/Director					
Operations Manager					
Assistant Manager					
Chief Customer Officer					
Chief Revenue Officer					
Customer Success Manager					
Customer Analytics Manager					
Platform Infrastructure Mgr.					
Fashion Buyers					
Service Account Specialists					
Sales Associates					
Style Consultants					
Seamstresses					
Software Engineers					
F/T Stock/Deliver					
Marketing Manager					
Bookkeeper					
P/T Janitor					
Other					
Total People: Headcount					
Total Annual Payroll					
Payroll Burden (Fringe Benefits)		(+)			
Total Payroll Expense		(=)			

10.0 Risk Factors

Risk management is the identification, assessment, and prioritization of risks, followed by the coordinated and economical application of resources to minimize, monitor, and control the probability and/or impact of unfortunate events or to maximize the realization of opportunities. For the most part, our risk management methods will consist of the following elements, performed, more or less, in the following order.
1. Identify, characterize, and assess threats
2. Assess the vulnerability of critical assets to specific threats
3. Determine the risk (i.e. the expected consequences of specific types of attacks on

specific assets)
4. Identify ways to reduce those risks
5. Prioritize risk reduction measures based on a strategy

Types of Risks:

_____ (company name) faces the following kinds of risks:

1. Financial Risks

Our quarterly revenues and operating results are difficult to predict and may fluctuate significantly from quarter to quarter as a result of a variety of factors. Among these factors are:
- Changes in our own or competitors' pricing policies.
- A downturn in the local economy, resulting in less disposable income available to our target markets.
- Fluctuations in expected revenues from advertisers, sponsors and strategic relationships.
- Timing of costs related to acquisitions or payments.

2. Legislative / Legal Landscape.

Our participation in the fashion arena presents unique risks:
- Product and other related liability.
- Federal and State regulations on licensing, privacy and insurance.

3. Operational Risks

For the past __ (#) years the owner has been dealing with computers, so he is comfortable with technology and understands a wide array of software applications. However, the biggest potential problem will be equipment malfunction and software virus attacks. To minimize the potential for problems, the owner will be taking equipment repair and virus removal training and will learn basic troubleshooting techniques. Beyond that, we have identified a service technician who is located close-by.

To attract and retain client to the _____ (company name) community, we must continue to provide differentiated and quality services. This confers certain risks including the failure to:
- Anticipate and respond to consumer preferences for partnerships and service.
- Attract, excite and retain a large audience of members to our community.
- Create and maintain successful strategic alliances with quality partners.
- Deliver high quality, customer service.
- Build our brand rapidly and cost-effectively.
- Compete effectively against better-established Dress Rental Companies.
- Problems generating visibility and product positioning.

4.   Worst case scenarios would include:
- Determining that the business cannot support itself on an ongoing basis.
- Having to liquidate assets to cover liabilities.

5.   Human Resource Risks

The most serious human resource risk to our business, at least in the initial stages, would be my inability to operate the business due to illness or disability. The owner is currently in exceptional health and would eventually seek to replace himself on a day-to-day level by developing systems and a management team to support the growth of the business.

6.   Marketing Risks

Advertising is our most expensive form of promotion and there will be a period of testing headlines and offers to find the one that works the best. The risk, of course, is that we will exhaust our advertising budget before we find an ad that works. Placing greater emphases on sunk-cost marketing, such as on existing referral relationships through direct selling will minimize our initial reliance on advertising to bring in a large percentage of business in the first year.

7.   Business Risks

A major risk to retail service businesses is the performance of the economy and the small business sector. Since economists are predicting subscription rentals as the fastest growing sector of the economy, our risk of a downturn in the short-term is minimized. The entrance of one of the major clothing retail chains into our marketplace is a risk. They offer more software driven personalization, provide a wider array of garments and accessories, competitive rental prices and faster turnaround service. This situation would force us to lower our prices in the short-term until we could develop an offering of higher margin, value-added services not provided by the large chains. It does not seem likely that the relative size of our market today could support the overhead of these other operators. Projections indicate that this will not be the case in the future and that leaves a window of opportunity for ___ (company name) to aggressively build a loyal client base. We will also not pursue big-leap, radical change misadventures, but rather strive to hit stepwise performance benchmarks, with a planned and controlled consistency over a long period of time.

To combat the usual start-up risks we will do the following:
1. Utilize our industry experience to quickly establish desired strategic relationships.
2. Pursue business outside of our immediate market area.
3. Diversify our range of packaged product and service offerings.
4. Develop multiple sales distribution channels.
5. Monitor our competitor actions.
6. Stay in touch with our members and suppliers.
7. Watch for fashion trends which could potentially impact our business.
8. Continuously optimize and scrutinize all business processes.

9. Institute daily financial controls using Business Ratio Analysis.
10. Create pay-for-performance compensation and training programs to reduce employee turnover.

Further, to attract and retain members the Company will need to continue to expand its market offerings, utilizing third party strategic relationships. This could lead to difficulties in the management of relationships, competition for specific services and products, and/or adverse market conditions affecting a particular partner.
The Company will take active steps to mitigate risks. In preparation of the Company's pricing, many factors will be considered. The Company will closely track the activities of all third parties and will hold monthly review meetings to resolve issues and review and update the terms associated with strategic alliances.

Additionally, we will develop the following kinds of contingency plans:
Disaster Recovery Plan
Business Continuity Plan
Business Impact and Gap Analysis
Testing & Maintenance

The Company will utilize marketing and advertising campaigns to promote brand identity and will coordinate all expectations with internal and third-party resources prior to release. This strategy should maximize customer satisfaction while minimizing potential costs associated with unplanned expenditures and quality control issues.

10.1 Business Risk Reduction Strategy

We plan to implement the following strategies to reduce our start-up business risk:
1. Implement our business plan based on go, no-go stage criteria.
2. Develop employee cross-training programs.
3. Regularly back-up all computer files/Install ant-virus software.
4. Arrange adequate insurance coverage with higher deductibles.
5. Develop a limited number of prototype samples.
6. Test market offerings to determine level of market demand and appropriate pricing strategy.
7. Thoroughly investigate and benchmark to competitor offerings.
8. Research similar franchised businesses for insights into successful prototype business/operations models.
9. Reduce operation risks by flowcharting all structured systems.
10. Use market surveys to listen to customer needs and priorities.
11. Purchase used equipment to reduce capital outlays.
12. Use leasing to reduce financial risk.
13. Outsource manufacturing to job shops to reduce capital at risk.
14. Use subcontractors to limit fixed overhead salary expenses.
15. Ask manufacturers about profit sharing arrangements.
16. Pay advertisers with a percent of revenues generated.
17. Develop contingency plans for identified risks.

18. Set-up procedures to control employee theft.
19. Do criminal background checks on potential employees.
20. Take immediate action on delinquent accounts.
21. Only extend credit to established account with D&B rating
22. Get regular competitive bids from alternative suppliers.
23. Check that operating costs as a percent of rising sales are lower as a result of productivity improvements.
24. Request bulk rate pricing on fast moving supplies.
25. Don't tie up cash in slow moving inventory to qualify for bigger discounts.
26. Reduce financial risk by practicing cash flow policies.
27. Reduce hazard risk by installing safety procedures.
28. Use financial management ratios to monitor business vitals.
29. Make business decisions after brainstorming sessions.
30. Focus on the products with biggest return on investment.
31. Where possible, purchase off-the-shelf components.
32. Request manufacturer samples and assistance to build prototypes.
33. Design production facilities to be flexible and easy to change.
34. Develop a network of suppliers with outsourcing capabilities.
35. Analyze and shorten every cycle time, including product development.
36. Develop multiple sources for every important input.
37. Treat the business plan as a living document and update it frequently.
38. Conduct a SWOT analysis and use determined strengths to pursue opportunities.
39. Conduct regular customer satisfaction surveys to evaluate performance.

10.2   Reduce Customer Perceived Risk Tactics

We will utilize the following tactics to help reduce the new customer's perceived risk of starting to do business with our company.

Status

1. Publish a page of testimonials. _____
2. Secure Opinion Leader written endorsements. _____
3. Offer an Unconditional Satisfaction Money Back Guarantee. _____
4. Long-term Performance Guarantee (Financial Risk). _____
5. Guaranteed Buy Back (Obsolete time risk) _____
6. Offer free trials and samples. _____
7. Brand Image (consistent marketing image and performance) _____
8. Patents/Trademarks/Copyrights _____
9. Publish case studies _____
10. Share your expertise (Articles, Seminars, etc.) _____
11. Get recognized Certification _____
12. Conduct responsive customer service _____
13. Accept Installment Payments _____
14. Display product materials composition or ingredients. _____
15. Publish product test results. _____
16. Publish sales record milestones. _____
17. Foster word-of-mouth by offering an unexpected extra. _____

18. Distribute factual, pre-purchase info. _____
19. Reduce consumer search costs with online directories. _____
20. Reduce customer transaction costs. _____
21. Facilitate in-depth comparisons to alternative services. _____
22. Make available prior customer ratings and comments. _____
23. Provide customized info based on prior transactions. _____
24. Become an Accredited Better Business Bureau member. _____
25. Publish overall customer satisfaction survey results. _____
26. Offer plan options that match niche segment needs. _____
27. Require client sign-off before proceeding to next phase. _____
28. Document procedures for dispute resolution. _____
29. Offer the equivalent of open source code. _____
30. Stress your compatibility features (avoid lock-in fear). _____
31. Create detailed checklists & flowcharts to show processes _____
32. Publish a list of frequently asked questions/answers. _____
33. Create a community that enables members to connect with each other and share common interests. _____
34. Inform members as to your stay-in-touch methods. _____
35. Conduct and handover a detailed needs analysis worksheet. _____
36. Offer to pay all return shipping charges and/or refund all original shipping and handling fees. _____
37. Describe your product testing procedures prior to shipping. _____
38. Highlight your competitive advantages in all marketing materials. _____

11.0   Financial Plan

About _____ (50%-70) % of sales are projected as credit card sales, in-line with actual experience of retail stores in _____ (city). Credit card collection is typically short, and this plan assumes a one-day collection time. Distributors terms are 30 days, although substantial discounts can be secured with earlier payments. The long-term interest rate basis is the current SBA guideline of prime plus _____ (2.25?) % for a _____ (seven) year loan. The short-term interest rate basis is the fed funds rate plus _____ (2.5?) %

Manufacturers and distributors reward volume purchases with lower costs. The company plans to take advantage of volume discounts and will pass along these savings to consumers in the form of sales and special rental promotions to stimulate loyalty and further growth. Gross margins will be maintained in the _____ (30-33)% range, which would put our business in-line with the competition in the _____ (city) metro area.

The over-all financial plan for growth allows for use of the significant cash flow generated by operations. We are basing projected sales on the market research, industry analysis and competitive environment. ___ (company name) expects a profit margin of over __ % starting with year one. By year two, that number should slowly increase as the law of diminishing costs takes hold, and the day-to-day activities of the business become

less expensive. Sales are expected to grow at __% per year, and level off by year _____.
Our financial statements will show consistent growth in earnings, which provides notice of the durability of our company's competitive advantage.

The initial investment in _____ (company name) will be provided by _____ (owner name) in the amount of $ _____. The owner will also seek a ___ (#) year bank loan in the amount of $ _____ to provide the remainder of the required initial funding. The funds will be used to renovate the space and to cover initial operating expenses. The owner financing will become a return on equity, paid in the form of dividends to the owner. We expect to finance steady growth through cash flow. The owners do not intend to take any profits out of the business until the long-term debt has been satisfied.

Our financial plan includes:
Moderate growth rate with a steady cash flow.
Investing residual profits into company expansion.
Company expansion will be an option if sales projections are met.
Marketing costs will remain below ___ (5?) % of sales.
Repayment of our loan calculated at a high A.P.R. of ___ (10?) percent and at a
     5-year-payback on our $_____ loan.

11.1   Important Assumptions

Since this is a start-up operation, a steady increase in sales is forecast over three years, as consumer awareness and regular repeat business grows with a strong and consistent increase in the local population, from an initial _____ residents to about _____ residents upon completion. A solid business plan and the management skills and experience of the managing partners should be sufficient to orchestrate the necessary growth to make this a successful launch with steady increases in sales over the first three years.

Operating expenses are based on an assessment of operational needs for a store of this size. Observations of _____ (city) retail Subscription Clothing Rental Company staffing, direct experience at ___ stores, and interviews with store owners and suppliers are the basis for these projections. Rent is based on negotiated lease agreement with the landlord. Other estimates are based on experience in operating a __ square foot ___(city) storefront business, and on vendor quotes and estimates. Collection days should remain fairly short, given the substantial cash revenues, and standard credit card collection periods.

Financial Plan Assumptions

1. All operating costs are based on the management's research of similar operating companies.
2. Automated informational systems will reduce the staff requirements.
3. Developmental start-up costs are amortized over a five-year period.
4. Home office or other apartment expenses are not included.
5. Overhead and operations costs are calculated on an annual basis.
6. The founders' salary is based on a fixed monthly salary expense basis.
7. All fixed and variable labor costs are scheduled to rise annually at ___ (5?) percent.
8. All revenues are figured to rise annually at ___ (10?) percent.
9. Administrative and office expenses rise at an annual rate of 2.5 percent.
10. Operating costs increase at ___ (5) percent annually.
11. Loan amount interest rate at ____ (10) percent.

Other Assumptions:

1. The economy will grow at a steady slow pace, without another major recession.
2. There will be no major changes in the industry, other than those discussed in the trends section of this document.
3. The State will not enact 'impact' legislation on our industry.
4. Sales are estimated at minimum to average values, while expenses are estimated at above average to maximum values.
5. Staffing and payroll expansions will be driven by increased sales.
6. Materials expenses will not increase dramatically over the next several years, but will grow at a rate that matches increasing consumption.
7. We assume access to equity capital and financing sufficient to maintain our financial plan as shown in the tables.
8. The amount of the financing needed from the bank will be approximately $_____ and this will be repaid over the next 10 years at $_____ per month.
9. We assume that the area will continue to grow at present rate of ___ % per year.
10. Interest rates and tax rates are based on conservative assumptions.

Revenue Assumptions:

	Year	Sales/Month	Growth Rate
1.			
2.			
3.			

Resource:
www.score.org/resources/business-plans-financial-statements-template-gallery

11.2 Break-even Analysis

Break-Even Analysis will be performed to determine the point at which revenue received equals the costs associated with generating the revenue. Break-even analysis calculates what is known as a margin of safety, the amount that revenues exceed the break-even point. This is the amount that revenues can fall while still staying above the break-even point. The two main purposes of using the break-even analysis for marketing is to (1) determine the minimum number of sales that is required to avoid a loss at a designated sales price and (2) it is an exercise tool so that you can tweak the sales price to determine the minimum volume of sales you can reasonably expect to sell in order to avoid a loss.

Definition: Break-Even Is the Volume Where All Fixed Expenses Are Covered.
Three important definitions used in break-even analysis are:
- **Variable Costs** (Expenses) are costs that change directly in proportion to changes in activity (volume), such as raw materials, labor and packaging.
- **Fixed Costs** (Expenses) are costs that remain constant (fixed) for a given time period despite wide fluctuations in activity (volume), such as rent, loan payments, insurance, payroll and utilities.
- **Unit Contribution Margin** is the difference between your product's unit selling price and its unit variable cost.
  Unit Contribution Margin = Unit Sales Price - Unit Variable Cost

For the purposes of this breakeven analysis, the assumed fixed operating costs will be approximately $ _____ per month, as shown in the following table.

Averaged Monthly Fixed Costs:		**Variable Costs:**	
Payroll	_____	Cost of Inventory Sold	_____
Rent	_____	Labor	_____
Insurance	_____	Supplies	_____
Utilities	_____	Direct Costs per Patient	_____
Security.	_____	Other	_____
Legal/Technical Help	_____		
Other	_____		
Total:	_____	Total	_____

A break-even analysis table has been completed on the basis of average costs/prices. With monthly fixed costs averaging $___, $____ in average sales and $_____ in average variable costs, we need approximately $____ in sales per month to break-even. Based on our assumed ___ % variable cost, we estimate our breakeven sales volume at around $ _____ per month. We expect to reach that sales volume by our _____ month of operations. Our break-even analysis is shown in further detail in the following table.

Breakeven Formulas:
Break Even Units = Total Fixed Costs / (Unit Selling Price - Variable Unit Cost)
_____ = _____ / (_____ - _____)

·**BE Dollars = (Total Fixed Costs / (Unit Price – Variable Unit Costs))/ Unit Price**
_____ = (_____ / (_____ - _____)) / _____

·**BE Sales = Annual Fixed Costs / (1- Unit Variable costs / Unit Sales Price)**

_____ = _____ / (1 - _____ / _____)

Table: Break-even Analysis

Monthly Units Break-even   _____
Monthly Revenue Break-even $ _____
Assumptions:
Average Per-Unit Revenue $ _____
Average Per-Unit Variable Cost $ _____
Estimated monthly Fixed Cost $ _____

Ways to Improve Breakeven Point:
1. Reduce Fixed Costs via Cost Controls
2. Raise unit sales prices.
3. Lower Variable Costs by improving employee productivity or getting lower competitive bids from suppliers.
4. Broaden designer lines to generate multiple revenue streams.

11.3 Projected Profit and Loss

Pro forma income statements are an important tool for planning our future business operations. If the projections predict a downturn in profitability, we can make operational changes such as increasing prices or decreasing costs before these projections become reality.

We expect losses in the first year, because it will take time for the store to build momentum and generate traffic. However, once sales increase, the results are positive because many of the other expenses will remain fixed. In fact, we expect that sample inventory costs will actually go down in years to come. Some designers will provide sample inventory at deep discounts and/or provide the samples free of charge once good credit terms are established. As a result, the annual expenditures for sample inventory should decrease. Our monthly profit for the first year varies significantly, as we aggressively seek improvements and begin to implement our marketing plan. However, after the first ___ months, profitability should be established.

We predict advertising costs will go down in the next three years as word-of-mouth about our Subscription Clothing Rental Company gets out to the public and we are able to find what has worked well for us and concentrate on those advertising methods, and corporate affiliations generate sales without the need for extra advertising. Our net profit/sales ratio will be low the first year. We expect this ratio to rise at least ___ (15?) percent the second year. Normally, a startup concern will operate with negative profits through the first two years. We will avoid that kind of operating loss on our second year by knowing our competitors and having a full understanding of our target markets.

Our projected profit and loss is indicated in the following table. From our research of the fashion industry, our annual projections are quite realistic and conservative, and we prefer this approach so that we can ensure an adequate cash flow.

Key P & L Formulas:
Gross Profit Margin = Total Sales Revenue - Cost of Goods Sold
Gross Margin % = (Total Sales Revenue - Cost of Goods Sold) / Total Sales Revenue
This number represents the proportion of each dollar of revenue that the company retains as gross profit.
EBITDA =Revenue - Expenses (exclude interest, taxes, depreciation & amortization)
PBIT = Profit (Earnings) Before Interest and Taxes = EBIT
A profitability measure that looks at a company's profits before the company has to pay corporate income tax and interest expenses. This measure deducts all operating expenses from revenue, but it leaves out the payment of interest and tax. Also referred to as "earnings before interest and tax ".
Net Profit = Total Sales Revenues - Total Expenses

Pro Forma Profit and Loss

	Formula	2019	2020	2021
Gross Revenue:				
Registration Fees				
Clothing Rentals				
Clothing Sales				
Other Accessories Sales				
Style Consulting Fees				
Other Revenue				
Total Revenue	A			
Cost of Sales				
Cost of Goods Sold				
Other				
Total Costs of Sales	D			
Gross Margin	A-D=E			
Gross Margin %	E / A			
Operating Expenses:				
Payroll				
Payroll Taxes				
Sales & Marketing				
Conventions/Trade Shows				
Depreciation				
License/Permit Fees				
Dues and Subscriptions				
Rent				
Utilities				
Deposits				

Repairs and Maintenance
Janitorial Supplies
Office Supplies
Leased Equipment
Buildout Costs
Insurance
Location Rental
Van Expenses
Software Maintenance
Professional Development
Resource Library
Merchant Fees
Bad Debts
Miscellaneous
Total Operating Expenses   F

Profit Before Int. & Taxes   E - F = G
Interest Expenses   H
Taxes Incurred   I
Net Profit   G - H - I = J
Net Profit / Sales   J / A = K

11.3.1 Proposed Subscription Income Statement

Annual Recurring Revenue (ARR)
ARR = Starting ARR + New ACV – Churn = Ending ARR
Growth Expense = Sales & Marketing Expenses
Growth Efficiency Index
GEI = Sales & Marketing Expenses / New Annual Contract Value (ACV)
Recurring Profit Margin
RPM = Starting ARR – COGS – G&A – R&D) / Starting ARR
Notes:
Annual Recurring Revenue (ARR) is used almost exclusively in B2B subscription businesses. ARR = 12 x MRR.

Monthly Recurring Revenue (MRR) is used exclusively in B2C and is the most popular for B2B subscription businesses as well.
Source:
www.slideshare.net/Zuora/saas-business-model-and-operating-plan/37-Extra_slides37
www.saasoptics.com/saaspedia/arr

11.3.2 Subscription Income Statement Worksheet

	Formula	Example	Actual
ARR	A	60,000	

Churn	B	-7,000	_____
Net ARR	A - B = C	53,000	_____
Cost of Subscription Revenue	D	11,985	_____
Research & Development	E	10,149	_____
General & Admin	F	15,122	_____
Recurring Expenses	D+E+F = G	37,256	_____
Recurring Profit	C – G = H	15,744	_____
Recurring Profit Margin	H / A = I	26.2%	_____
Growth Expense	J	45,773	_____
Growth Efficiency Index (GEI)		0.9	_____
Net New ARR	J / (GEI) = K	50,859	_____
Ending ARR	C + K = L	103,859	_____

11.4 Projected Cash Flow

The Cash Flow Statement shows how the company is paying for its operations and future growth, by detailing the "flow" of cash between the company and the outside world. Positive numbers represent cash flowing in, negative numbers represent cash flowing out. We are positioning ourselves in the market as a medium-risk concern with steady cash flows. Accounts payable is paid at the end of each month while sales are in cash and short-term credit card collectibles. Cash balances will be used to reduce outstanding line of credit balances or will be invested in a low-risk liquid money market fund to decrease the opportunity cost of cash held. Surplus cash balances during the critical first year of operations will function as protection against unforeseen changes in the timing of disbursements required to fund operations.

The cash flow of _____ (company name) is somewhat unique. For items that are sold off the floor, the cash flow and revenue recognition is traditional, in that full payment is received at the time of the sale, and the customer takes possession of the item at that time. This is how most of the shoe sales will take place, as well as some of the other accessory purchases. However, most of the other items in the store have a different flow. Let's use a dress as an example. The customer will try on a sample in the store, and when she decides to purchase the item, she will most likely have to order it in the size and color of her choosing. For this process to begin, the customer must provide a deposit of at least 50% of the total price of the item (note: while some members may choose to pay the full amount at the time the order is placed, these illustrations assume that everyone will choose the 50% option). The remaining balance will be due within thirty days of when the item arrives in our store. This timing issue has also been taken into consideration for the costs of goods sold. The store will be billed for items when the items are shipped, thus cash outflow for the cost of the item will closely match the cash inflow of the customer paying the balance on the item.

The first year's monthly cash flows are will vary significantly, but we do expect a solid cash balance from day one. We expect that the majority of our sales will be done in cash or by credit card and that will be good for our cash flow position. Additionally, we will stock only slightly more than one month's inventory at any time. Consequently, we do not anticipate any problems with cash flow, once we have obtained sufficient start-up funds. A __ year commercial loan in the amount of $_____, sought by the owner will be used to cover our working capital requirement. Our projected cash flow is summarized in the following table and is expected to meet our needs. In the following years, excess cash will be used to finance our growth plans.

Cash Flow Management:
We will use the following practices to improve our cash flow position:
1. Perform credit checks and become more selective when granting credit.
2. Seek deposits or multiple stage payments.
3. Reduce the amount/time of credit given to members.
4. Reduce direct and indirect costs and overhead expenses.
5. Use the 80/20 rule to manage inventories, receivables and payables.
6. Invoice as soon as the project has been completed.
7. Generate regular reports on receivable ratios and aging.
8. Establish and adhere to sound credit practices.
9. Use more pro-active collection techniques.
10. Add late payment fees where possible.
11. Increase the credit taken from suppliers.
12. Negotiate purchase prices and extended credit terms from vendors.
13. Use some barter arrangements to acquire goods and service.
14. Use leasing to gain access to the use of productive assets.
15. Covert debt into equity.
16. Regularly update cash flow forecasts.
17. Defer projects which cannot achieve acceptable cash paybacks.
18. Require a 50% deposit upon the signing of the contract and the balance in full, due five days before the event.
19. Speed-up the completion of projects to get paid faster.
20. Ask for extended credit terms from major suppliers.
21. Put ideal bank balances into interest-bearing (sweep) accounts.
22. Charge interest on client installment payments.
23. Check the accuracy of invoices to avoid unnecessary rework delays.
24. Include stop-work clauses in contracts to address delinquent payments.

Cash Flow Formulas:
Net Cash Flow = Incoming Cash Receipts - Outgoing Cash Payments
Equivalently, net profit plus amounts charged off for depreciation, depletion, and amortization. (also called cash flow).
Cash Balance = Opening Cash Balance + Net Cash Flow
We are positioning ourselves in the market as a medium risk concern with steady cash flows. Accounts payable is paid at the end of each month, while sales are in cash, giving our company an excellent cash structure.

Pro Forma Cash Flow

	Formula	**2019**	**2020**	**2021**

Cash Received
Cash from Operations
Cash Sales   A   _____
Cash from Receivables   B   _____
Subtotal Cash from Operations   A + B = C   _____

Additional Cash Received
Non-Operating (Other) Income   _____
Sales Tax, VAT, HST/GST Received   _____
New Current Borrowing   _____
New Other Liabilities (interest fee)   _____
New Long-term Liabilities   _____
Sales of Other Current Assets   _____
Sales of Long-term Assets   _____
New Investment Received   _____
Total Additional Cash Received   D   _____
Subtotal Cash Received   C + D = E   _____

Expenditures
Expenditures from Operations
Cash Spending   F   _____
Payment of Accounts Payable   G   _____
Subtotal Spent on Operations   F + G = H   _____
Additional Cash Spent
Non-Operating (Other) Expenses   _____
Sales Tax, VAT, HST/GST Paid Out   _____
Principal Repayment Current Borrowing   _____
Other Liabilities Principal Repayment   _____
Long-term Liabilities Principal Repayment   _____
Purchase Other Current Assets   _____
Dividends   _____
Total Additional Cash Spent   I   _____
Subtotal Cash Spent   H + I = J   _____
Net Cash Flow   E - J = K   _____
Cash Balance   _____

11.5   Projected Balance Sheet

Pro forma Balance Sheets are used to project how the business will be managing its assets in the future. As a pure start-up business, the opening balance sheet may contain no values. As the business grows, our investment in inventory increases. This reflects sales volume increases and the commensurate ability to secure favorable volume discount terms with our distributors. The projected accounts receivable position is relatively low and steady due to the nature of the business, in which up to _____ (50) % of our sales are cash, and the balance are consumer credit card purchases. No other consumer credit terms are envisioned or necessary for the operation of this business.

Capital assets of $_____ are comprised of a quoted $_____ for the build-out of the store (depreciating straight line over the 15 year term of the lease), $_____ for start-up costs (amortized over five years), and $_____ for the landlord's security deposit (about eight months' rent). Long-term liabilities are projected to decrease steadily, reflecting re-payment of the original seven-year term loan required to finance the business. It is important to note that part of the retained earnings may become a distribution of capital to the owners, while the balance would be reinvested in the business to replenish depreciated assets and to support further growth. **Note**: The projected balance sheets must link back into the projected income statements and cash flow projections.

_____ (company name) does not project any real trouble meeting its debt obligations, provided the revenue predictions are met. We are very confident that we will meet or exceed all our objectives in the Business Plan and produce a slow but steady increase in net worth. All our tables will be updated monthly to reflect past performance and future assumptions. Future assumptions will not be based on past performance but rather on economic cycle activity, regional industry strength, and future cash flow possibilities. We expect a solid growth in net worth by the year _____.

The Balance Sheet table for fiscal years 2019, 2020, and 2021 follows. It shows managed but sufficient growth of net worth, and a sufficiently healthy financial position.
Excel Resource:
www.unioncity.org/ED/Finance%20Tools/Projected%20Balance%20Sheet.xls

Key Formulas:

Paid-in Capital = Capital contributed to the corporation by investors on top of the par value of the capital stock.
Retained Earnings = The portion of net income which is retained by the corporation and used to grow its net worth, rather than distributed to the owners as dividends.
Retained Earnings = After-tax net earnings - (Dividends + Stock Buybacks)
Earnings = Revenues - (Cost of Sales + Operating Expenses + Taxes)
Net Worth = Total Assets - Total Liabilities
Also known as 'Owner's Equity'.

Pro Forma Balance Sheet

	Formulas	2019	2020	2021
Assets				
Current Assets				
Cash				
Accounts Receivable				
Inventory				
Other Current Assets				
Total Current Assets	A			

Long-term Assets
Long-term Assets   B   _____
Accumulated Depreciation   C   _____
Total Long-term Assets   B - C = D   _____
Total Assets   **A + D = E**   _____

Liabilities and Capital
Current Liabilities
Accounts Payable   _____
Current Borrowing   _____
Other Current Liabilities   _____
Subtotal Current Liabilities   **F**   _____

Long-term Liabilities
Notes Payable   _____
Other Long-term Liabilities   _____
Subtotal Long-term Liabilities   **G**   _____
Total Liabilities   **F + G = H**   _____

Capital
Paid-in Capital   I   _____
Retained Earnings   J   _____
Earnings   K   _____
Total Capital   I - J + K = L   _____
Total Liabilities and Capital   **H + L = M**   _____
Net Worth   **E - H = N**   _____

11.6 Business Ratios

The following table provides significant ratios for the personal services industry. The final column, Industry Profile, shows ratios for this industry as it is determined by the Standard Industrial Classification, SIC 5621, for comparison purposes. Our comparisons to the SIC Industry profile are very favorable and we expect to maintain healthy ratios for profitability, risk and return.

Key Business Ratio Formulas:

EBIT = Earnings Before Interest and Taxes
EBITA = Earnings Before Interest, Taxes & Amortization. (Operating Profit Margin)
Sales Growth Rate =((Current Year Sales - Last Year Sales)/(Last Year Sales)) x 100
Ex: Percent of Sales = (Advertising Expense / Sales) x 100
Net Worth = Total Assets - Total Liabilities
Acid Test Ratio = Liquid Assets / Current Liabilities
Measures how much money business has immediately available. A ratio of 2:1 is good.
Net Profit Margin = Net Profit / Net Revenues
The higher the net profit margin is, the more effective the company is at converting

revenue into actual profit.

Return on Equity (ROE) = Net Income / Shareholder's Equity
The ROE is useful for comparing the profitability of a company to that of other firms in the same industry. Also known as "return on net worth" (RONW).

Debt to Shareholder's Equity = Total Liabilities / Shareholder's Equity
A ratio below 0.80 indicates there is a good chance the company has a durable competitive advantage, with the exception of financial institutions, which are highly leveraged institutions.

Current Ratio = Current Assets / Current Liabilities
The higher the current ratio, the more capable the company is of paying its obligations. A ratio under 1 suggests that the company would be unable to pay off its obligations if they came due at that point.

Quick Ratio = Current Assets - Inventories / Current Liabilities
The quick ratio is more conservative than the current ratio, because it excludes inventory from current assets.

Pre-Tax Return on Net Worth = Pre-Tax Income / Net Worth
Indicates stockholders' earnings before taxes for each dollar of investment.

Pre-Tax Return on Assets = (EBIT / Assets) x 100
Indicates much profit the firm is generating from the use of its assets.

Accounts Receivable Turnover = Net Credit Sales / Average Accounts Receivable
A low ratio implies the company should re-assess its credit policies in order to ensure the timely collection of imparted credit that is not earning interest for the firm.

Net Working Capital = Current Assets - Current Liabilities
Positive working capital means that the company is able to pay off its short-term liabilities. Negative working capital means that a company currently is unable to meet its short-term liabilities with its current assets (cash, accounts receivable and inventory).

Interest Coverage Ratio = Earnings Before Interest & Taxes /Total Interest Expense
The lower the ratio, the more the company is burdened by debt expense. When a company's interest coverage ratio is 1.5 or lower, its ability to meet interest expenses may be questionable. An interest coverage ratio below 1 indicates the company is not generating sufficient revenues to satisfy interest expenses.

Collection Days = Accounts Receivables / (Revenues/365)
A high ratio indicates that the company is having problems getting paid for services.

Accounts Payable Turnover = Total Supplier Purchases/Average Accounts Payable
If the turnover ratio is falling from one period to another, this is a sign that the company is taking longer to pay off its suppliers than previously. The opposite is true when the turnover ratio is increasing, which means the firm is paying of suppliers at a faster rate.

Payment Days = (Accounts Payable Balance x 360) / (No. of Accounts Payable x 12)
The average number of days between receiving an invoice and paying it off.

Total Asset Turnover = Revenue / Assets
Asset turnover measures a firm's efficiency at using its assets in generating sales or revenue - the higher the number the better.

Sales / Net Worth = Total Sales / Net Worth
Dividend Payout = Dividends / Net Profit
Assets to Sales = Assets / Sales

Current Debt / Totals Assets = Current Liabilities / Total Assets
Current Liabilities to Liabilities = Current Liabilities / Total Liabilities

Business Ratio Analysis

	2019	2020	2021

Sales Growth
Percent of Total Assets
Accounts Receivable
Inventory
Other Current Assets
Total Current Assets
Long-term Assets
Total Assets
Current Liabilities
Long-term Liabilities
Total Liabilities
Net Worth
Percent of Sales
Sales
Gross Margin
Selling G& A Expenses
Advertising Expenses
Profit Before Interest & Taxes
Main Ratios
Current
Quick
Total Debt to Total Assets
Pre-tax Return on Net Worth
Pre-tax Return on Assets
Additional Ratios
Net Profit Margin
Return on Equity
Activity Ratios
Accounts Receivable Turnover
Collection Days
Inventory Turnover
Accounts Payable Turnover
Payment Days
Total Asset Turnover
Inventory Productivity
Sales per sq/ft.
Gross Margin Return on Inventory (GMROI)
Debt Ratios
Debt to Net Worth

Current Liabilities to Liabilities _____
Liquidity Ratios
Net Working Capital _____
Interest Coverage _____
Additional Ratios
Assets to Sales _____
Current Debt / Total Assets _____
Acid Test _____
Sales / Net Worth _____
Dividend Payout _____
Business Vitality Profile
Sales per Employee _____
Survival Rate _____

Specialized Subscription Business Ratios

Churn is the number of customers that cancel the service in a given month or the sum of canceled contracts.

Churn Rate = # of customers who canceled ÷ total customers at the start of the month

_____ = _____ / _____

Gross MRR Churn Rate (GMCR)
Reports the rate at which you are losing MRR through contractions and cancellations.
GMCR =
(Sum of Cancelled Contracts MRR Churn / MRR at the beginning of the period) x 100

Net MRR Churn rate

(SUM of Churn & Contraction MRR - SUM of Expansion & Reactivation MRR) / MRR at start of period.

Monthly Recurring Revenue
MMR =   Total billings from existing customers paid in given month _____
           First month payments from new customers   + _____
                                                                     = _____

Total Recurring Revenue
ARR = Subscription Revenue +   Fee-based Support   + Value-added Recurring
                                & Adoption Services   Services

____ = _____ + _____ + _____

ARPU (average revenue per user/customer) is the average revenue received per customer on an average month.

ARPU   =   Monthly Recurring Revenue (MRR) / Total number of customers
_____ = _____ / _____

LTV (lifetime value)
Tracks the expected revenue from an average customer over the entire time that they have subscribed to our service.

$$LTV = ARPU / \text{Customer Churn Rate}$$

Note: Assumes that a typical customer pays the same amount every month over the lifetime of their subscription.

CAC (Customer Acquisition Cost)

Indicates what it costs to acquire a typical customer. To calculate CAC, just divide your total sales and marketing expenses in a given month by the number of customers added during that month:

CAC = (Total monthly sales + Marketing Expenses) / Number of new customers added during the month

____ = (_____ + _____) / _____

Note: CAC must be lower than LTV to make more from customers than paid to acquire them.

LTV-CAC Ratio
Provides insight into the startup's profitability and future potential (the good value range is 3 to 4).

LTV-CAC Ratio = Life Time Value / Customer Acquisition Cost

_____ = _____ / _____

Second Year Renewal Rate (SYRR)
Indicates how many new customers are retained early in their relationship with the company.

SYRR=
   (No. of New Subscription Plans Renewed / Total No. of New Subscription) x 100
    Into the second term in current year   Sold in the Prior Year

____ =(_____ / _____) x 100

Net Revenue Retention (NRR)
It measures the total change in recurring revenue from a certain pool of customers over time and is calculated as follows:

NRR = The Current MMR / MRR from One Year Ago

Note: MRR = Monthly Recurring Revenue

Source: www.saas-capital.com/blog/essential-saas-metrics-revenue-retention-fundamentals/

12.0 Summary

_____ (company name) will be successful. This business plan has documented that the establishment of _____ (company name) is feasible. All of the critical factors, such as industry trends, marketing analysis, competitive analysis, management expertise and financial analysis support this conclusion.

Project Description: (Give a brief summary of the product, service or program.)
_____
Description of Favorable Industry and Market Conditions.
(Summarize why this business is viable.) _____
Summary of Earnings Projections and Potential Return to Investors: _____
Summary of Capital Requirements: _____
Security for Investors & Loaning Institutions: _____
Summary of expected benefits for people in the community beyond the immediate business concern: _____
Means of Financing:
A. Loan Requirements: $_____
B. Owner's Contribution: $ $_____
C. Other Sources of Income: $_____
Total Funds Available: $_____

13.0　　Potential Exit Scenarios

Two potential exit strategies exist for the investor:
1. **Initial Public Offering. (IPO)**
   We seek to go public within ___ (#) years of operations. The funds used will both help create liquidity for investors as well as allow for additional capital to develop our _____ (international/national?) roll out strategy.
2. **Acquisition Merger with Private or Public Company.**
   Our most desirable option for exit is a merger or buyout by a large corporation. We believe with substantial cash flows and a loyal customer base our company will be attractive to potential corporate investors within five years. Real value has been created through the novel combination of home health care services as well as partnering with key referral groups.

APPENDIX

Purpose: Supporting documents used to enhance your business proposal.
- Tax returns of principals for the last three years, if the plan is for new business
- A personal financial statement, which should include life insurance and endowment policies, if applicable
- A copy of the proposed lease or purchase agreement for building space, or zoning information for in-home businesses, with layouts, maps, and blueprints
- A copy of licenses and other legal documents including partnership, association, or shareholders' agreements and copyrights, trademarks, and patents applications
- A copy of résumés of all principals in a consistent format, if possible
- Copies of letters of intent from suppliers, contracts, orders, and miscellaneous.
- In the case of a franchised business, a copy of the franchise contract and all supporting documents provided by the franchisor
- Newspaper clippings that support the business or the owner, including something about you, your achievements, business idea, or region

Promotional literature for your company or your competitors
Product/Service Brochures of your company or competitors
Photographs of your product. equipment, facilities, etc.
Market research to support the marketing section of the plan
Trade and industry publications when they support your intentions
Quotations or pro-forma invoices for capital items to be purchased, including a list of fixed assets, company vehicles, and proposed renovations
References/Letters of Recommendation
All insurance policies in place, both business and personal
Operation Schedules
Organizational Charts
Job Descriptions
Additional Financial Projections by Month
Customer Needs Analysis Worksheet
Sample Sales Letters
Copies of Software Management Reports
Copies of Standard Business Forms
Equipment List
Personal Survival Budget

Helpful Resources:

Associations:
Association of Wedding Gown Specialists
www.weddinggownspecialists.com/friends.htm

Miscellaneous:

Vista Print Free Business Cards	www.vistaprint.com
Free Business Guides	www.smbtn.com/businessplanguides/
Open Office	http://download.openoffice.org/
US Census Bureau	www.census.gov
Federal Government	www.business.gov
US Patent & Trademark Office	www.uspto.gov
US Small Business Administration	www.sba.gov
National Association for the Self-Employed	www.nase.org
International Franchise Association	www.franchise.org
Center for Women's Business Research	www.cfwbr.org

Some sites for USA business:
http://sbinformation.about.com/
http://www.business.gov/
http://www.sba.gov/regions/states.html
http://freeadvice.com/
http://www.government-grants-101.com/
http://www.pueblo.gsa.gov/
http://www.smallbusinessnotes.com/sitemap.html

Printed in Great Britain
by Amazon